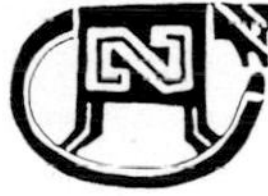

To find peace, we must find harmony.
We should respect Mother Earth and all her creatures.
When we do, our souls will realize our oneness,
our relationship, and our dependence to the land.
As long as the sun shines and the rivers flow,
the land will be here to give us life.

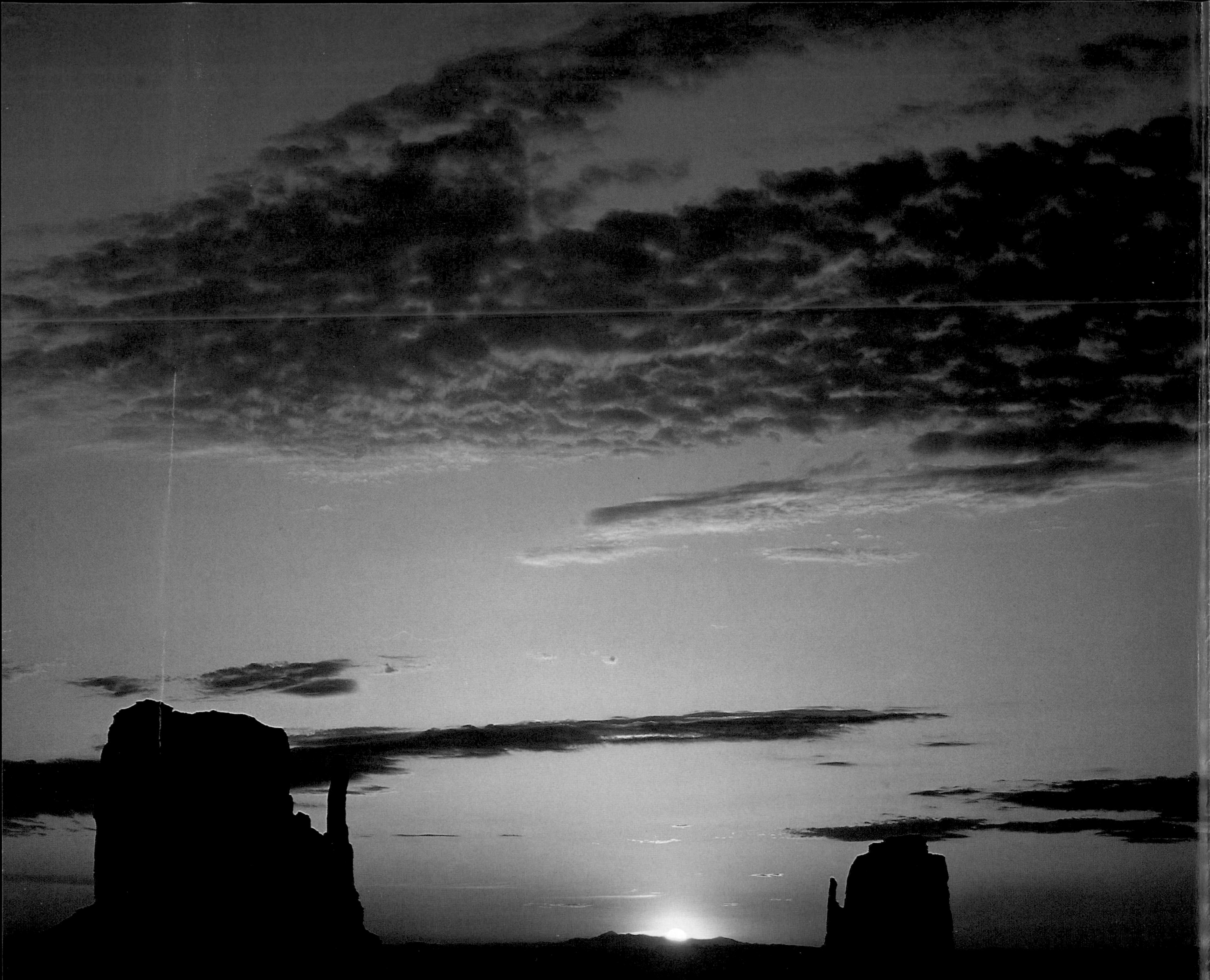

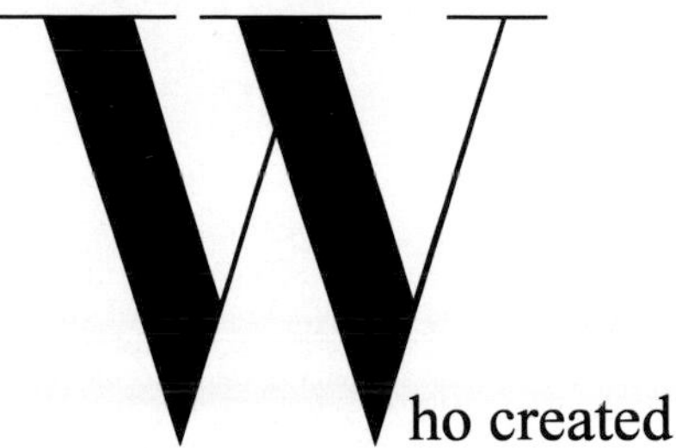ho created this world we do not know. Only through something like the sun, powering and radiant,

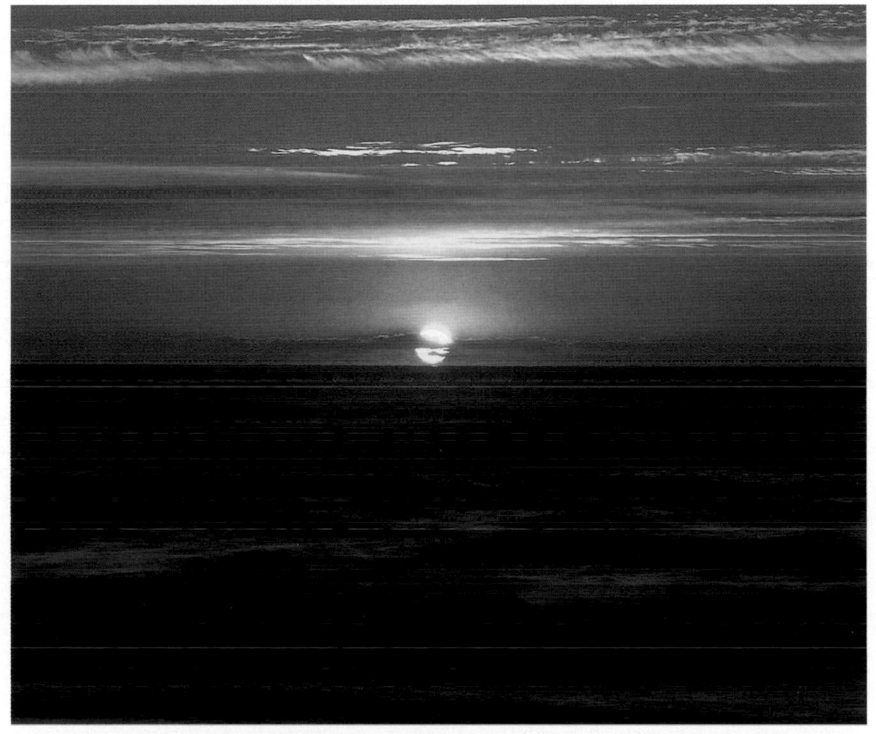

can we sense the Creator. Every morning my grandfathers and grandmothers awakened early to greet the sun. At that special time they sang their prayer songs. They sent their prayers through the rays of the sun to the creator.

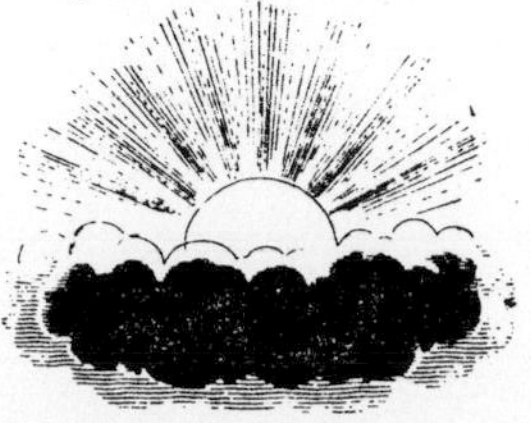

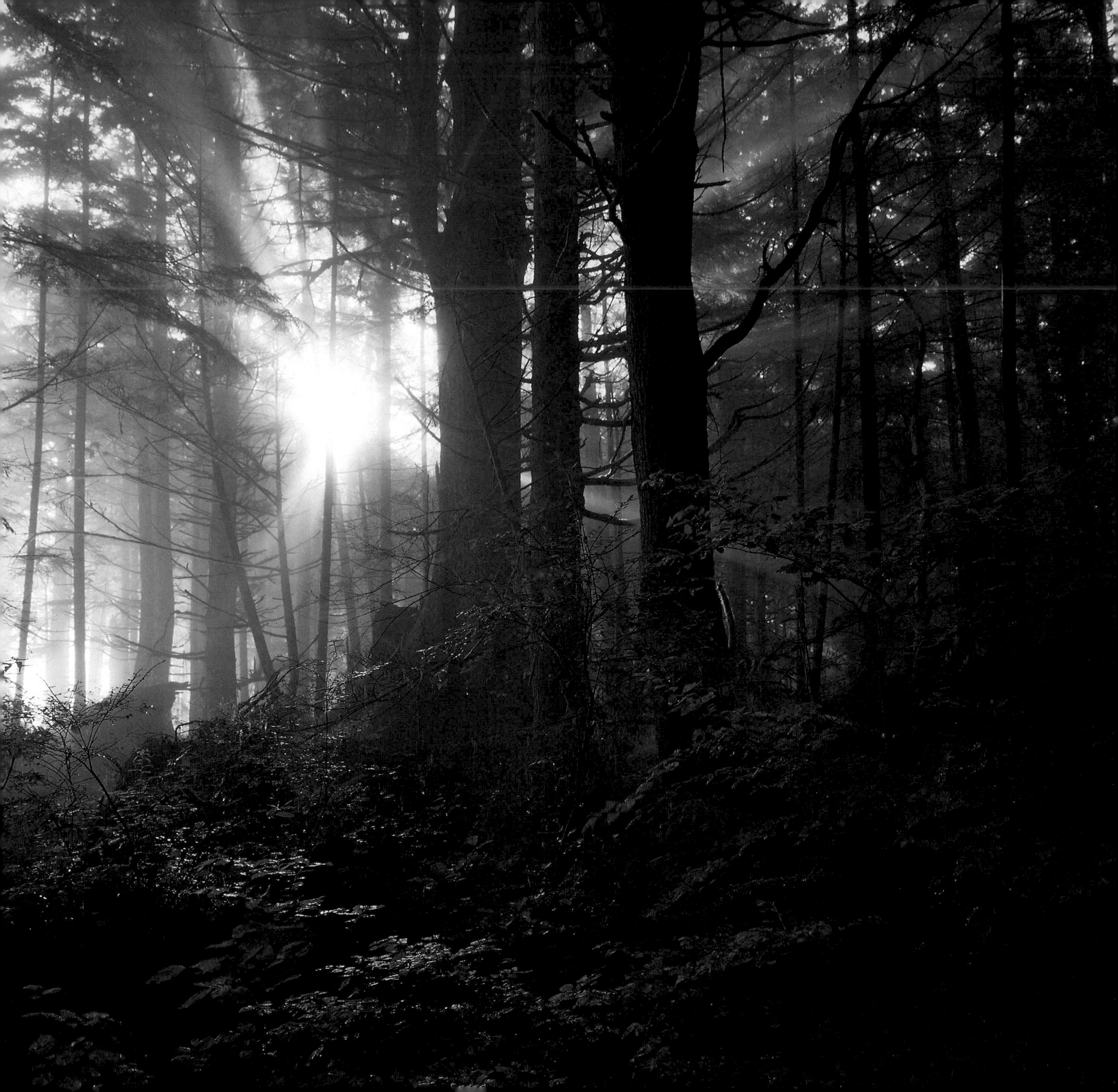

IN THE SPIRIT OF

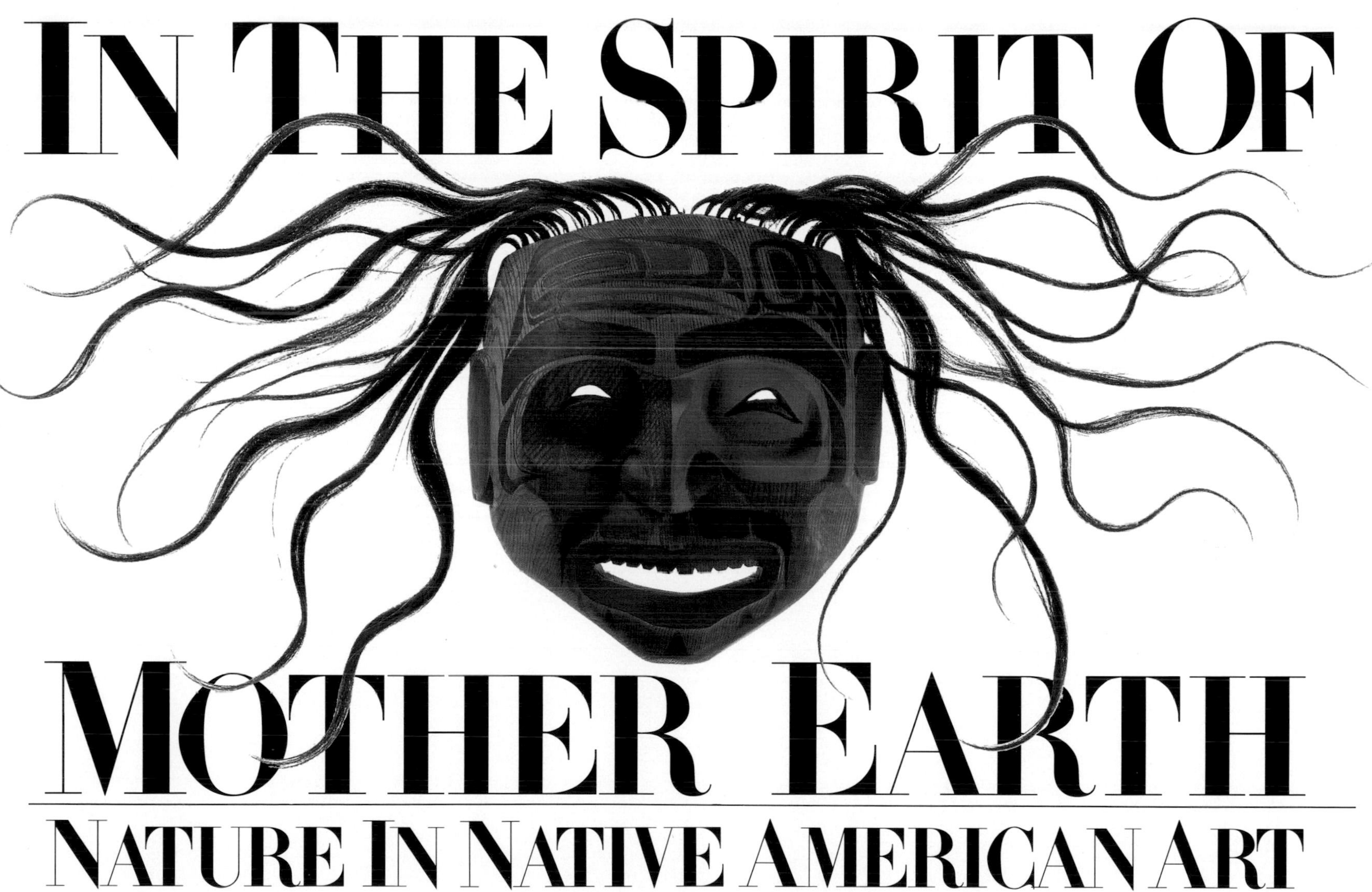

MOTHER EARTH

NATURE IN NATIVE AMERICAN ART

Created and Produced by McQuiston & McQuiston
Text by Jeremy Schmidt and Captions by Laine Thom

CHRONICLE BOOKS
SAN FRANCISCO

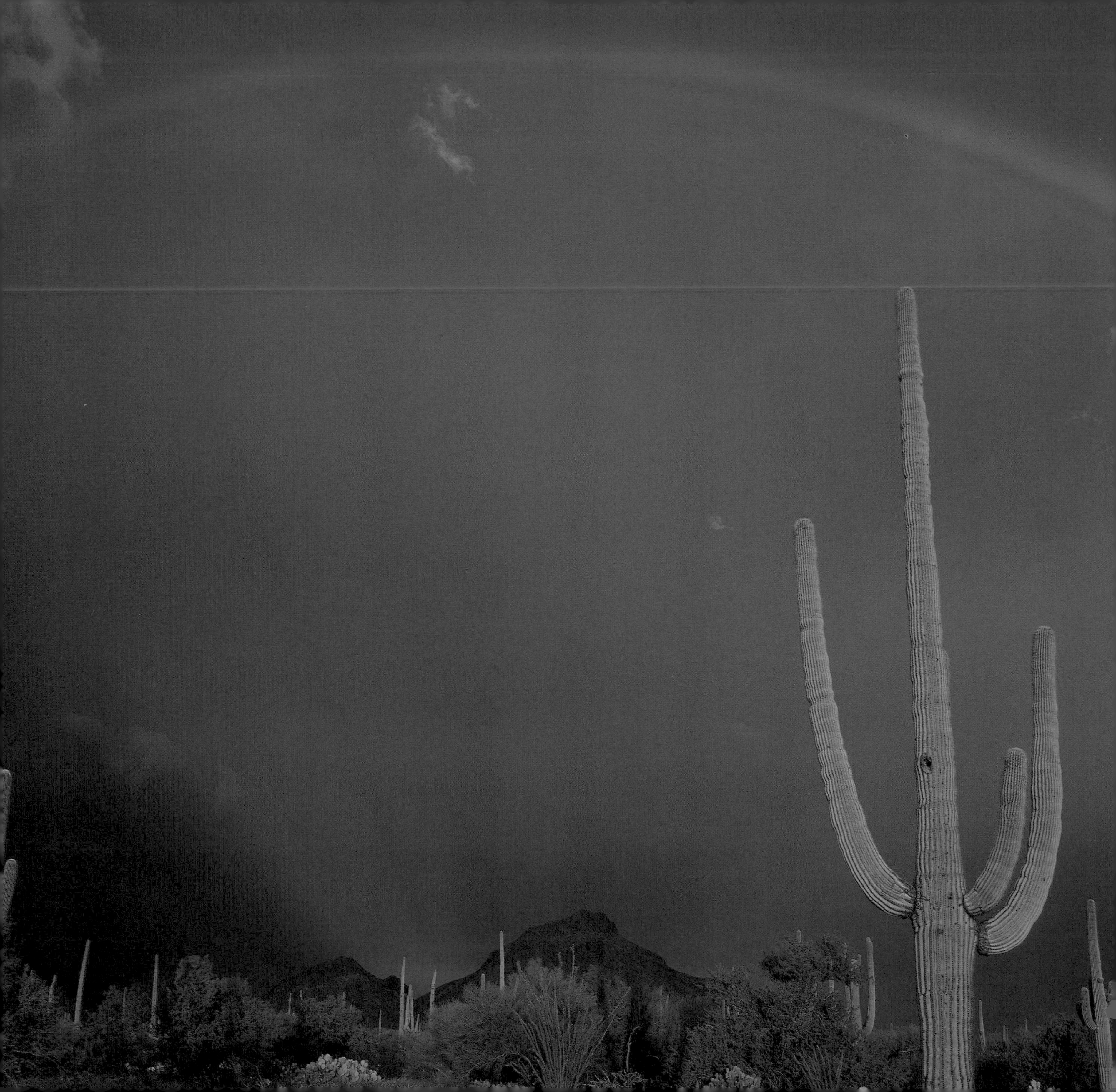

Dedicated to the lasting, living spirit of Native Americans.

This book could not have been produced without the assistance and help of many people. We are grateful to the staff at the San Diego Museum of Man for their invaluable help. Special thanks are due to Grace Johnson, Assistant Curator, who helped us select the artifacts and historical photos, to Ken Hedges, Chief Curator, and Stefani Salkeld, Curator. Many thanks are due to the Teton County Historical Center in Jackson, Wyoming, especially Larry Kummer, Director, and Jo Anne Bryd, Rita Verley, and Amy Kiessling for their helpfulness at the Center's library, and Stephanie Ivic, her family, and Debbie Lind for their hospitality in Jackson, Wyoming. Special thanks to Jack Jensen, Drew Montgomery, Charlotte Stone, and Michael Carabetta of Chronicle Books for their continual support. And last but not least, to Laine Thom's mother, Ardis Brown, who inspired Laine with her beautiful floral beadwork and encouraged him to continue the traditional Great Basin–Plateau beadwork and the sharing of native knowledge and wisdom to other Native Americans and the world.

Produced by McQuiston & McQuiston; artifact photography by John Oldenkamp; computer composition by Joyce Sweet and Jeremy Schmidt; printed in Hong Kong by South Sea International Press.

Library of Congress
Cataloging-in-Publication Data:
Schmidt, Jeremy.
In the spirit of mother earth: nature in Native American art / Jeremy Schmidt, Laine Thom.
p. cm.
Includes bibliographical references and index.
ISBN 0-8118-0529-8
ISBN 0-8118-0501-8 (pbk).
1. Indians of North America—Art.
2. Nature (Aesthetics)
I. Thom, Laine, 1952- . II. Title.
E98.A7S358 1994
730'. 089'97—dc20 93- 43280
CIP

10 9 8 7 6 5 4 3 2 1

Distributed in Canada by Raincoast Books
112 East Third Avenue
Vancouver, British Columbia V5T 1C8

Chronicle Books
275 Fifth Street
San Francisco, California 94103

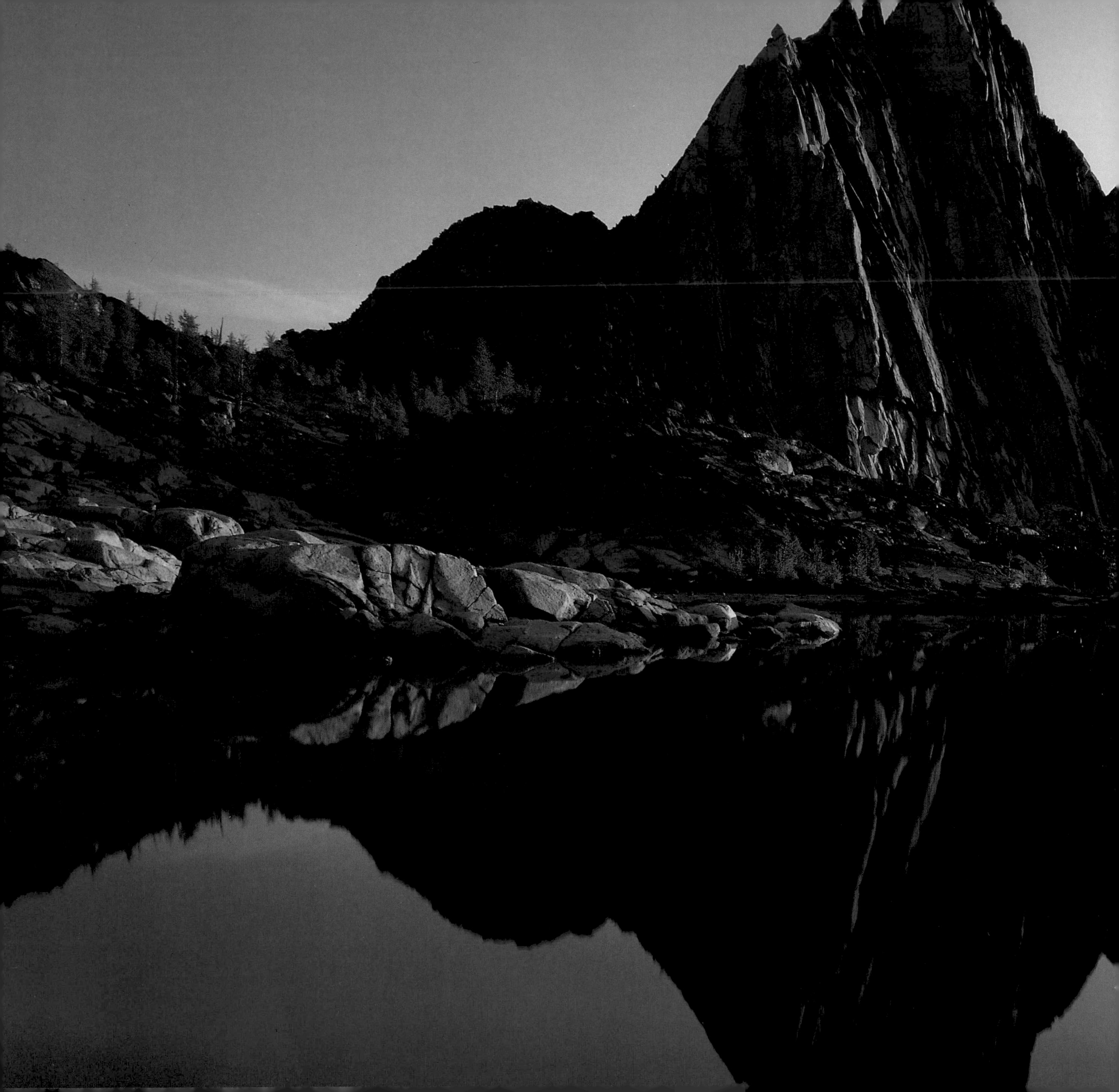

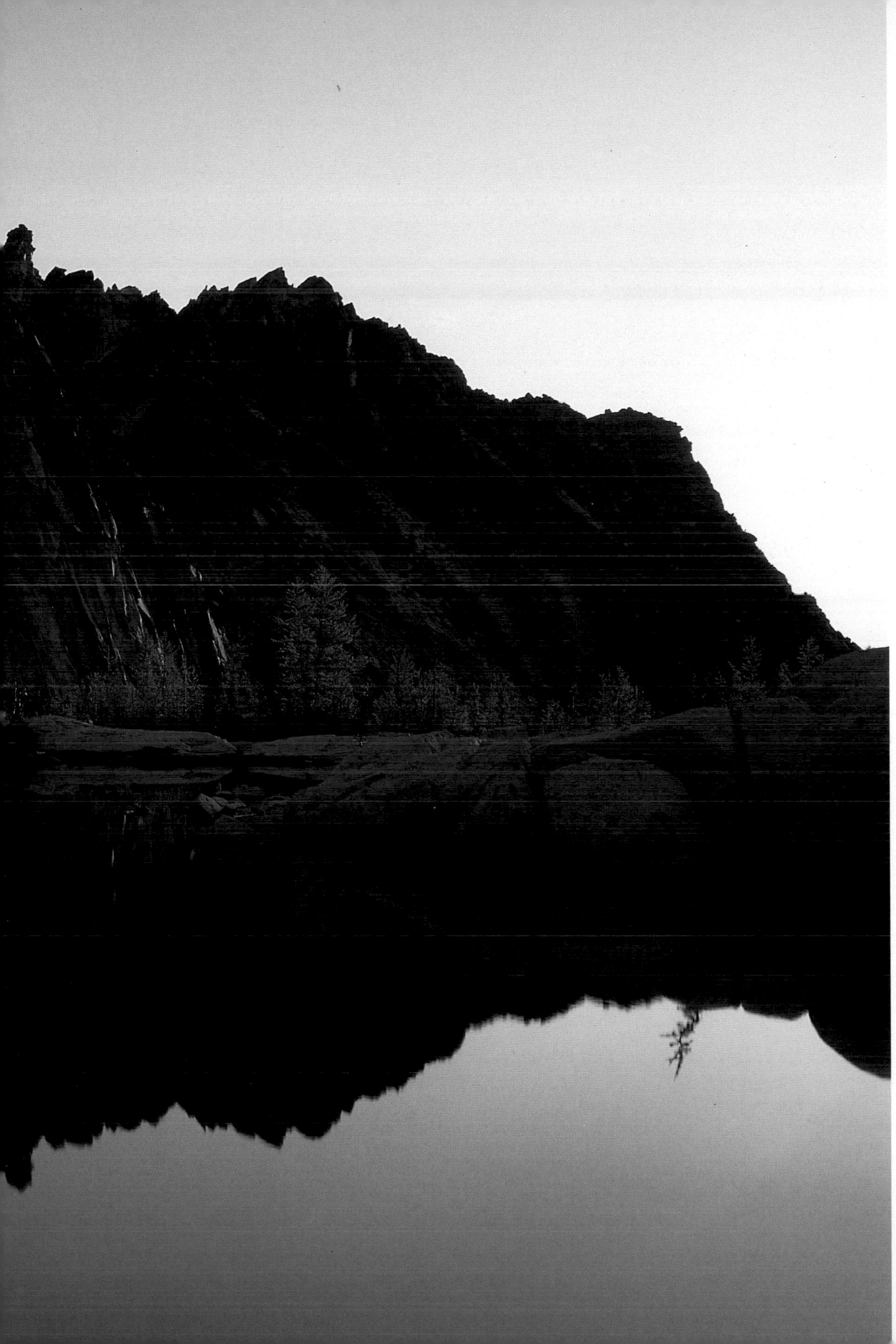

As I walk along the shore of a lake near the mountains I feel the spirit of my ancestors who often visit this special place. Their voices and songs are heard in the wind. It reminds me to respect the land we call our Mother and all the living things upon it. The plants and animals, they are my brothers and sisters.

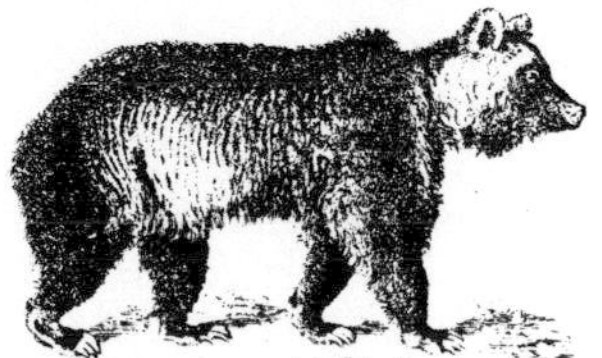

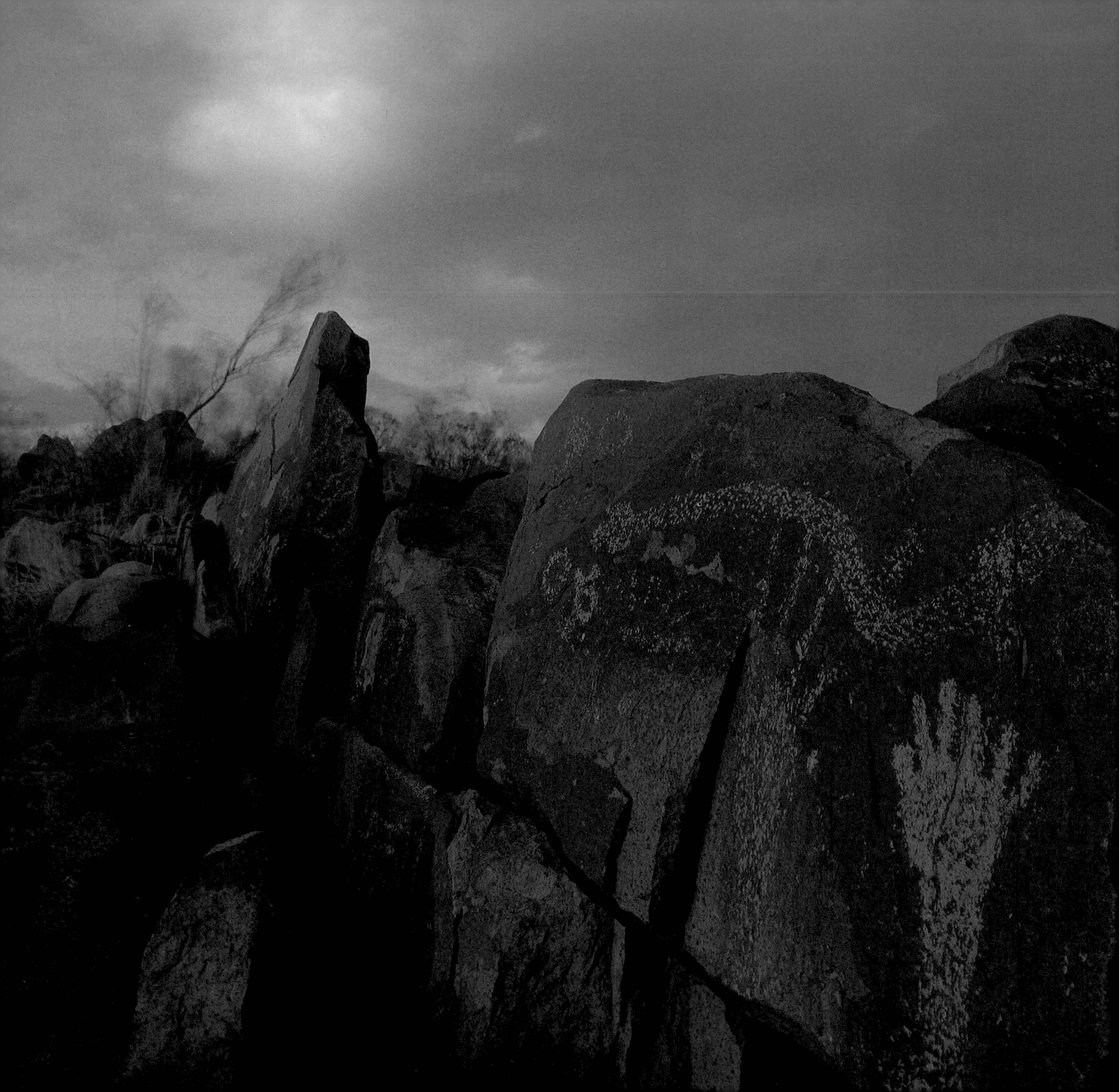

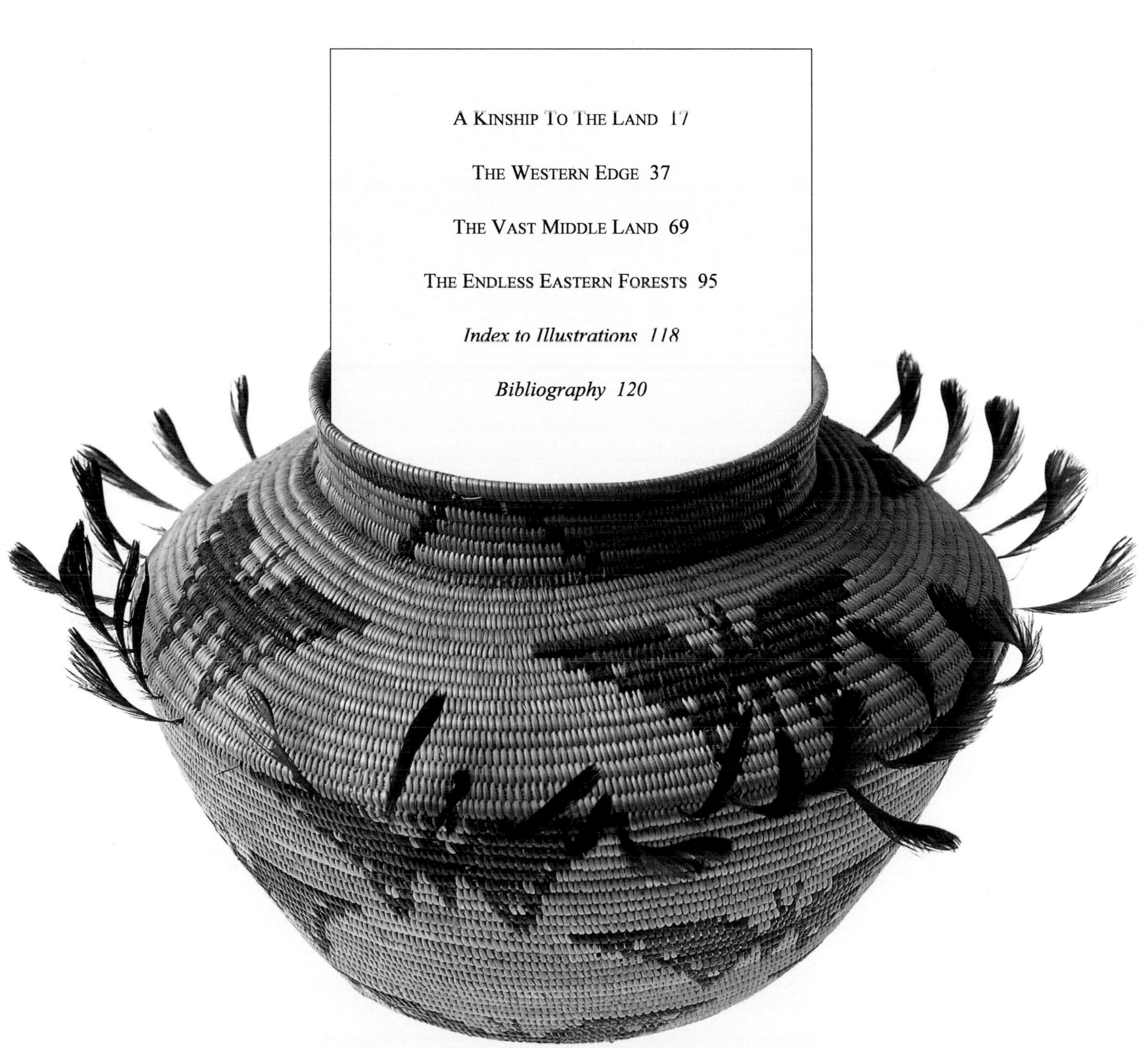

Yokut basket

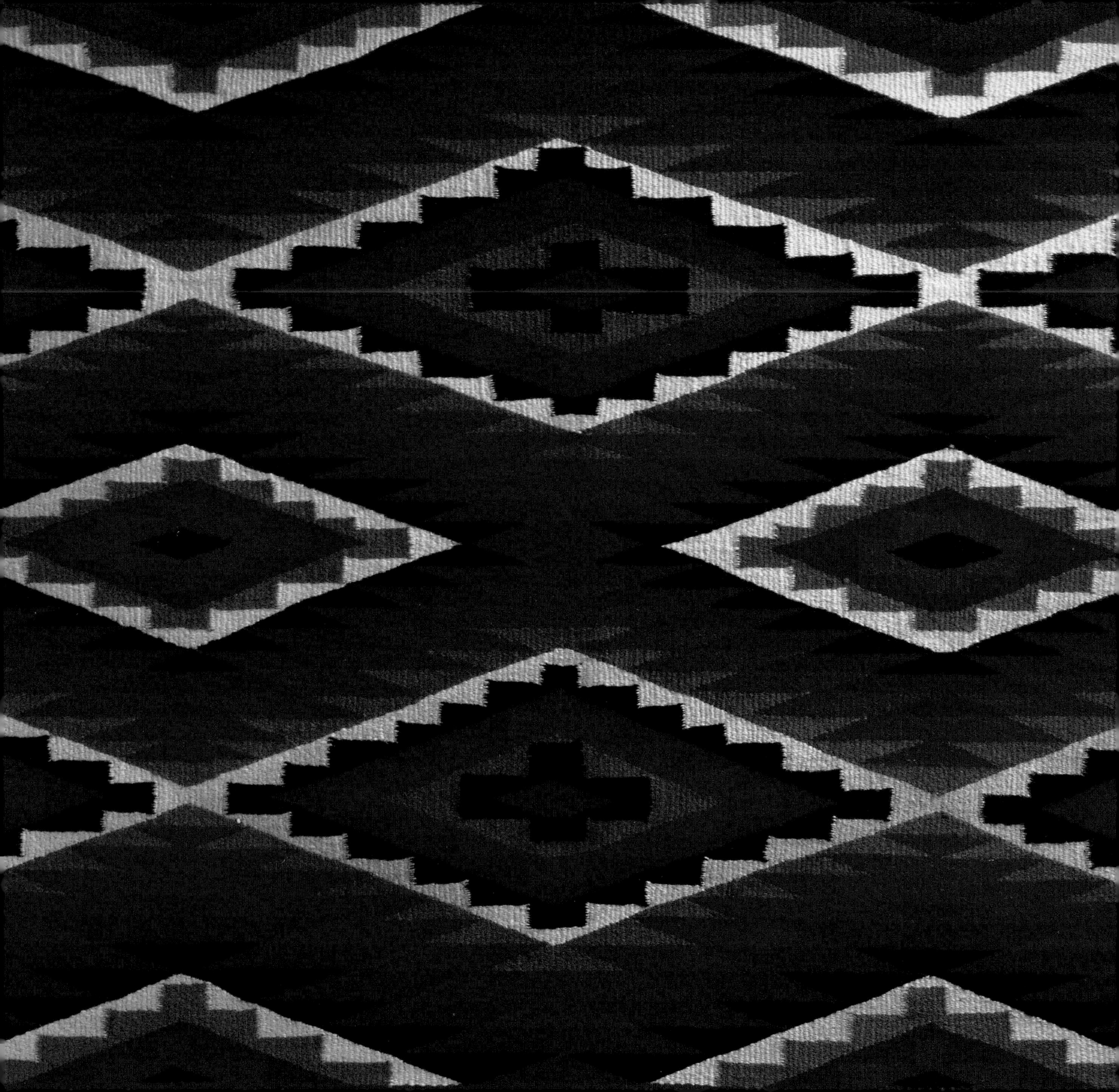

O our Mother
the Earth, O our Father the Sky,
Your children are we, and with tired backs
We bring you the gifts you love.
Then weave for us a garment of brightness:

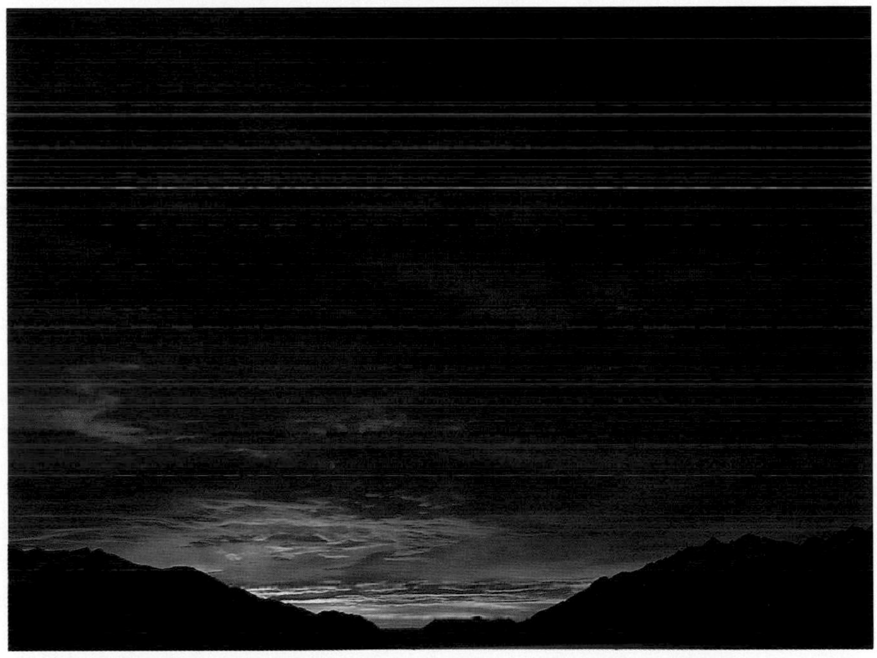

May the warp be the white light of morning,
May the weft be the red light of evening,
May the fringes be the falling rain,
May the border be the standing rainbow.
Thus weave for us a garment of brightness,
That we may walk fittingly where birds sing,
That we may walk fittingly where grass is green,
O our Mother the Earth, O our Father the Sky.

Navajo saddle cover

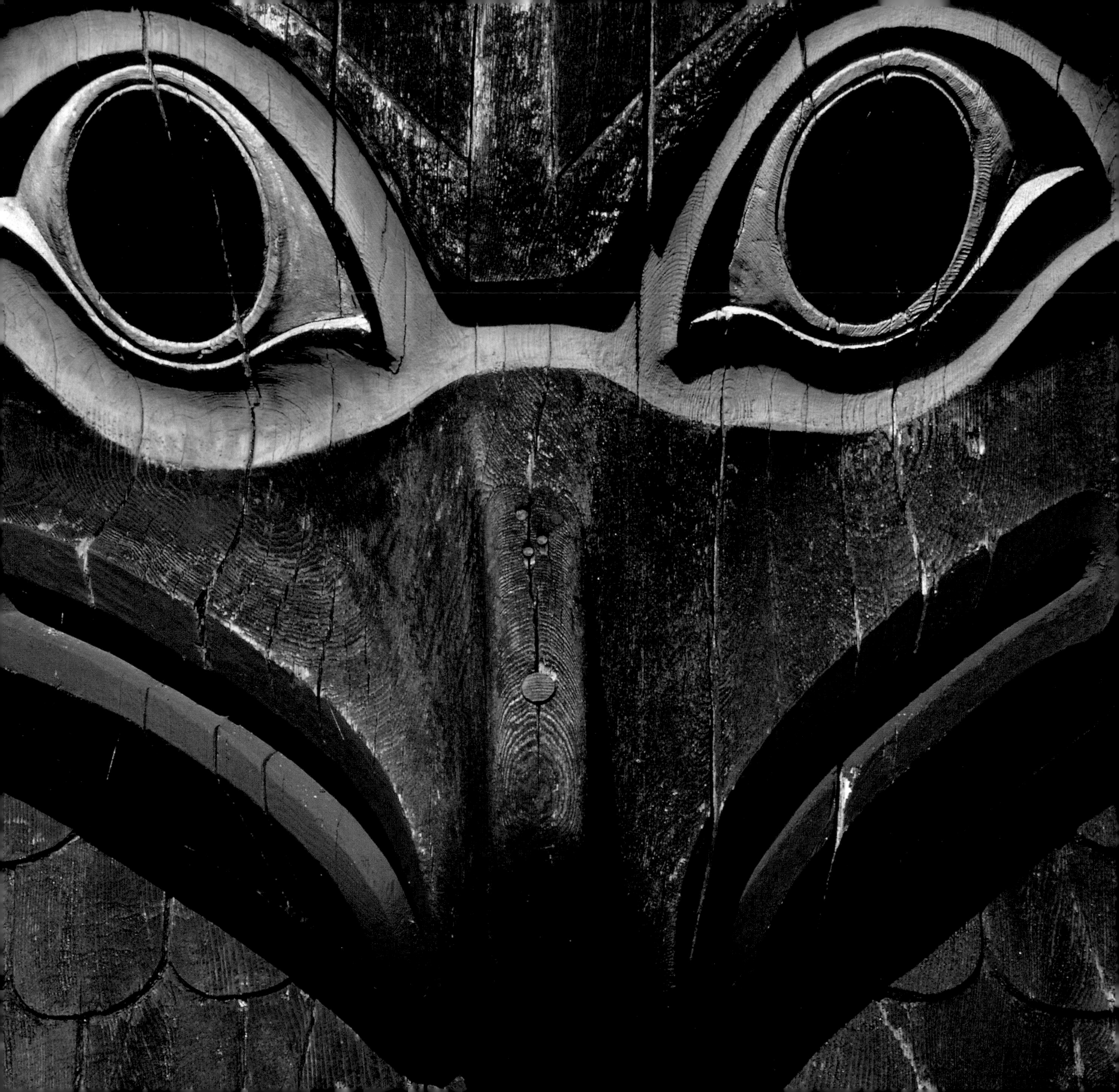

The Great Mystery gave the earth and all living things a spirit.

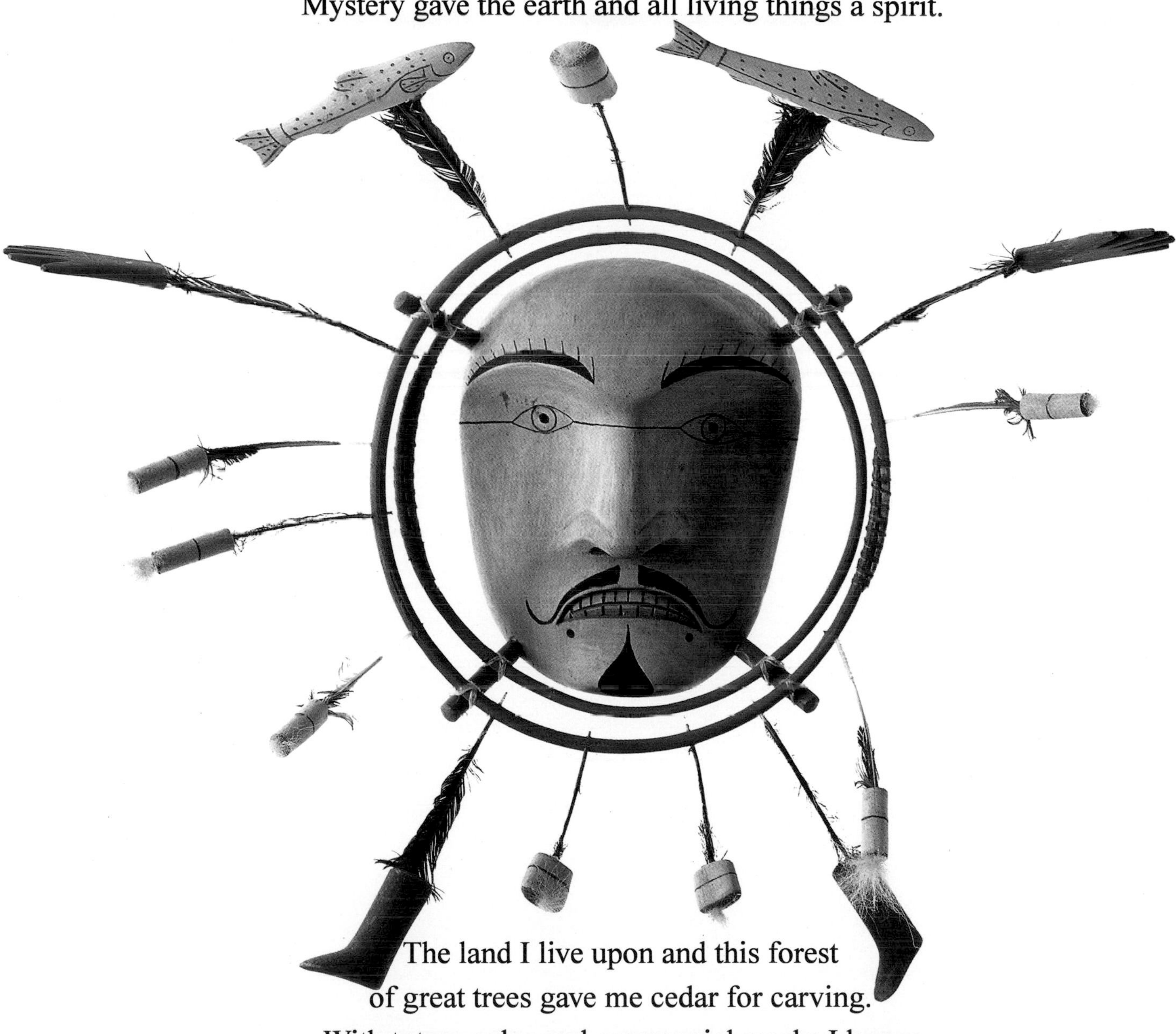

The land I live upon and this forest of great trees gave me cedar for carving. With totem poles and ceremonial masks I honor the spirits of animal beings: raven, bear, whale, and salmon.

Chief Kadashan totem pole (left)
Eskimo face mask (above)

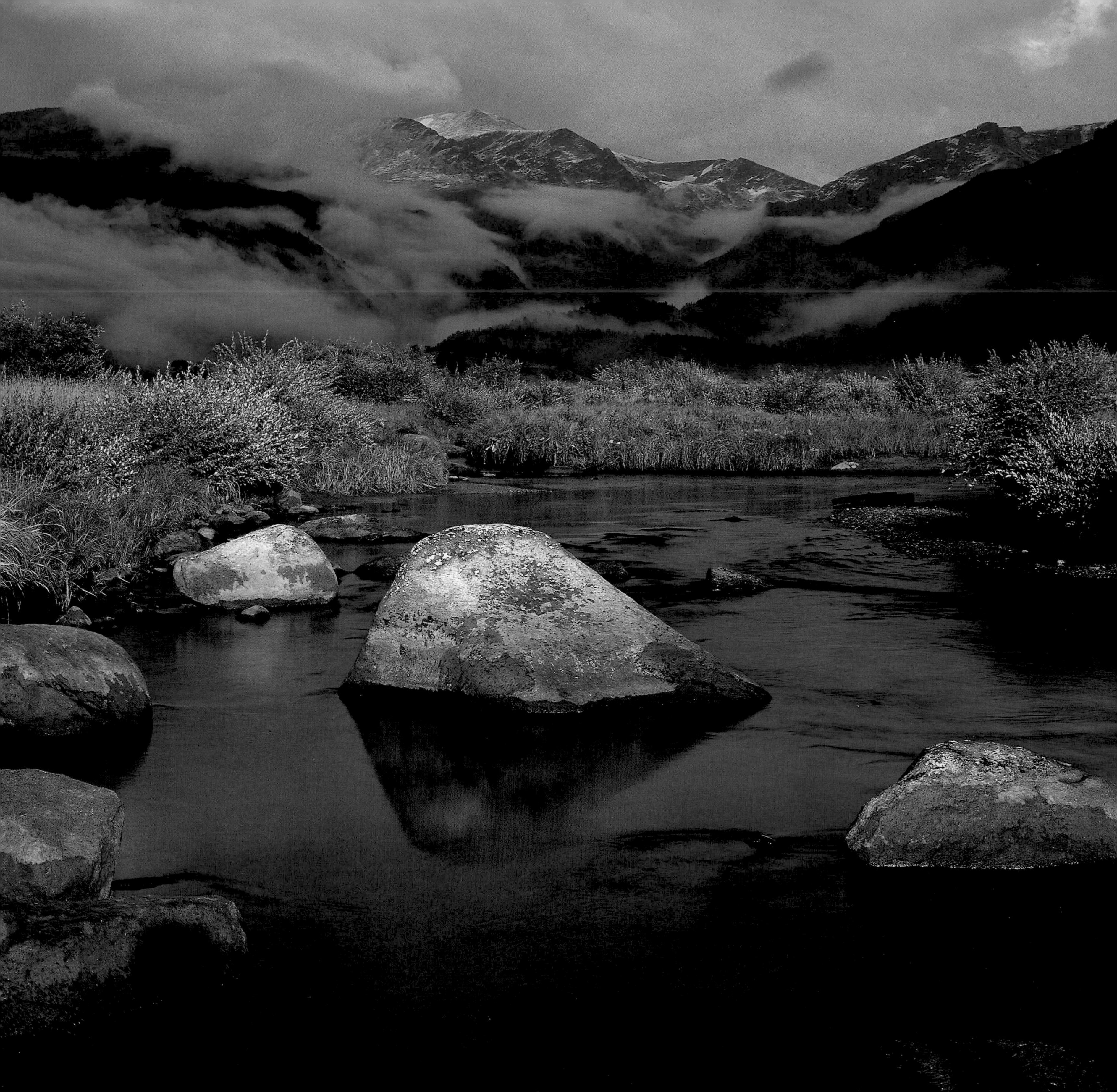

A KINSHIP TO THE LAND

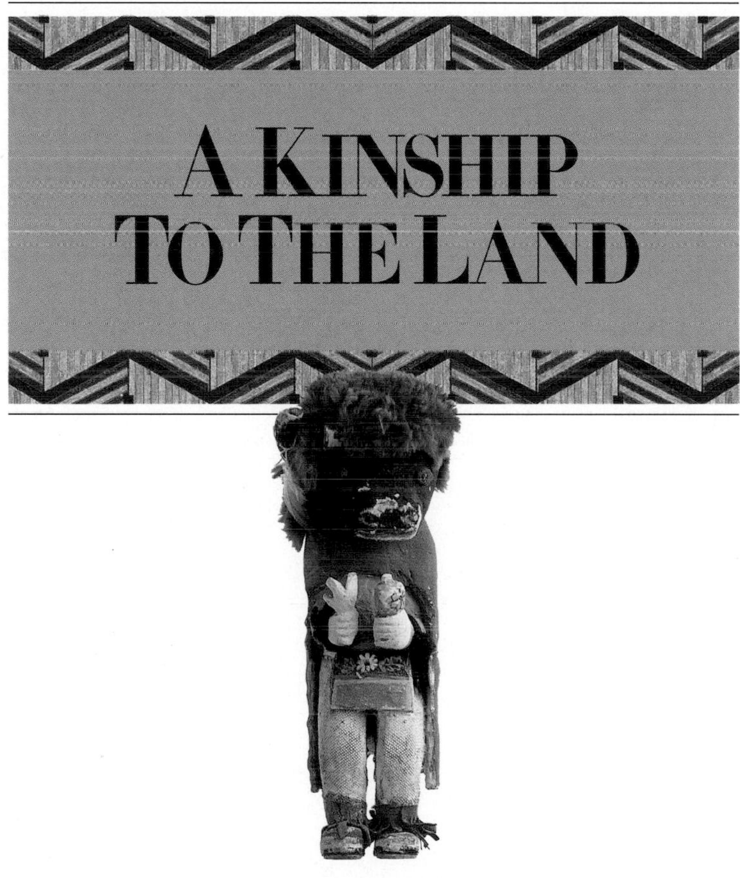

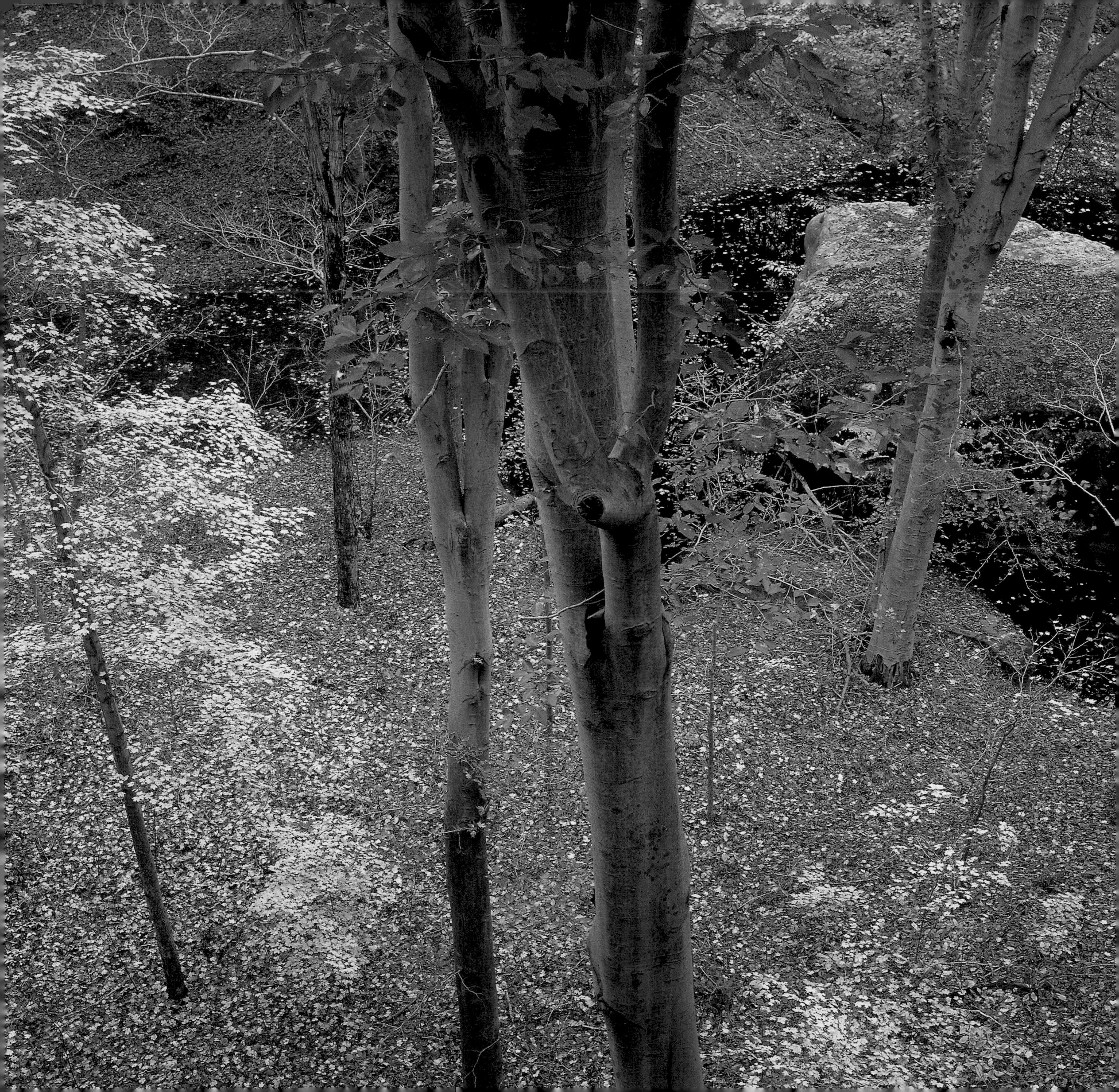

A Kinship To The Land

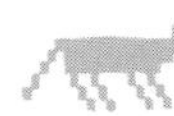
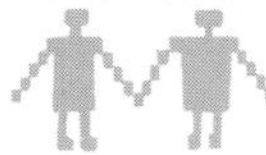
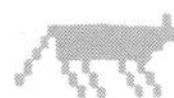

In the time before European settlers changed the face of the continent, the native peoples of North America had a relationship to the land that might never be recreated. For thousands of years they lived in close contact with the earth. Their art was inspired by nature; their lives were lived in accord with nature. Between people and nature there was no clear distinction, for each was part of the other, and all parts were sacred.

North America was then a glorious land in the fullness of its spiritual and natural power. Unchecked by dams, its rivers ebbed and flowed with the seasons as they had always done. Vast wetlands lay undrained, supporting millions of ducks, geese, cranes, swans, and shorebirds. As autumn moved south across the continent so did the birds, lifting up from the marshes and prairies and forests, streaming southward with the annual tide of migration. In the spring, back they would come, calling and spiraling down from the sky as their ancestors had done for thousands of years. On the western plains beyond the hundredth meridian, the sod was broken only by the hooves of native animals — deer, elk, pronghorn, and most notably, buffalo. Salmon swarmed the headwaters of cold-

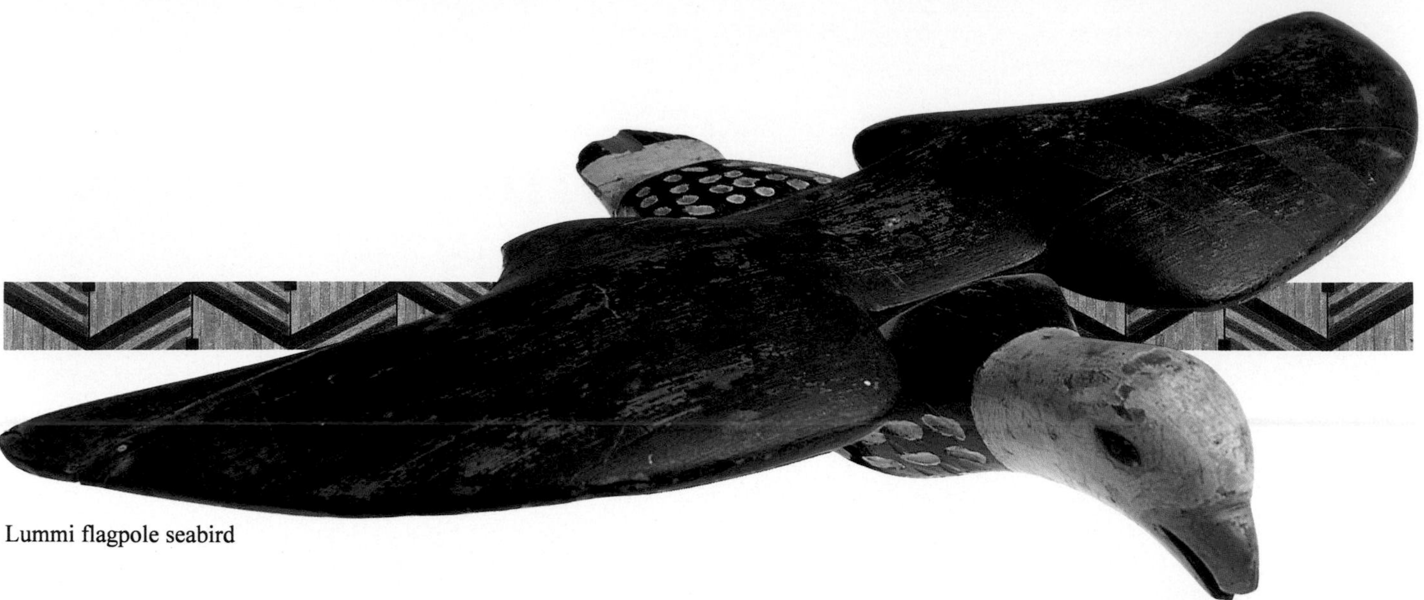

Lummi flagpole seabird

water rivers on both coasts. The plants themselves grew according to the dictates of rock, wind, rain, and the cycle of seasons. In the night sky, the brightest object was the moon.

The earth spoke with a strong voice, and the people fashioned their lives according to what they heard. As the Mohawk said,

Our Grandparents of old, they are saying, "Listen to her, all, to the Earth our Mother, to what she is saying." People, listen all.

What they heard were some of life's most basic lessons: All motions are circular; no action is free of consequence; all life begins from the ground beneath our feet; all living and non-living things are related in flesh and spirit; and for human beings, solace comes from alignment with natural forces, not from the attempt to conquer, overcome, or bend those forces to one's will. These lessons, once dismissed by European science and philosophy as primitive superstition, have acquired a new relevance in the sciences of ecology and physics. At a time when the relationship between people and the earth seems to have reached a critical juncture, the ancient knowledge of Native Americans has begun to sound like wisdom for the future.

This is not to say that life close to nature was idyllic, as if it were an Eden where the earth provided abundantly and there was no pain, no conflict, no death. On the contrary, people then as now experienced hunger and discomfort. Work was hard, crops failed, wildlife became scarce, fishermen came home with boats empty of fish, loved ones died, friends could be cruel, enemies attacked without warning. Like a stern but loving parent, the earth provided not only pleasurable things but hard lessons, tests of courage, strength, endurance, and patience. With joy came sorrow; with life there was death.

Life was a mystical adventure, a continuous ceremony lived in a landscape that itself had spirit. From the time a young man (and in some tribes a young woman) went alone on his first vision quest until the time he died, he sought a sacred relationship with all things, from the buffalo and the sun to the smallest insects. All these things had spirits of their own. They were also manifestations of the divine, named by various tribes the Great Spirit, Creator, Great Mystery Power, the Grandfather Spirit, and others.

Native Americans valued all living things as fellow creatures, and many as kin. For example, salmon in the northwest rivers were embodiments of an immortal race of humans who had turned themselves into fish for the benefit of the peo-

Qagyuhl dancers in war canoes

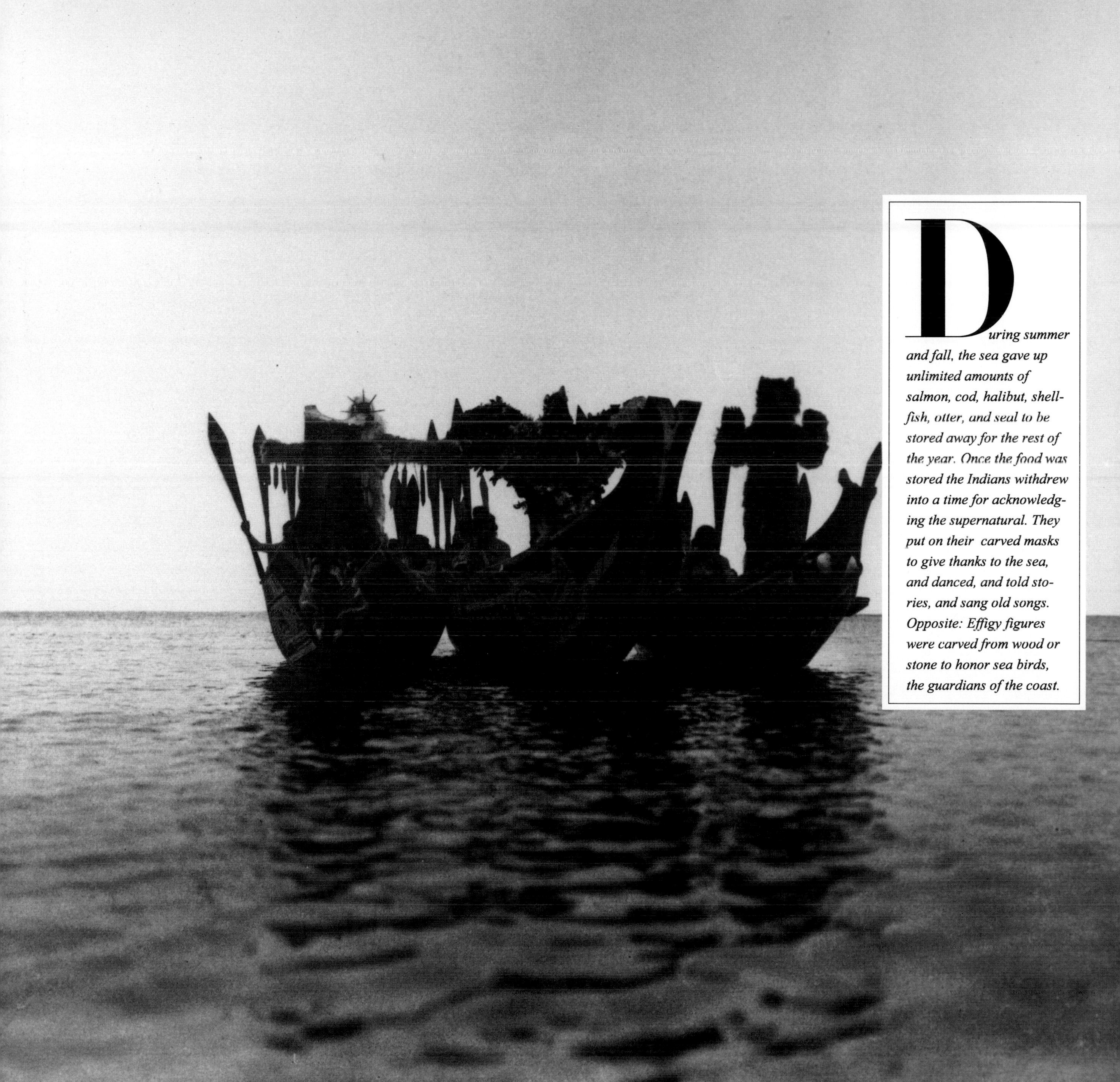

During summer and fall, the sea gave up unlimited amounts of salmon, cod, halibut, shellfish, otter, and seal to be stored away for the rest of the year. Once the food was stored the Indians withdrew into a time for acknowledging the supernatural. They put on their carved masks to give thanks to the sea, and danced, and told stories, and sang old songs. Opposite: Effigy figures were carved from wood or stone to honor sea birds, the guardians of the coast.

ALEUTIANS

ple. Clan names reflected alliances or kinships with particular animals. Along the Northwest Coast, people saw themselves as direct descendants of otters, bears, ravens, and other animals.

These were reciprocal relationships. Game animals gave themselves willingly, or were given by a higher spirit, only when the hunter observed proper respect for the animal, offering propitiatory gestures for having taken a life. Before the hunt, and again afterwards, he would speak ritually to an animal, explaining his need, apologizing to his fellow creature, and speeding the animal spirit back to its home, where it would again acquire a physical form and return for another hunt. For example, when the Makah of the Pacific Northwest killed a whale, they would celebrate. A single whale would feed an entire village for many days, and the hunters were respected for their prowess. At the same time, the spirit of the whale was thanked and acknowledged, as in this Makah song:

Whale, I have given you what you wish to get — my good harpoon. Please hold it with your strong hands. . . . Whale, tow me to the beach of my village, for when you come ashore there young men will cover your great body with blue-bill duck feathers and the down of the great eagle.

Death was seen as an intrinsic part of life, as was the taking of plants and animals. As a deer ate grass and made it into a warm pelt, a person took the deer's pelt to shelter his or her naked skin. But never without giving thanks, and never without pondering the mingled fates of all creatures. It is possible, after all, to kill an animal, to eat its flesh, to sew clothing

Since the landing of Columbus in 1492, the original people of North America have witnessed enormous changes in the natural landscape, and have suffered cultural cataclysms of the sort that few societies survive. Yet in most of the fundamental aspects of native life, the continuity of centuries remains unbroken. Traditional values, spiritual concepts, and religious ceremonies still form the backbone of native culture. This can be seen in the Sun Dance of the Shoshone, the Hopi Kachina, the Iroquois False Face Society, Navajo tales of Spider Woman, and a thousand other aspects of modern Indian life.

Although this book is written from a historic perspective, and in past tense, it is dedicated to the lasting, living spirit of Native Americans.

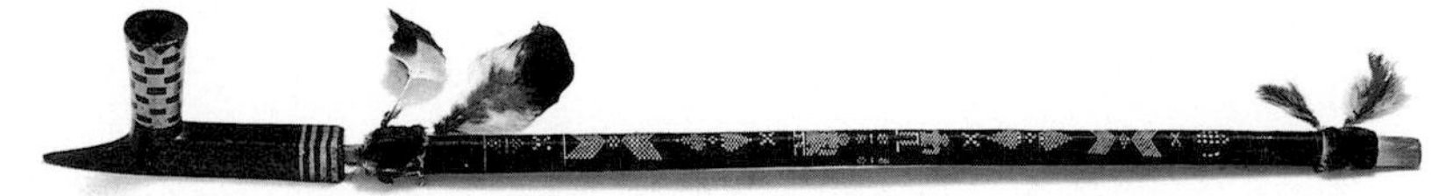

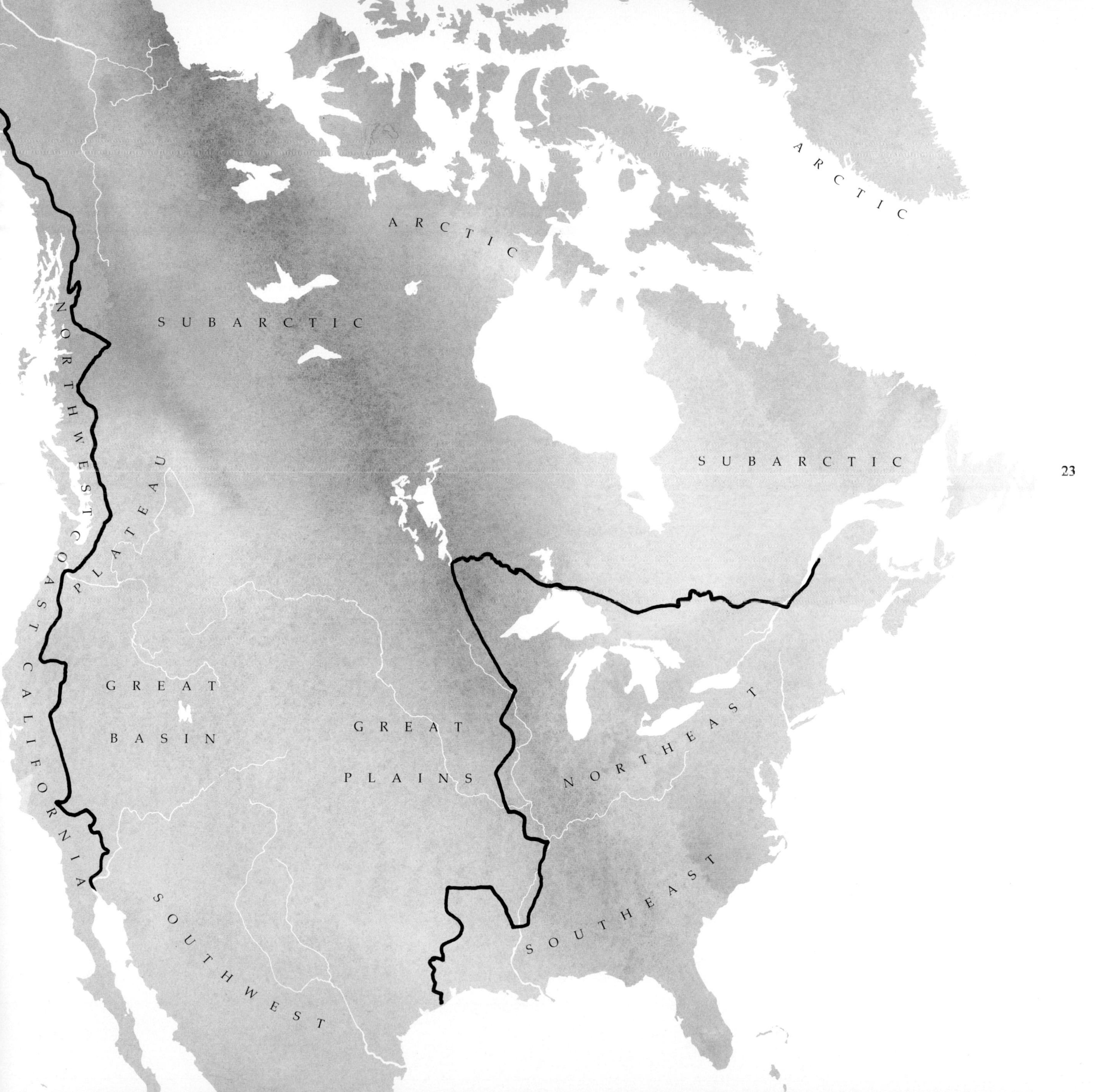
ARCTIC
ARCTIC
SUBARCTIC
SUBARCTIC
NORTHWEST COAST
PLATEAU
CALIFORNIA
GREAT BASIN
GREAT PLAINS
NORTHEAST
SOUTHWEST
SOUTHEAST

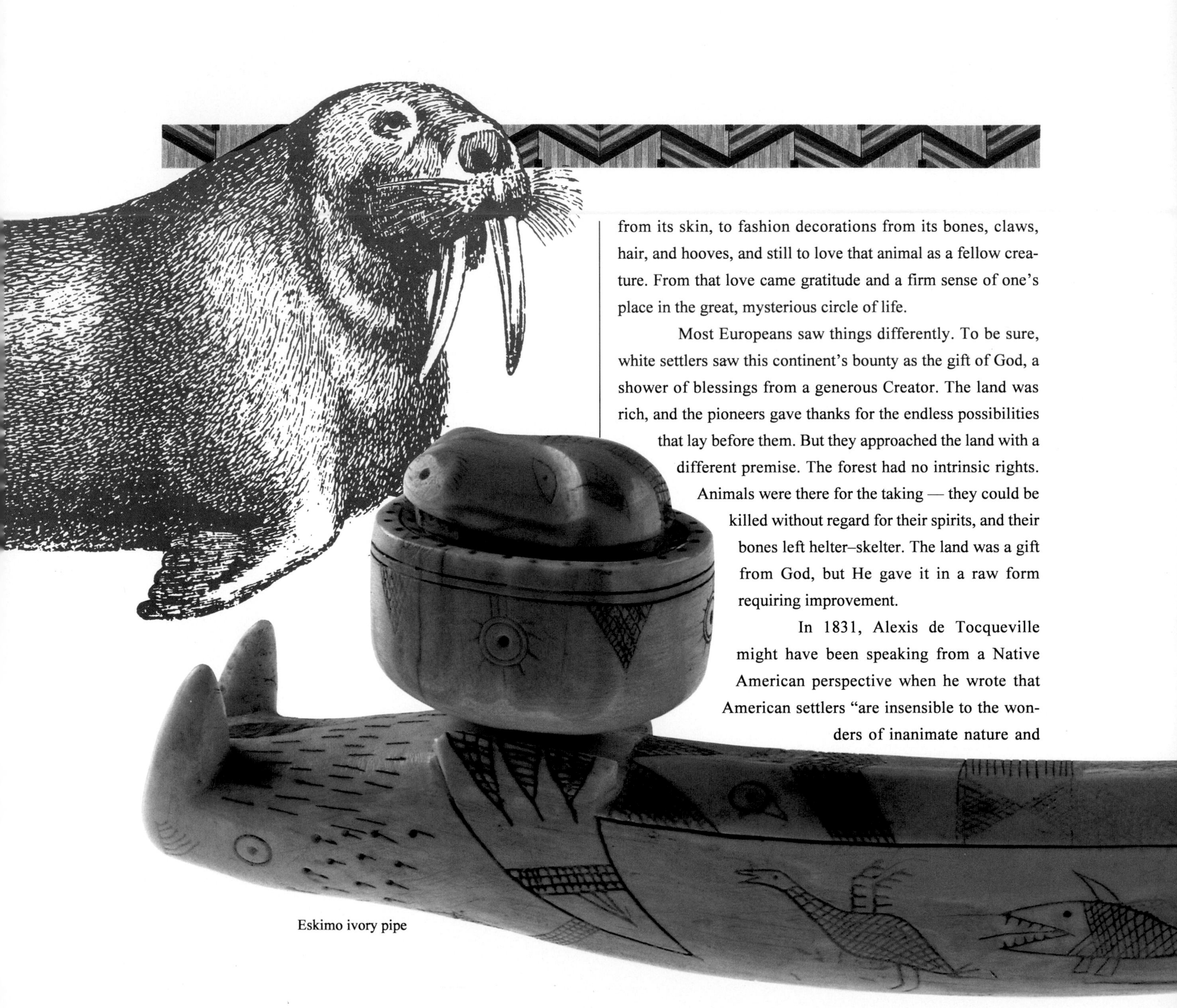

from its skin, to fashion decorations from its bones, claws, hair, and hooves, and still to love that animal as a fellow creature. From that love came gratitude and a firm sense of one's place in the great, mysterious circle of life.

Most Europeans saw things differently. To be sure, white settlers saw this continent's bounty as the gift of God, a shower of blessings from a generous Creator. The land was rich, and the pioneers gave thanks for the endless possibilities that lay before them. But they approached the land with a different premise. The forest had no intrinsic rights. Animals were there for the taking — they could be killed without regard for their spirits, and their bones left helter–skelter. The land was a gift from God, but He gave it in a raw form requiring improvement.

In 1831, Alexis de Tocqueville might have been speaking from a Native American perspective when he wrote that American settlers "are insensible to the wonders of inanimate nature and

Eskimo ivory pipe

they may be said not to perceive the mighty forests that surround them till they fall beneath the hatchet. Their eyes are fixed upon another sight, the . . . march across these wilds, draining swamps, turning the course of rivers, peopling solitudes, and subduing nature."

So much needed to be done. Marshes to be drained, prairies to be plowed, forests to be cut, river beds to be turned inside out in search of gold, wild buffalo to be destroyed and replaced by domestic cattle, predators to be exterminated. The invading culture went to work with vast energy — building roads and railroads and telegraph lines; canals, bridges, and dams; homes and churches and structures of state. It was seen as good, important work. As one Oregonian booster put it, "When improved and embellished . . . [Oregon would become] the loveliest and most envied country on earth."

In winter, when the sun traveled unseen in the south and the eerie curtain of the Aurora borealis hung in the starry sky, Eskimos moved toward the coast. During the dark months, seal and walrus became their staff of life. The walrus was their hardware store. Shoulder blades made snow shovels. Ivory tusks became ice picks, sled runners, harness swivels, buckles, weapons, and images. This pipe, in the shape of a walrus lying on its back holding the bowl, is made from an ivory tusk decorated with scrimshaw.

But to Native Americans, the earth was already a complete landscape, fully furnished with everything necessary to sustain both physical and spiritual life. Although they knew about building houses and — particularly in the East — taught the Europeans much about farming, it made no sense to erect a church when the earth itself was sacred and every action of one's life was an act of worship. Native Americans understood the unbreakable link between the spirit of a bison — the mysterious force that caused the great animal to stand upon its strong legs and breathe the clear air and race across the plains — and the souls of people. They understood that from the earth comes life, and that all life sustains all other

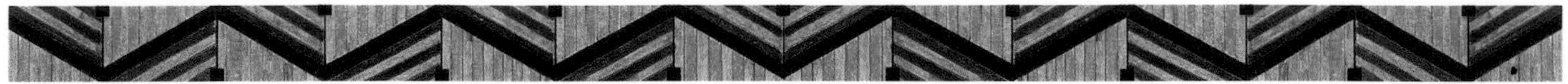

life, without rancor or jealousy or bitterness, because all beings are threads in the same great fabric.

Even today these lessons are everywhere. In the desert country of southern Arizona and California, the stony ground bakes beneath the summer sun, reaching temperatures of 160 degrees and higher. It is a fitting place for cacti, spiny lizards, rattlesnakes, and unexpectedly, toads. These soft-skinned amphibians require constant moisture to live. They breed and lay eggs in ponds. The eggs hatch into tadpoles, which must have a place to swim until they become adults with legs and lungs. The desert seems an unlikely place to find toads, yet toads occur in North American deserts in greater abundance and variety than anywhere else on the continent.

The explanation for this lies in thunderstorms and clay. Although summer is the hottest time of year, it is also the time of violent thunderstorms, when several inches of rain might fall in a matter of minutes, creating shallow ponds where hours before there was nothing but dried clay. The clay softens, and in the night the ponds fill with spadefoot toads. Named for their ability to dig their way backward into damp soil, they have spent months — up to two years — in underground dormancy, like seeds waiting for favorable conditions. Sensing abundant moisture, they force their way to the surface and launch themselves into a frenzy of rehydration, reproduction, and feeding. When the water dries up, the toads vanish back beneath the hardening clay like a desert mirage. The entire event might last only one night. Eggs might dry up before hatching. But for a brief time the clay produces toads by the hundreds and thousands. And although Western science can prove that wet clay does not spontaneously become a toad, in a metaphysical sense it is clear that toads and other things do arise from what southwestern tribes call Grandmother Clay — an expression of the earth's amazing ability to bring forth life.

If clay serves as a metaphor for the land, then all the objects pictured in this book find their origins in clay. The spirit of the earth shows itself through the hands of its people, and each object reflects the maker's closeness with and reverence for nature. For example, in carving a new mask for healing ceremonies, an Iroquois member of the False Face Society does not take just any chunk of wood. He carefully chooses a basswood tree and speaks to it. He requests a portion of its power before carving the mask into the living wood. The last act is to cut away the empowered mask without further damaging the tree.

These native rituals do not spring from simple superstitions, as if the tree spirit, like a ghost, will come haunt the mask maker if he does it wrong. The understanding goes far deeper than that. The only haunting comes from within one's own heart;

Sioux horn spoon

it is the self-inflicted pain of disharmony or imbalance. To perform these rituals correctly is to seek the sense of balance that comes from being right with the world. The Iroquois mask retains the power of the tree, and the act becomes a kind of communion.

To Native Americans, religion, art, and daily life are all the same thing. In fact, art is not a strictly accurate term. Many Indian languages lack a distinct word for art, since there is no distinction between art and life. Art is life. The two are inseparable. A life lived in balance is a work of art, and any object made by a balanced person is an object of art. Or to put it another way, an artfully crafted object reflects the true path of life being walked by its maker.

These objects also reflect the natural settings of their origins. The masks and totem poles and cedar boats of the Pacific Coast bring to mind images of ocean and coastal forests. Foaming surf pounds beaches of black volcanic sand. The smell of saltwater mingles with the pungent fragrance of ferns and rotting wood. Cold rivers brown with tannin pour across the tidal flats. They bring the scarred trunks of fallen fir and cedar trees to the sea, where they drift among seals, otters, orca, and migrating humpback whales.

Eastern objects reflect a drier forest where seasons are defined by the changing foliage of deciduous trees and shrubs: The leaves are light green in spring, darkly translucent come summer, flaming with cyanin pigments in autumn, and replaced by snow crystals in winter. Although the eastern woodland people were farmers (growing the highly valued

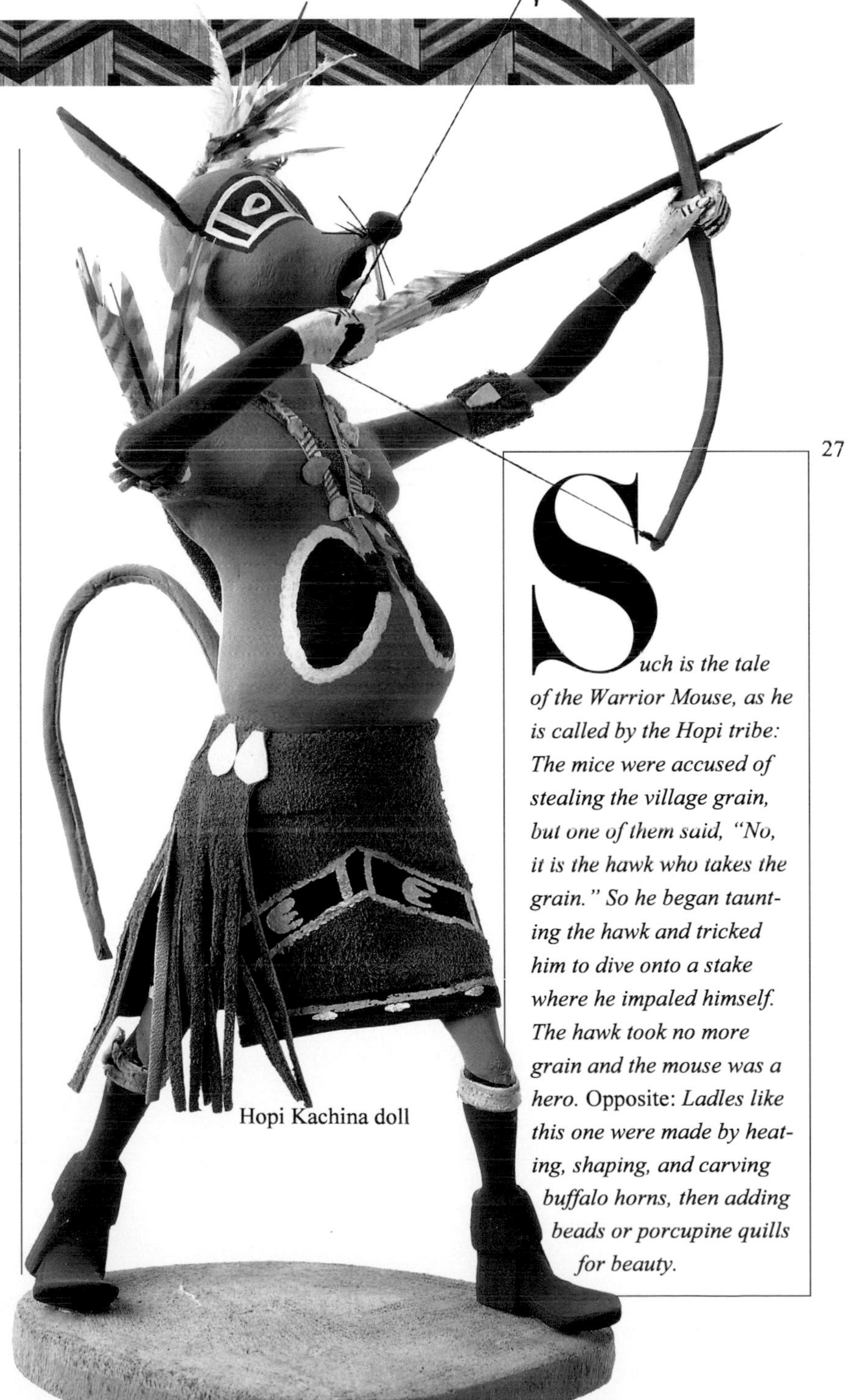

Hopi Kachina doll

Such is the tale of the Warrior Mouse, as he is called by the Hopi tribe: The mice were accused of stealing the village grain, but one of them said, "No, it is the hawk who takes the grain." So he began taunting the hawk and tricked him to dive onto a stake where he impaled himself. The hawk took no more grain and the mouse was a hero. Opposite: *Ladles like this one were made by heating, shaping, and carving buffalo horns, then adding beads or porcupine quills for beauty.*

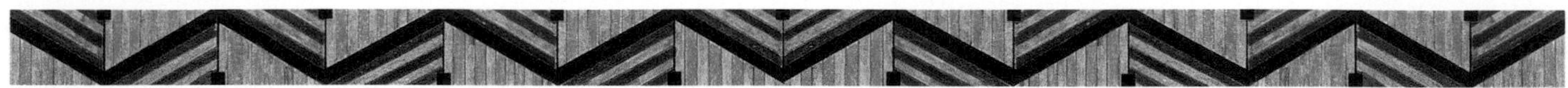

Three Sisters — corn, beans, and squash), they also lived by hunting white-tailed deer, wild turkeys, ducks, geese, and other animals. They took fish, freshwater mussels, and turtles from the rivers. Among building materials, the bark of birch trees stood preeminent; it was used in wigwams, tipis, canoes, cradleboards, containers, and more.

Between the mountains of the Pacific Coast and the eastern forests, the center of the continent had yet a different character. It was a generally arid region dominated by sun, sky, wind, and vast horizons. Second only to the sun, the great source of sustenance was the bison, the buffalo of western romance. These great animals supported plains cultures for centuries only to vanish in a matter of decades beneath the implacable demands and different values of the new settlers.

In many ways, the world that inspired the objects displayed in this book has disappeared. Bison herds no longer sail like cloud shadows over the grasslands of the Great Plains. The eastern hardwood forest lies dismembered and shrunken, its pieces scattered from Maine to Florida, from Texas to Minnesota. For the salmon that once turned the rivers red in their migrating millions, the land has become a place of death, not rebirth. Today their very survival hangs in the balance.

Understanding the inspiration for Native American art requires a view of North America as it appeared in its natural condition. Fortunately, many places remain on this continent — notably in our national parks and wilderness areas — where an illusion of pre-Columbian conditions survives. Although much has changed, it is still possible, by visiting the right places, to imagine the landscapes of a hundred or five hundred or more years ago. At the same time, it is necessary to do more than imagine lost scenes from pristine America. We have to remove things. Take away the roads, the dams, the powerlines and fences and administrative boundaries, which not only slice up the land but force our thinking into the short-term and rectilinear. We need to forget our map-view of states and rivers and mountain ranges and replace it with a ground-view, one derived from walking the trails and riding the open miles. We need to know how it was to move at a human, non-mechanical pace before there was an option. When we walk now, we know that we can also ride in a car. What must it have felt like to walk when walking was the only way?

The handworks of Native Americans can help. The beauty of these objects, what they reveal of the hearts and hands of the men and women who made them, can provide us with a human-crafted window on a world long gone. Like old photographs of vanished landscapes, or stories from dusty books, they tell of an ancient order based on the workings of nature and remind us that we are all children of the land.

Eskimo bear carving

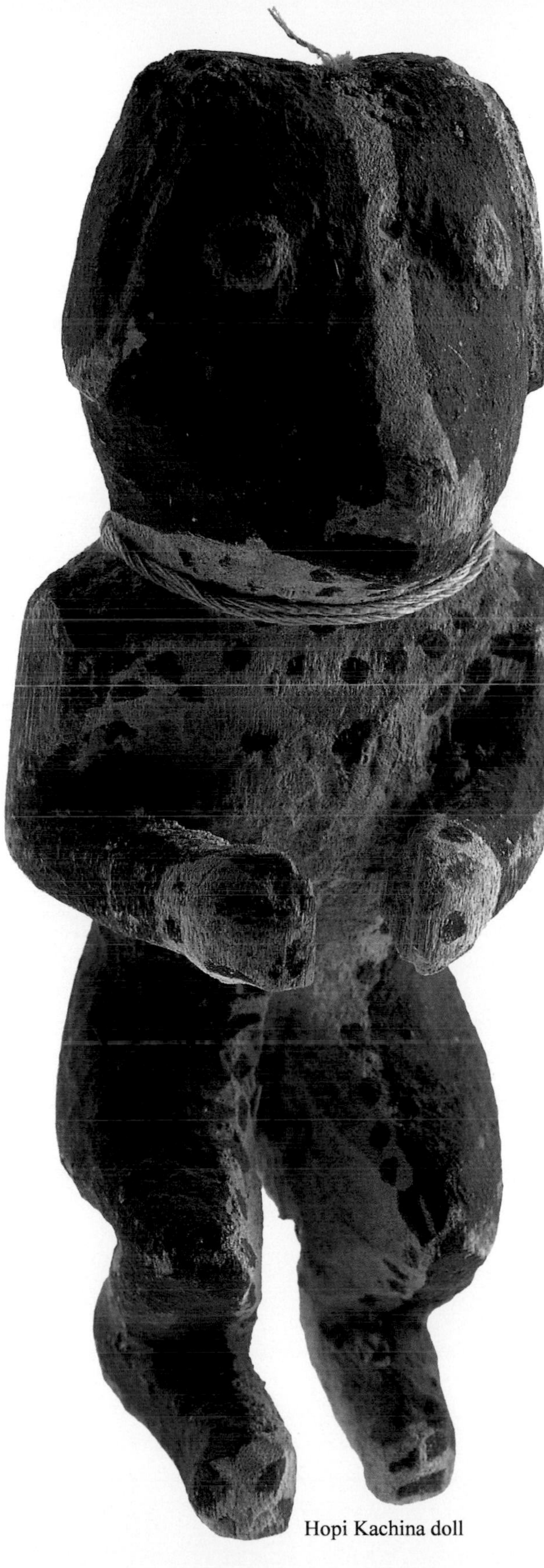

Hopi Kachina doll

The Indians' only domestic animal was the dog, protector and friend of every person in the world. The spirit of the dog said, "I shall always remain with the people. I shall be a guardian for all their belongings. I shall be a carrier of their burden." The nomadic plains Indians used dogs to transport their belongings on travois, wooden frames dragged along the ground. Even in the Pueblo villages of the southwest dogs came to greet the people. Opposite: *Carved figures like this soapstone bear served as good luck charms, for the bear's meat and fur were highly prized.*

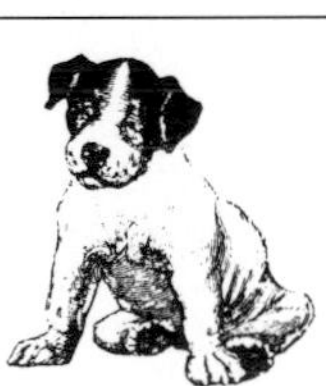

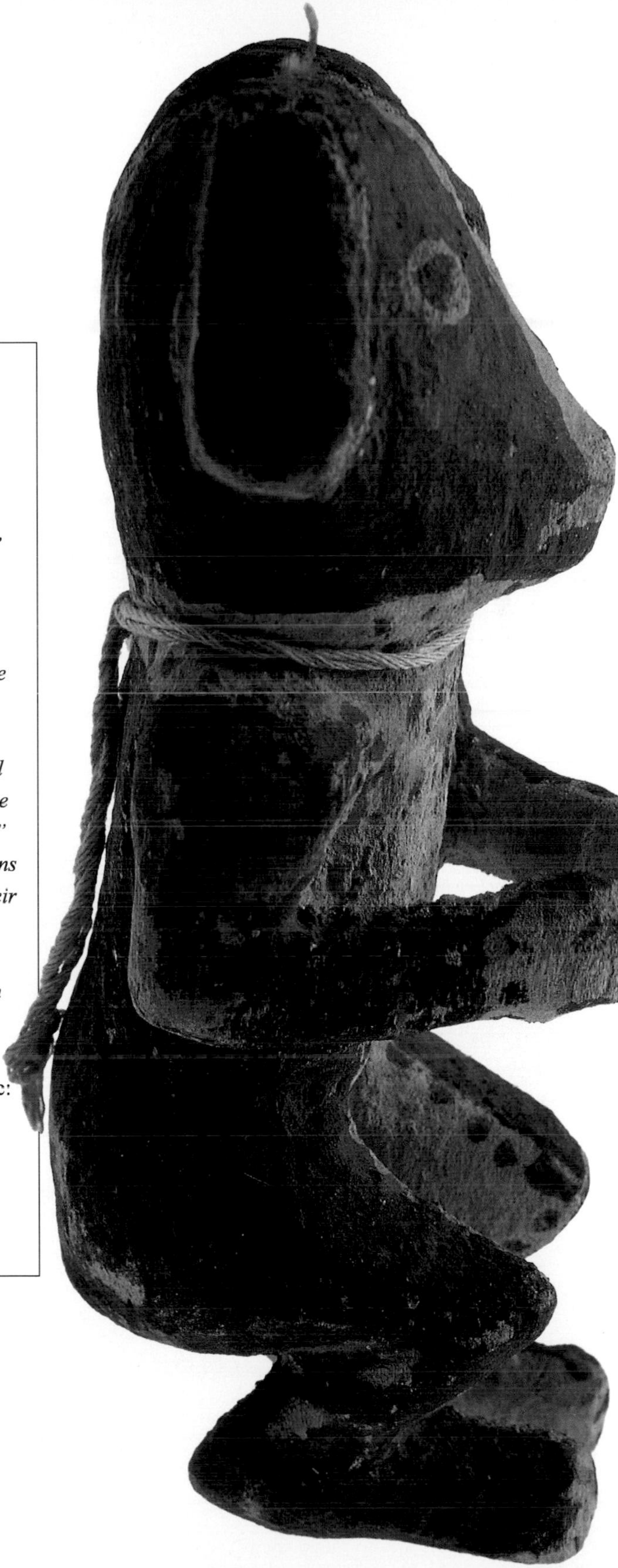

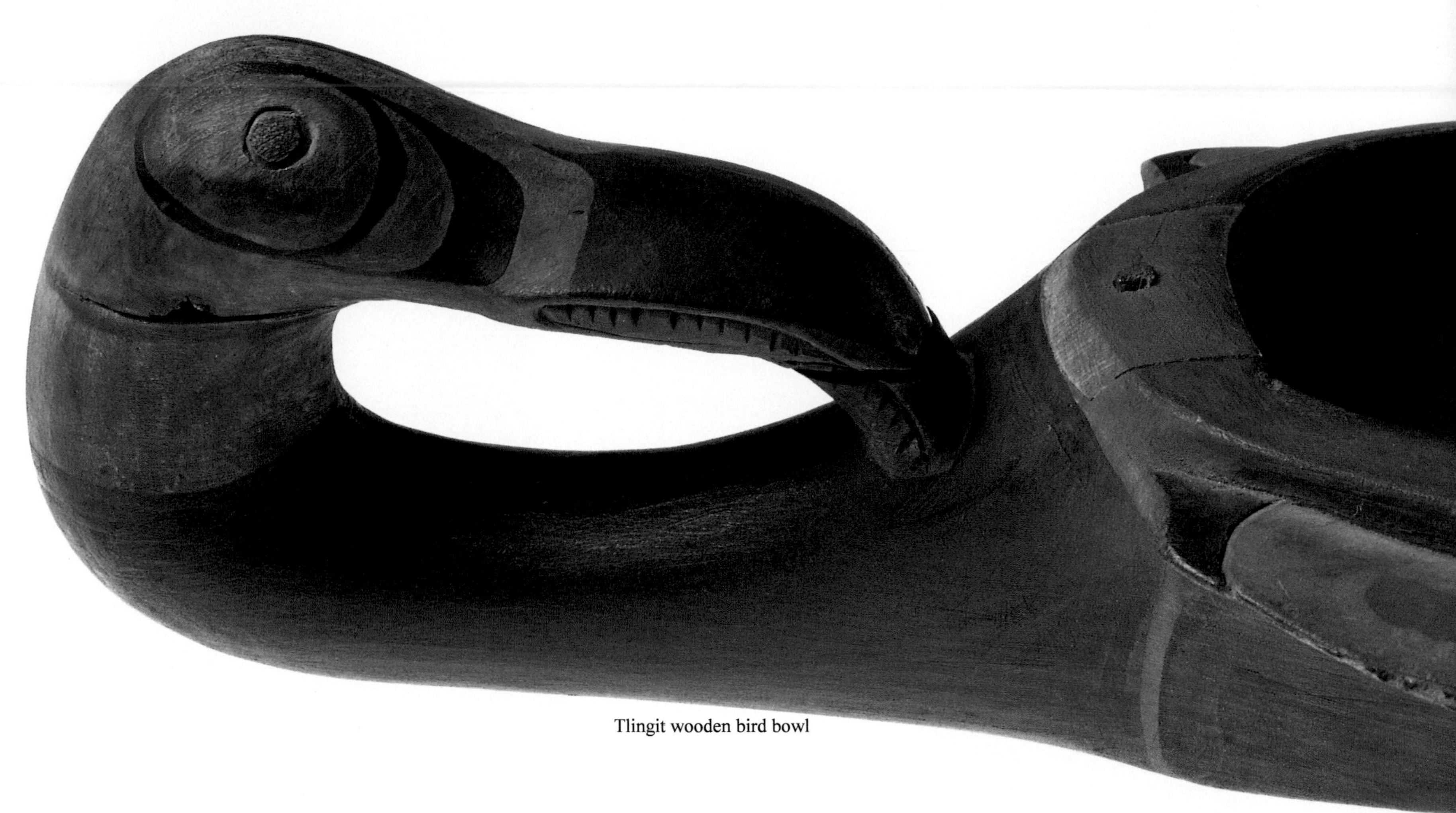

Tlingit wooden bird bowl

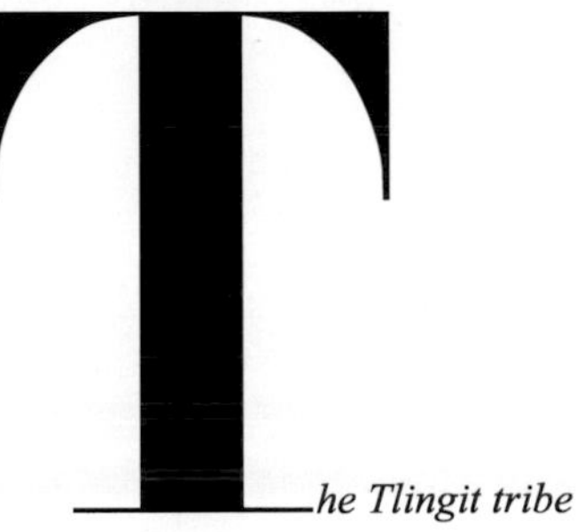

he Tlingit tribe believed that birds had supernatural powers and were friendly and concerned with everyday activities such as fishing and eating. This wooden bowl represents a merganser or fish duck. It was used as a dish for holding fish oil obtained by boiling eulachon, or candlefish, and skimming the oil from the surface of the cooking vessel. The oil was eaten as a dip with almost every meal, and in large amounts at potlatch ceremonies.

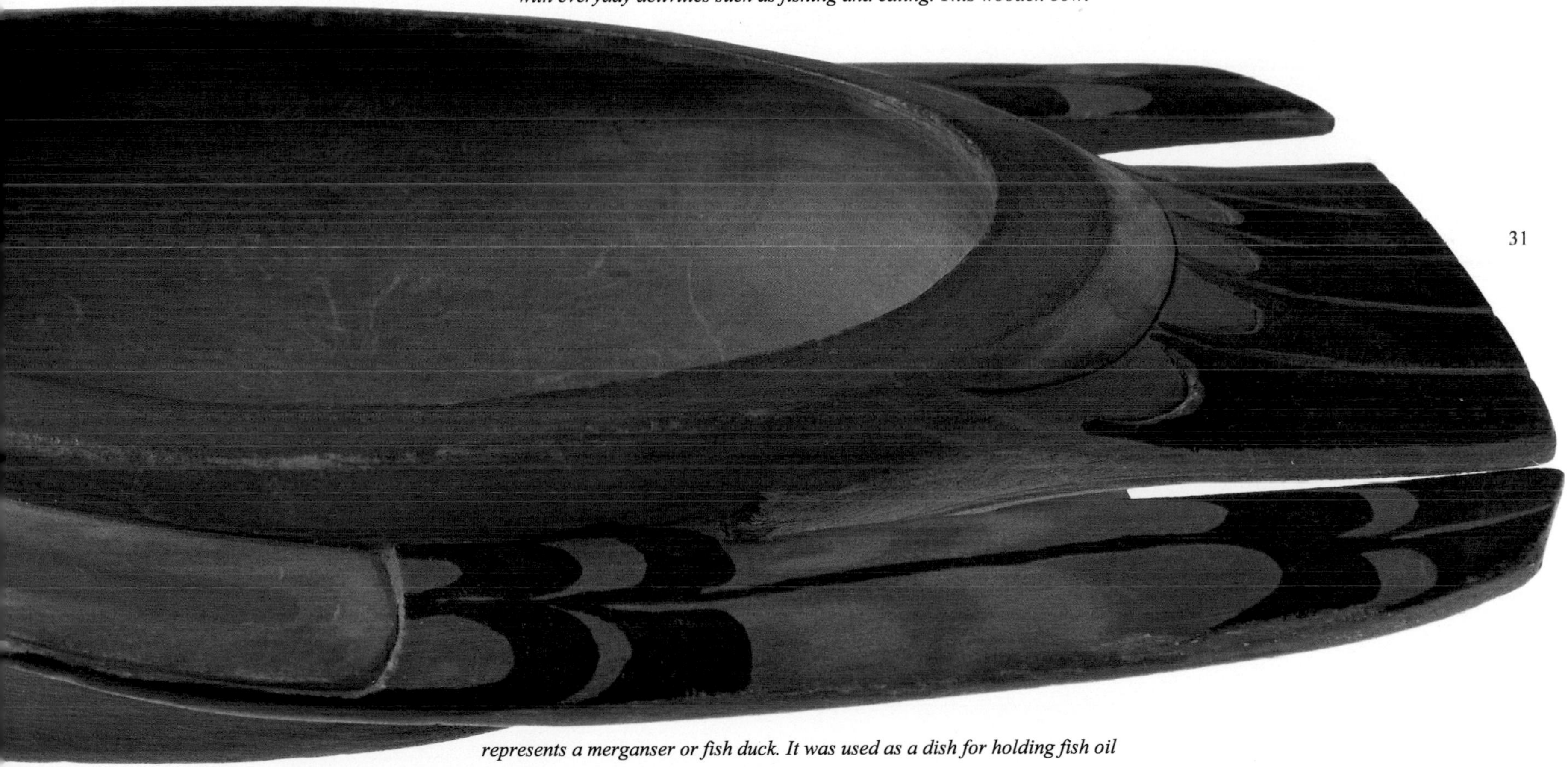

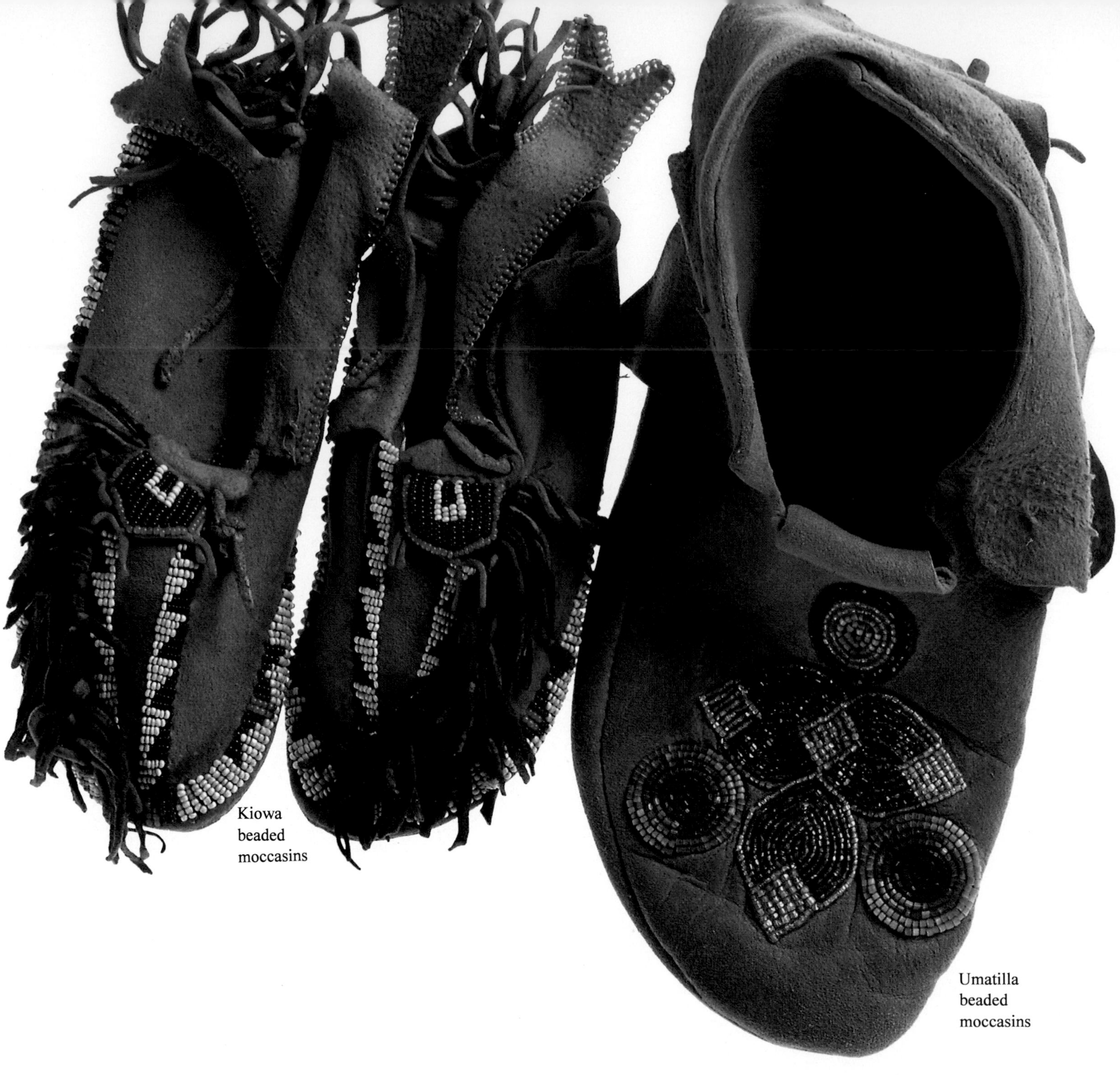

Kiowa beaded moccasins

Umatilla beaded moccasins

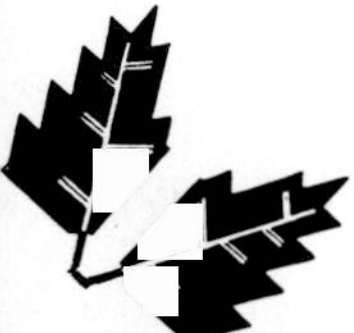

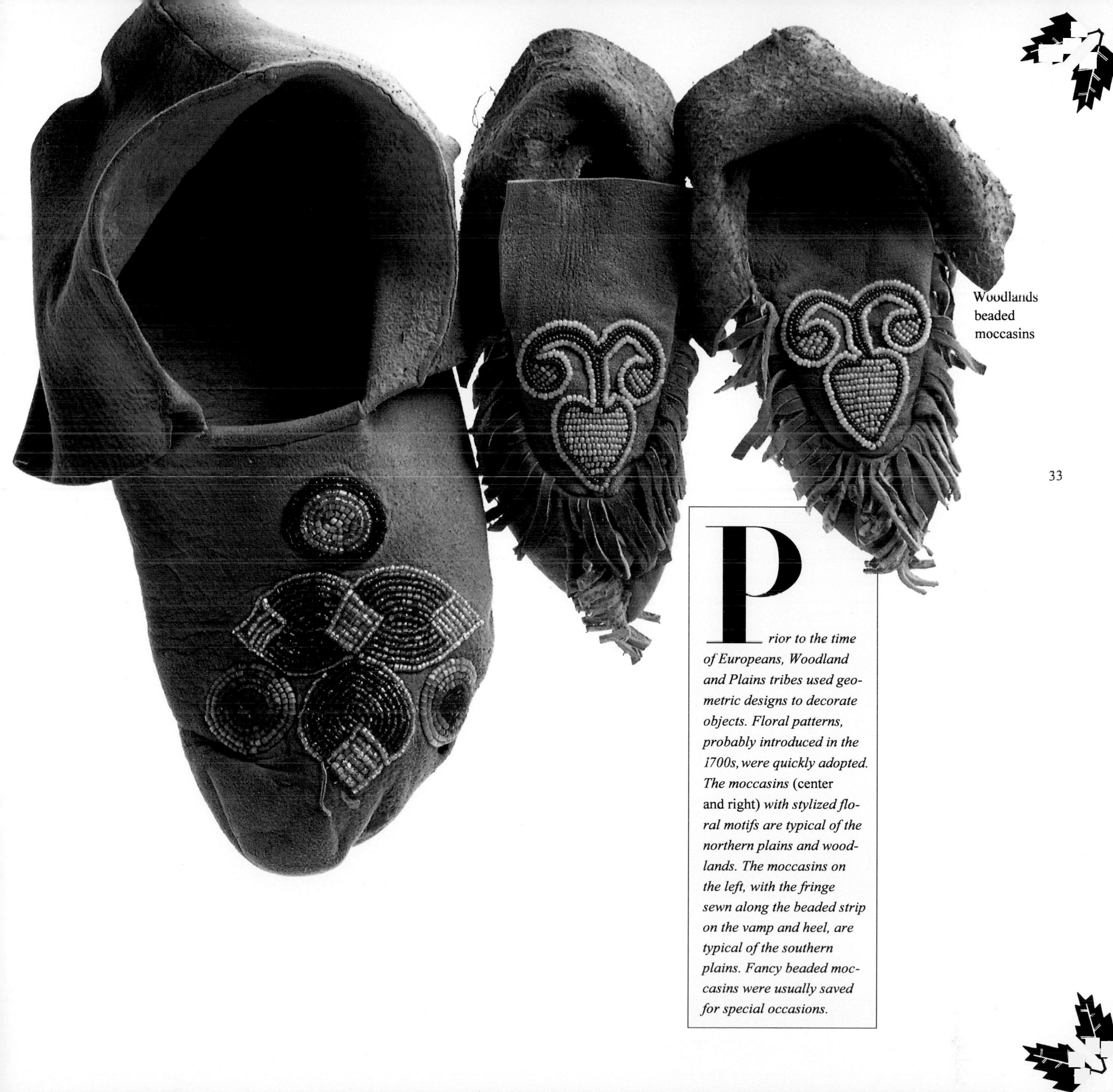

Woodlands beaded moccasins

Prior to the time of Europeans, Woodland and Plains tribes used geometric designs to decorate objects. Floral patterns, probably introduced in the 1700s, were quickly adopted. The moccasins (center and right) *with stylized floral motifs are typical of the northern plains and woodlands. The moccasins on the left, with the fringe sewn along the beaded strip on the vamp and heel, are typical of the southern plains. Fancy beaded moccasins were usually saved for special occasions.*

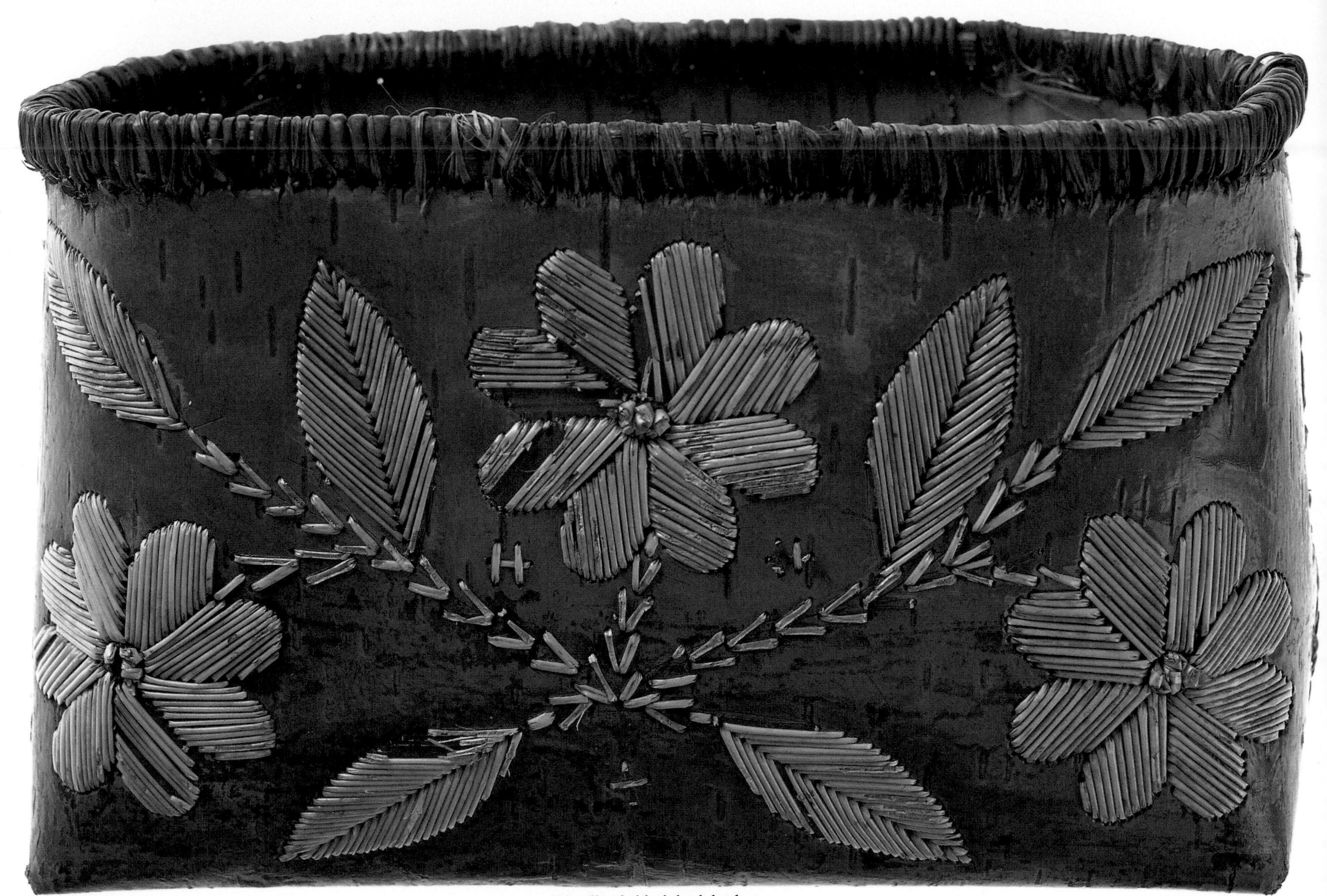

Woodlands birch bark basket

***B**irch bark* (opposite) *was one of the most important materials available to the tribes of the northern woodlands. Bark containers, often decorated with porcupine quills, were made in many different shapes including boxes, trays, and bowls.* Right: *After European traders introduced glass beads and velvet, women of the woodlands made stylized floral designs using an appliqué stitch, sewing and tacking down every three beads as with this colorful bag.*

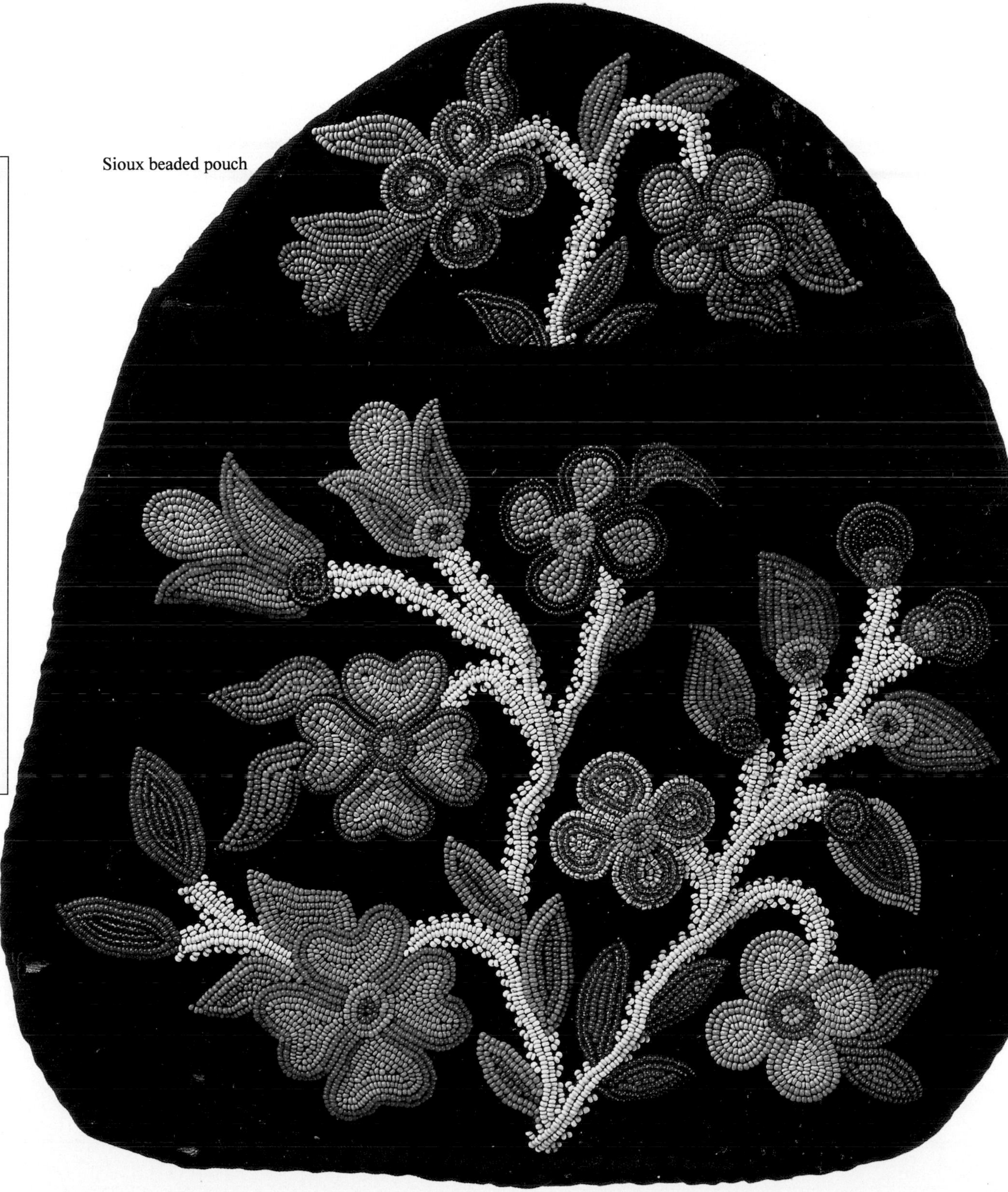

Sioux beaded pouch

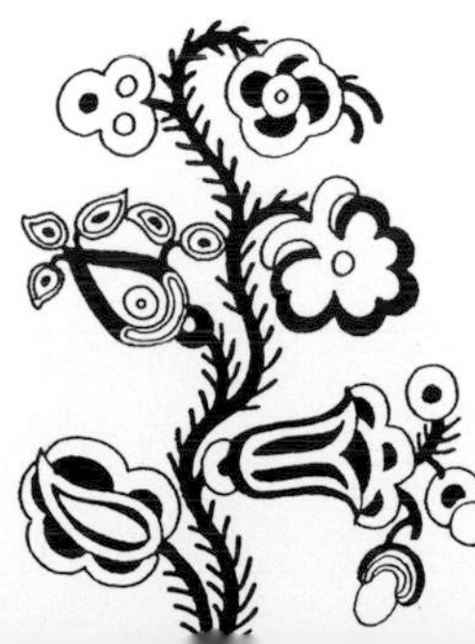

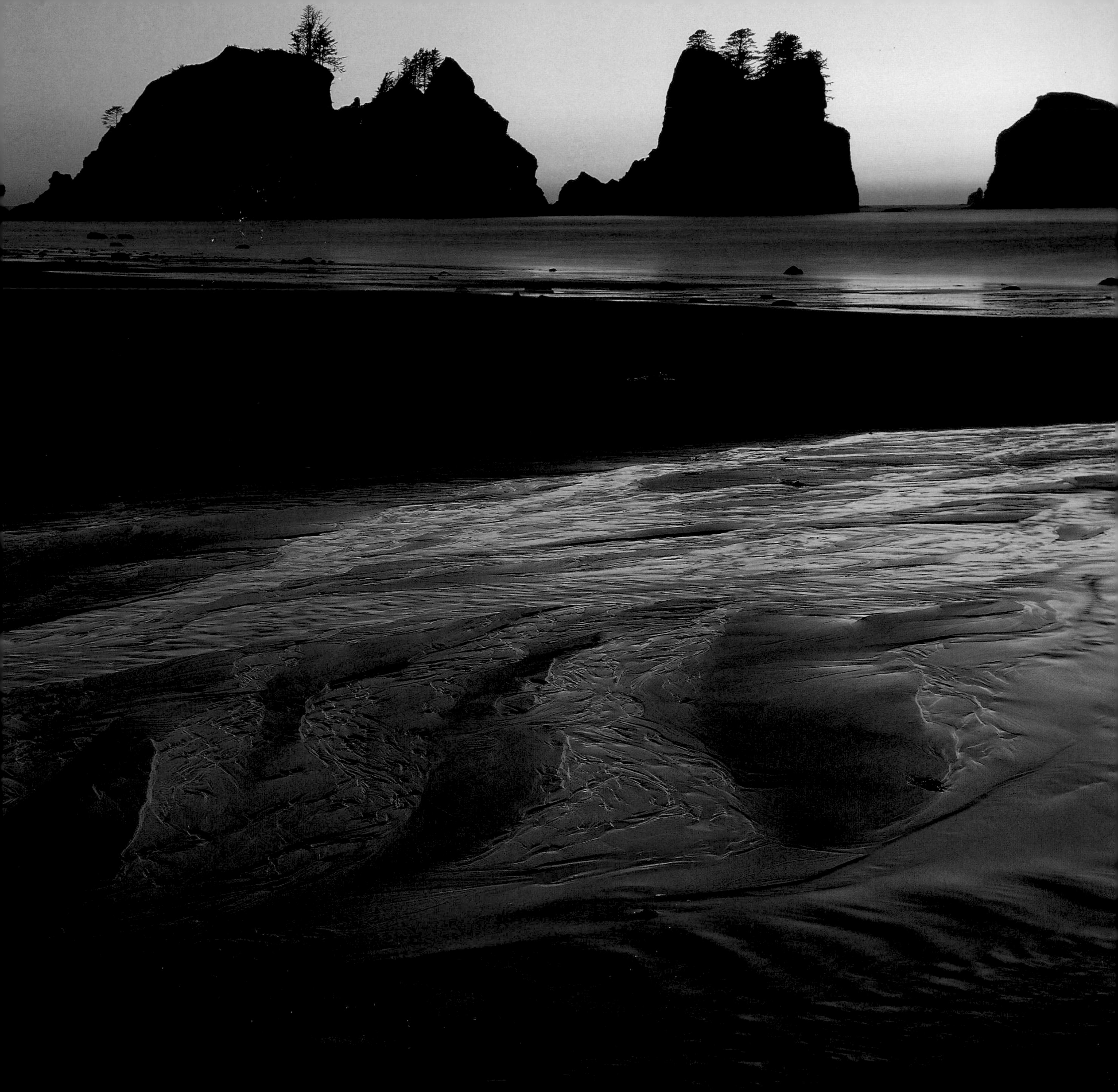

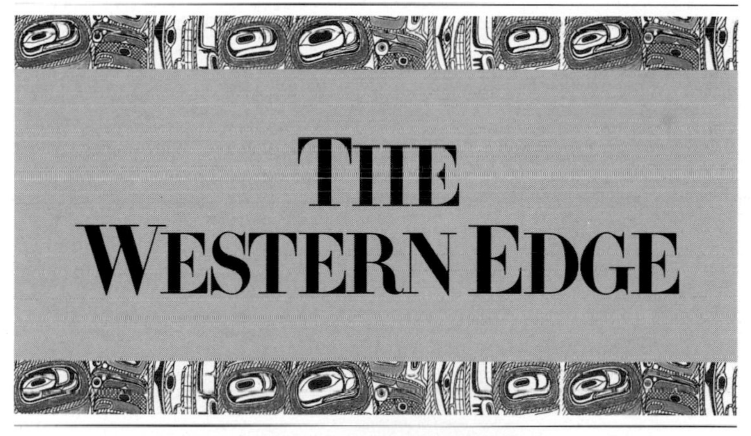
THE
WESTERN EDGE

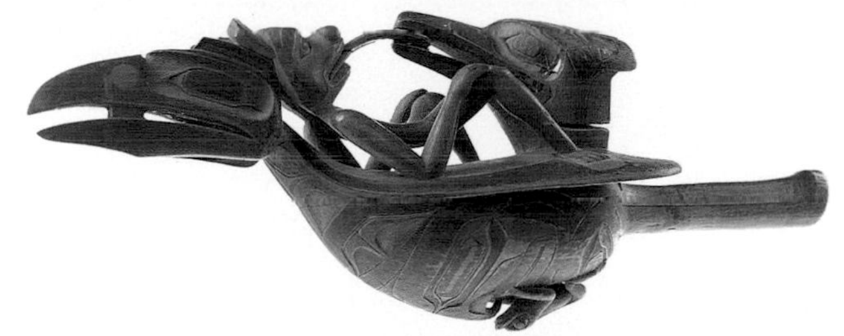

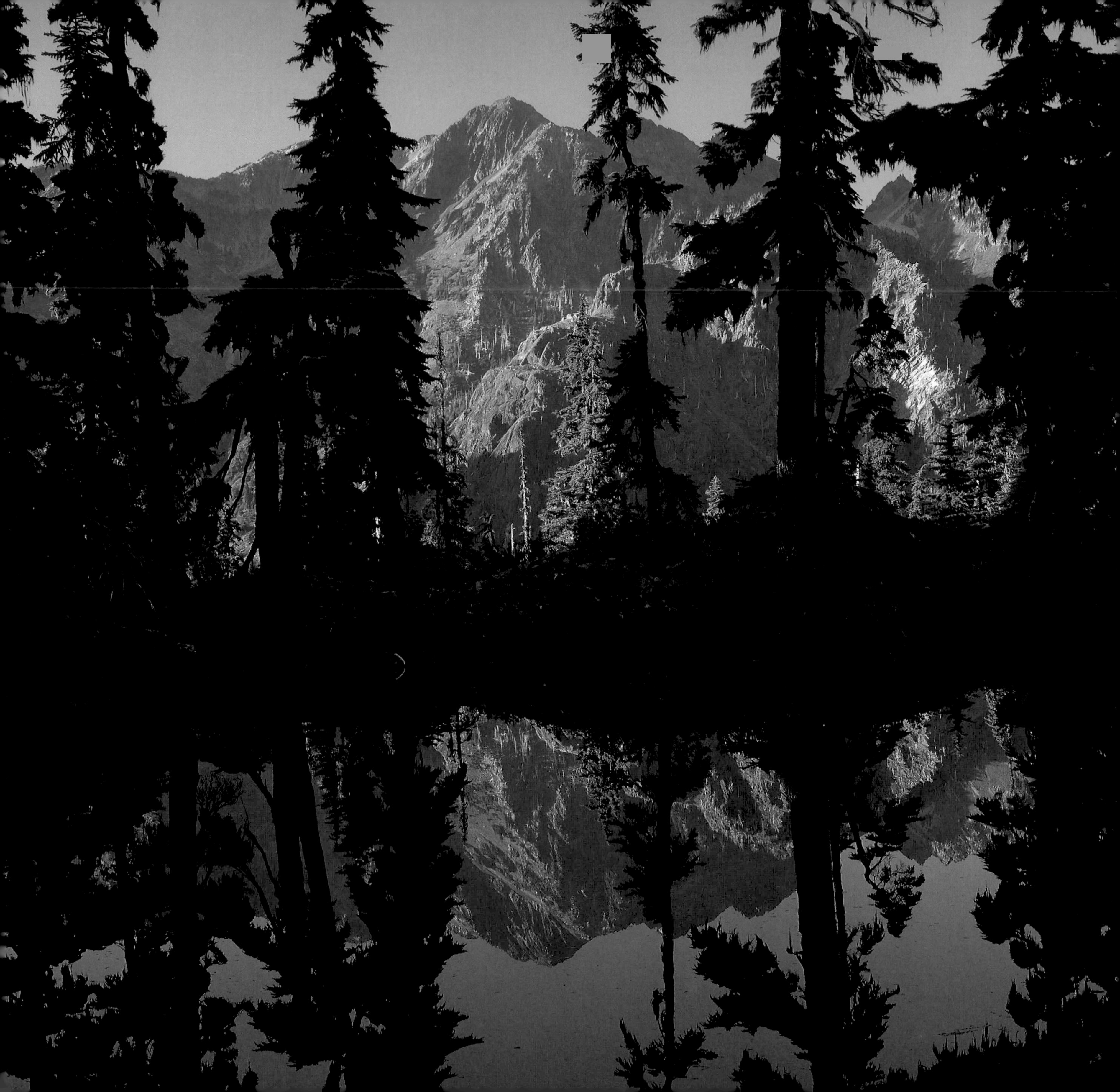

THE WESTERN EDGE

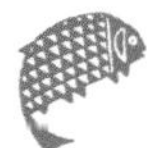 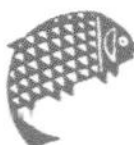 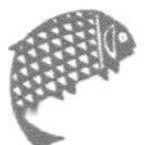

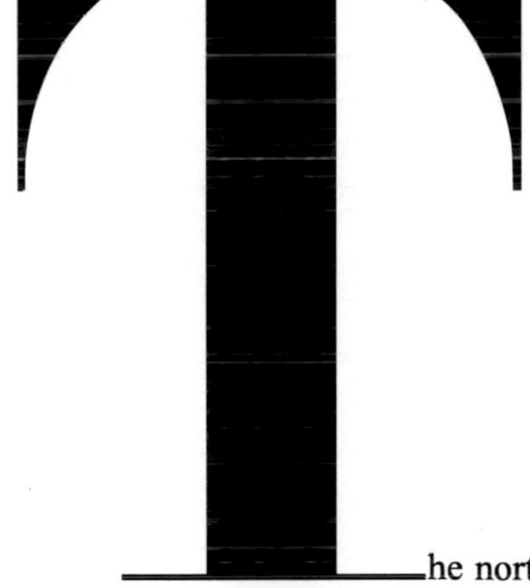

The northern Pacific Coast is a silver-grey landscape of moving water, where the ocean pounds against a rain-soaked shore and dark branches of conifers fade like dream figures into rolling billows of mist. The wind tears at lofty treetops, while far below, on the soft and silent forest floor, falls a gentle, filtered rain.

It is a complex, rugged coast. British Columbia alone measures about five hundred miles from one end to the other, but in that distance are folded some sixteen thousand miles of shoreline twisting through a maze of islands, rocky headlands, sand beaches, and sea stacks—natural rock pillars standing offshore like the ruins of flooded temples. From the sea, mountains rise sharply to frozen peaks that support the largest glaciers in North America.

In this land of mist and rain and the smell of the ocean, the climate is strongly affected by currents circulating in a clockwise direction in the northern Pacific Ocean. The currents bring not only moderate temperatures but also nutrient-rich waters to the coast. All around the world, coastal waters are more productive than waters in the deep

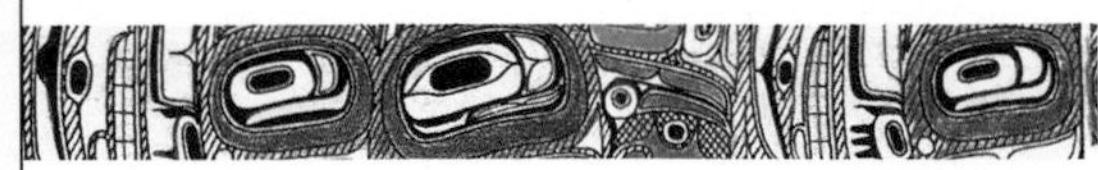

*W*orking with willow, redbark, bulrush root, and digger pine root fibers, the Pomo Indians of California's northern coast developed basketmaking into a high art. Their exquisite designs, incorporating feathers, beads, and shells, were highly prized even by visitors from different tribes. When gathering natural materials, the basket weaver always offered a prayer to the spirit of the land and the creator for taking what was needed.*

ocean, and the Northwest Coast has one of the richest fisheries on earth.

The land, too, is extraordinarily productive. Abundant melting snow and rain pour off high coastal mountains, feeding big rivers that teem with salmon returning to their place of birth. Sea birds populate the flyways: gulls, cormorants, ducks, puffins, auklets, murres, loons. Osprey and bald eagles take fish from the dark shadowed waters of coastal inlets, while the croak of ravens—sometimes somber, sometimes shouting with pleasure—is never silent. The offshore waters are populous with humpback whales, sea lions, porpoises, orca, and vast shoals of herring. Life here moves according to the ebb and flow of tides, the pound of waves, and the seasonal rhythms of migrating animals.

This place we call the Northwest Coast stretches from southeast Alaska to northern California. For centuries it has been the home of the Tlingit, Haida, Tsimshian, Makah, Kwakiutl, Chinook, and other tribes—people of the watery fringe, living on the coast just beyond the reach of winter storm waves or on the banks of large rivers, their backs to the forest, their faces toward the ocean.

Historically, some of their food came from the land. Native people hunted deer, elk, bear, and other animals, and they gathered plant foods, including the rich variety of berries for which the Northwest is still famous. But for the most part, they looked to the water for their needs and found them abundantly met.

From the ocean came halibut, cod, rockfish, perch, smelt, and eulachon, or candlefish, a small silver creature containing so much oil that its dried body could be threaded with a wick and lit like a candle. From sandy beaches, rocky outcrops, and tide pools there were clams to be dug, oysters and mussels and limpets to be pried loose, and other creatures to be caught by hook and line.

Most important of all were the salmon taken from coastal rivers. Caught with dipnets, impaled on three-pointed spears, or pulled from traps and weirs, some were eaten fresh but most were smoked and dried for winter. Salmon were considered no ordinary fish, but a race of immortal humans who had generously changed their forms to provide food for people.

Coastal people also hunted large mammals on the open sea: porpoises, sea lions, sea otters, harbor seals, and of enormous significance, whales. What an event it must have been: A single gray whale could feed a village for weeks and provide a variety of other materials as well. Every part had a use—the oil, the bone, the baleen. People even ate the barnacles attached to its skin. The size and value of whales was matched only by the difficulty of hunting them, an activity

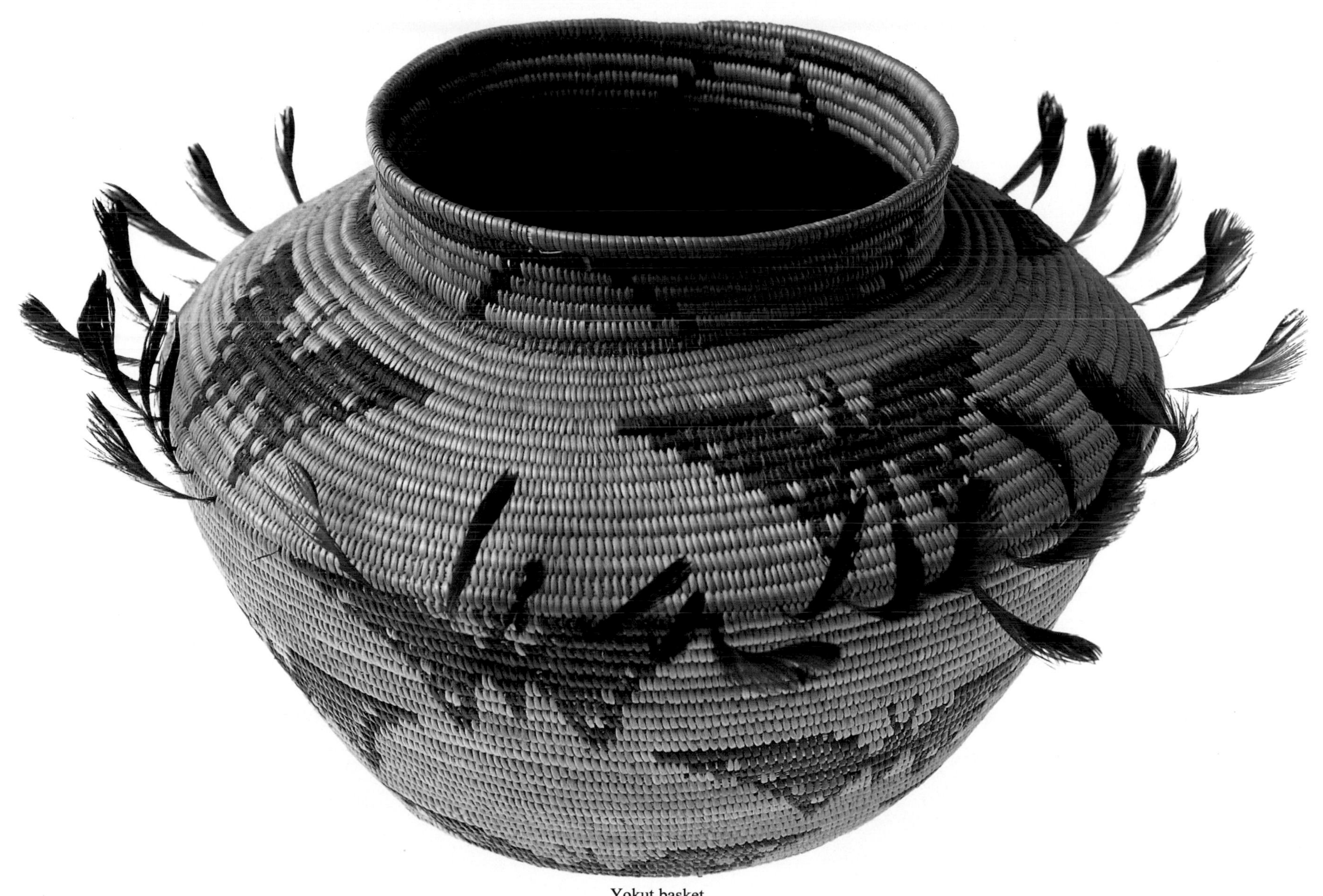

Yokut basket

that required sophisticated boats and navigational skills, elaborate preparations, both physical and spiritual in nature, and a coordinated community effort. The Makah and Kwakiutl, living around Vancouver Island and the northern coast of Washington, were the best whalers, capable of venturing onto the open sea in search of the biggest quarry. Their boats were more than fifty feet long. They used harpoons of yew tipped with sharpened shell points, and although just getting within contact range of a whale was a great accomplishment, the contest that followed was the stuff of winter tales. In went the harpoon and down went the whale, dragging a line of inflated sealskin floats hurriedly thrown overboard by men assigned just that task. If all went well, the floats would slow the animal and weary it enough for the paddlers to approach it again, this time to kill it with long lances. The chase might last for hours or days at a time might result in a triumphant return, dragging a whale. It might also end in tragedy when a boatload of men were caught by storm and swallowed by the sea.

Baskets decorated with woodpecker, quail, and duck feathers were used by the Pomo in religious ceremonies. Other baskets, decorated with sea shells and glass beads, were made for giving away.
Opposite: *Far to the north along the Alaskan coast, the Chilkat people wove blankets from cedar bark and mountain goat's wool. First sketched by men on wooden boards, stylized designs of animal eyes and fish fins were then woven into blankets by women. Such blankets were symbols of wealth and were worn at ceremonial gatherings.*

Northwest Coast people were not farmers; their only crop was tobacco, which they never planted in large quantities. But neither were they nomads. They were something unusual among the world's cultures, having developed a complex society based in permanent settlements without agriculture. Unlike the plains tribes, coastal people had no need to continually move in search of good hunting. The ocean was generous. It provided more food than they could use. In a few months of hard work, an entire year's food supply could be gathered and preserved. And although people might leave for weeks or months at a stretch—as they did during summer salmon runs—they would return in winter to coastal villages, some of which were occupied continuously for hundreds of years. This combination

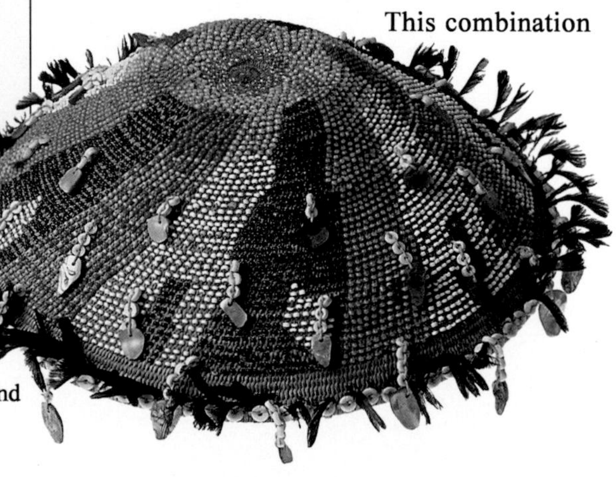

Pomo feather and shell baskets

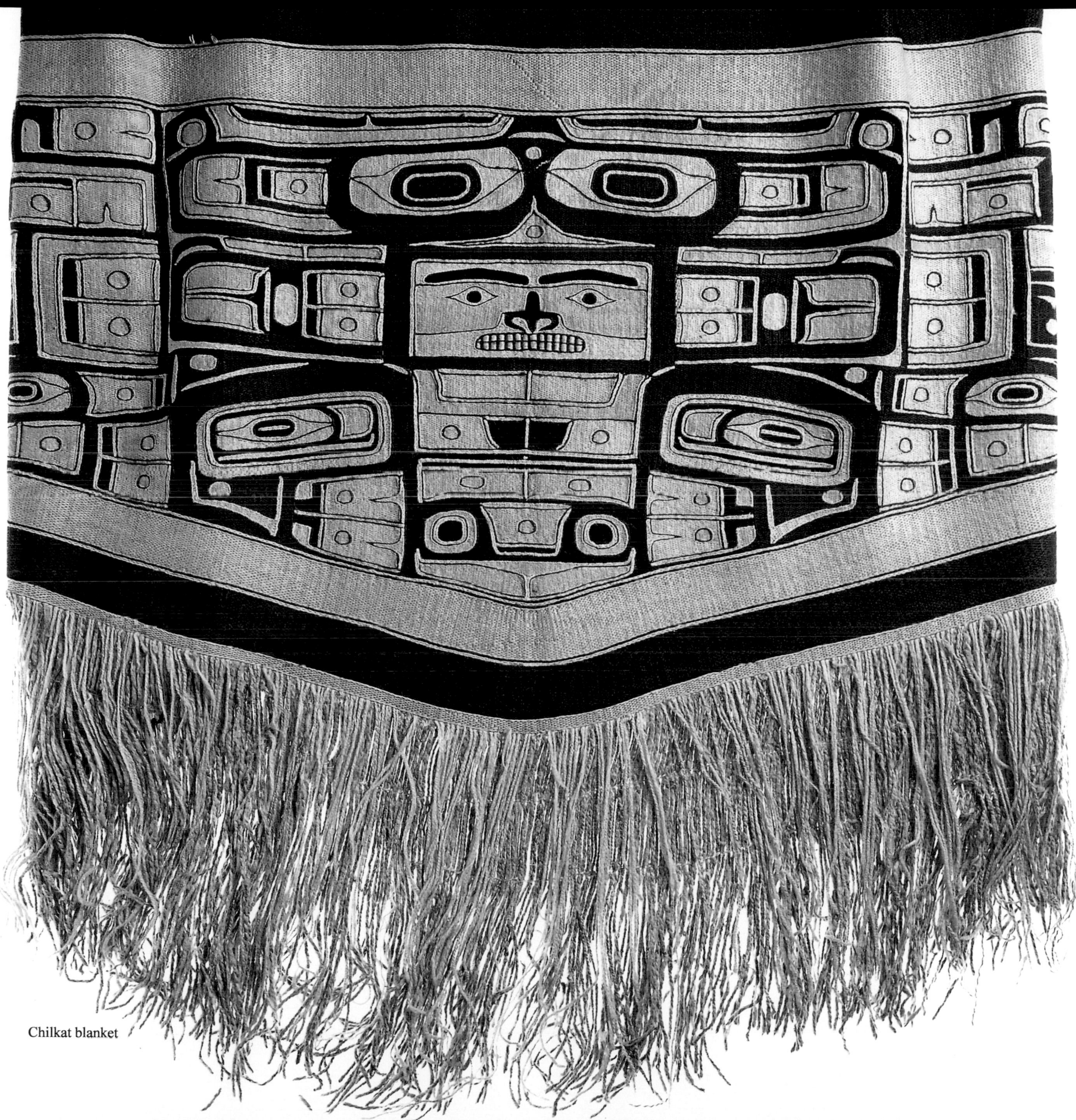

Chilkat blanket

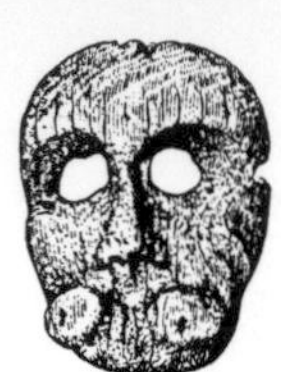

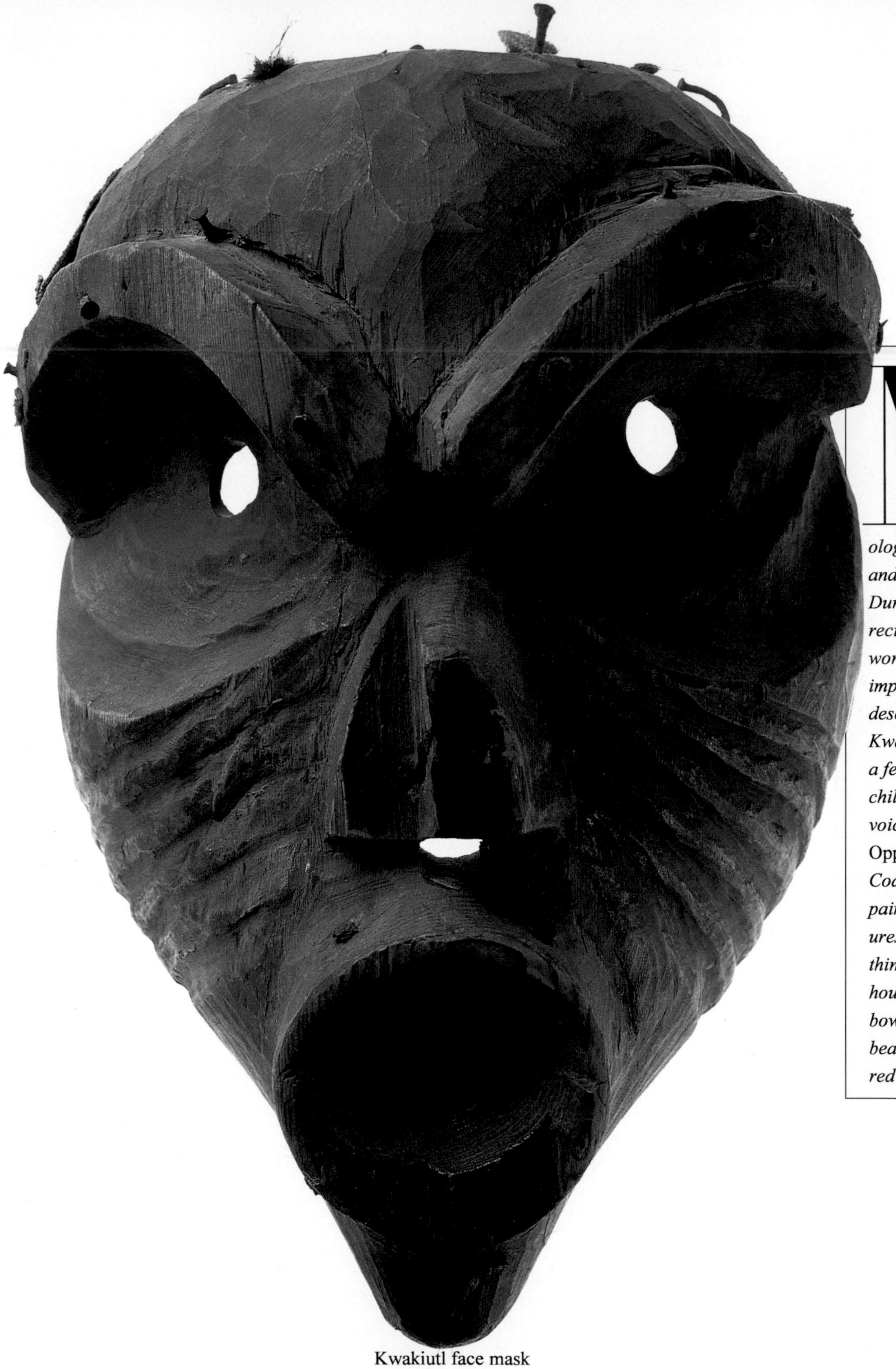

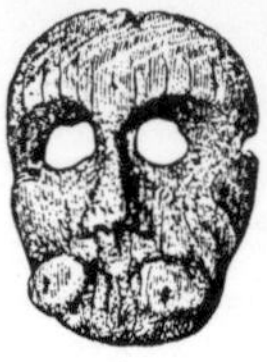

Mythology was based on nature and the natural world. During winter, storytellers recited myths while actors wore masks and robes to impersonate the characters described. On the left is a Kwakiutl mask representing a female ogre who devours children. Her whistling voice is heard in the forest. Opposite: *The Northwest Coast Indians carved and painted mythological figures on just about everything from the walls of houses to the smallest bowls, like this eagle-and-beaver oil dish carved from red cedar.*

Kwakiutl face mask

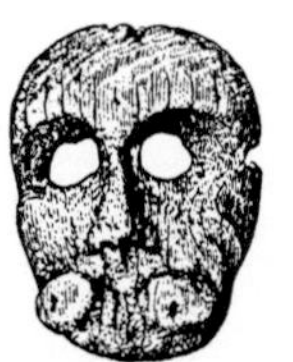

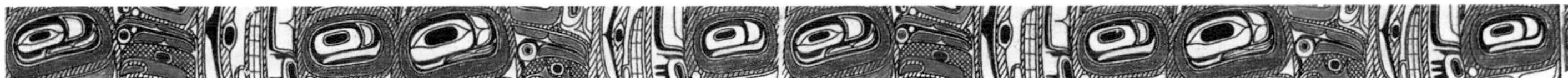

of a settled way of life and abundant food made it possible for people to build large houses and to fill them with possessions. It also gave them time to pursue activities such as trade, art, the development of ritual, and the acquisition of wealth. Coastal tribes developed distinct social classes in which the status of individuals and of families was defined by what they owned. This included not only physical belongings but titles, totems, privileges, hunting territories, and the rights to perform certain dances and songs. Some possessions were inherited, others could be earned, and still others were acquired at potlatches — complicated affairs during which wealthy persons would assert and reinforce their status by giving away much of what they owned.

While there were social reasons for acquiring things, good materials were also available for making them. From the forest came abundant wood, cedar ranking as the most important. An excellent carving wood, cedar splits easily into rot-resistant boards and shakes, makin it ideal for house construction. The bark, too, was useful woven into baskets, mats, and bags and pounded into a remark ably soft material for clothing (yet not so desirable or expen- sive as mountain goat wool). Besides cedar, there was yew, known for its strength and used for harpoon shafts, bows, and canoe paddles. Red alder, harder to split than cedar and less likely to crack, was chosen for bowls and food storage vessels.

Rough woodworking was done with stone wedges and mallets. Blades made of shell were capable of finer work, while finishing touches could be applied with sharkskin, which served as a natural sandpaper. Metal was essentially unknown, although copper, the most valued of all commodities, was mined by inland tribes and brought to the coast by Tlingit mid- dlemen. They even had some steel knife blades — obtained perhaps through trade or from the wrecks of Asian junks that drifted to North America on the same ocean currents

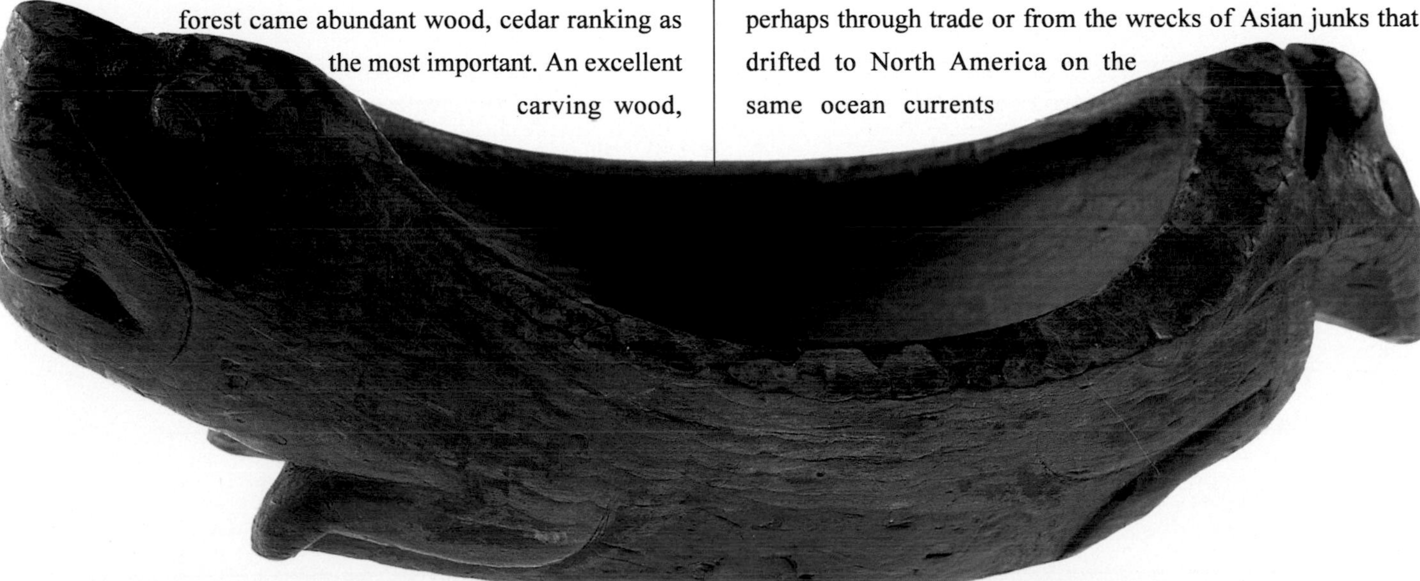

Haida oil dish

that today bring glass net floats to the beaches of Washington and British Columbia.

Other materials and finished objects they obtained through trade. For example, the Haida made the best canoes, and these they would exchange for baskets, blankets, abalone shells, and whale products from southern tribes. Or from northern people, they would get mountain goat horns and skins, Chilkat blankets, and ivory from northern sea mammals.

Elaborate carvings are symbolic of the Northwest Coast cultures—from the faces on totem poles to halibut hooks to elaborate masks used in rituals. Totem poles developed from the carved supporting pillars of longhouses. Nowhere was this more impressive than among the Haida, who combined the poles with doorways, so that people entering a house did so through a rounded opening in a massive carved pillar.

Although house designs varied with the tribe, basic building techniques were similar all along the coast—heavy frameworks of shaped, interlocking timbers were covered with slabs of wood or bark. Such houses resembled big, rectangular boxes. Nootka and Kwakiutl builders laid slabs of wood on the roof like overlapping tiles, weighting them down with stones to keep them in place during winter gales. In gentler seasons, the occupants could use long poles to shift the loose boards to let in light or to let out smoke. For walls, they fastened boards horizontally like clapboards and chinked the gaps with seaweed. Farther north, the Haida built walls with vertical planks set into grooved timbers at the tops and bottoms. Like so many aspects of these cultures, the sizes were larger than life. One house in the Puget Sound area (actually a number of houses joined together) was 540 feet long and 60 feet wide.

The Haida made large storage boxes from single boards that were scored across the grain at what would become corners and then steamed and folded to make the four sides. The bottom was another piece grooved so the sides could into it. The containers were tight enough to hold water or oil; some were used as cooking vessels by dropping hot rocks into the liquids they held.

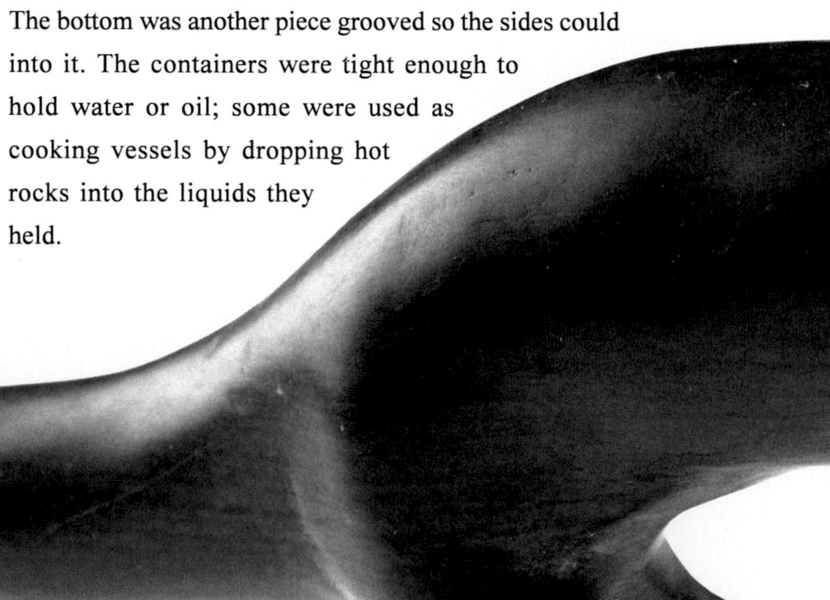

Great care went into the making of ritual masks. The Kwakiutl thought of humans and animals as primordial kin; at the time of creation, all creatures possessed both an animal and a human nature. Some removed their animal appearances, revealing human forms hidden beneath. Others kept both forms. Dancers with animal masks didn't simply pretend to be animals; they were acknowledging kinship with their animal ancestors. Expressing the same idea, transformation masks showing animal heads could be opened to reveal a carved human face beneath the first layer.

From the northern sea came riches: dentalium shells, walrus ivory, and sea otter skins prized by tribes throughout the west. Although the otter was an important animal, the early Eskimo, struggling to survive in the cruelest of environments, had little time for carving. Only recently did they build a strong artistic tradition using ivory and soapstone to make animated figurines of otters and others among their fellow creatures.

Perhaps the most impressive displays of woodworking were dugout canoes. They came in all sizes, depending on their function. The largest ones, used as whaling and cargo vessels, measured up to 65 feet long and were 7 feet wide at the beam. They were carved from enormous trunks of cedar, redwood, or fir. To hollow out a tree of such dimensions with little more than stone tools and carefully controlled fires would be a significant challenge all by itself, but making a good boat involves more than gouging out the insides of a log like a giant bowl. A boat must be shaped to slice through the waves without filling with water. It should remain upright and stable in rough water. The gunwales should be light, and the keel relatively heavy. Through centuries of practice, Northwest boat builders developed ingenious techniques and sophisticated designs for accomplishing these ends. For example, to achieve the desired thickness of wood in the finished craft, they drilled small holes to a specified depth from the outside of the dugout. These served as indicators for carvers working from the inside, who would stop carving when they uncovered the holes. Later, it was a simple

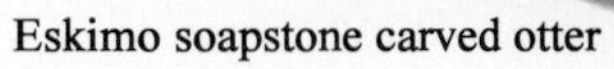

Eskimo soapstone carved otter

matter to plug the holes with paste. There was also the matter of shape. Rather than carve a complex curve from gunwale to keel, workers would fill the nearly completed boat with water and dump in hot rocks until the water boiled. This method softened the wood, allowing boat builders to spread the gunwales by hammering boards crosswise in the canoe, thus widening the beam, creating a more stable shape, and providing seats for paddlers in the process.

Southward, along the California coast, both the climate and the shoreline change character. While mist and rain saturate the northern forests, sunshine warms the south. The north is a land of silver and subdued green; the south is blue and hot yellow. Made of softer sedimentary materials, the coastal rock erodes to form a less intricate shoreline. Instead of islands and fjords, beaches and sea cliffs form long graceful arcs between headlands with few natural harbors.

Here lived the Luisenos, the Gabrielinos, and the Chumash, the Miwok, the Pomo, and other tribes. Typically, there were no large tribal organizations; it was more like extended families living in small villages scattered throughout the region. In California the land was gentler than farther north, where impenetrable rain forests hindered travel and made hunting difficult. As white settlers were to learn, California west of the Sierras was a golden, bountiful land; the original inhabitants took full advantage of the relaxed life that was possible there. White oaks provided acorns in huge quantities; there were deer, elk, antelope, bear, sheep, rabbits, beaver, and other animals. It was not hard for these tribes to make a living on dry land.

Yet for people living along the coast itself, the sea was still the dominant aspect of life, especially for the Chumash, who lived in the area of modern Santa Barbara. They built sleek canoes from pine planks and traveled to offshore islands and for miles out to sea in their hunt for swordfish, tuna, halibut, sardines, seals, and otters. Theirs was an ocean environment as rich as that of the Northwest Coast, occupied by many of the same species. Vast underwater forests of kelp provided habitat for over a hundred species of fish and various sea mammals.

Their best craftwork had to do with the sea. From planks and driftwood, they built good boats, responsive to the paddle and capable of traveling miles from shore. Using bone and shell, they carved fish hooks with the grace and beauty of jewelry. Yet in the warmer climate, their houses and other accoutrements were simple—a fact that deceived the first white settlers into thinking the people were primitive.

How wrong they were is demonstrated by the Pomo, who lived north of San Francisco Bay. They developed basket-making into a high art, with intricate, sophisticated shapes and gorgeous decorations of feathers, beads, shells, and other items. These baskets take their place beside the best of their kind from anywhere in the world and demonstrate well how nature inspires some of the most pleasing of human creations.

Haida potlatch ladle

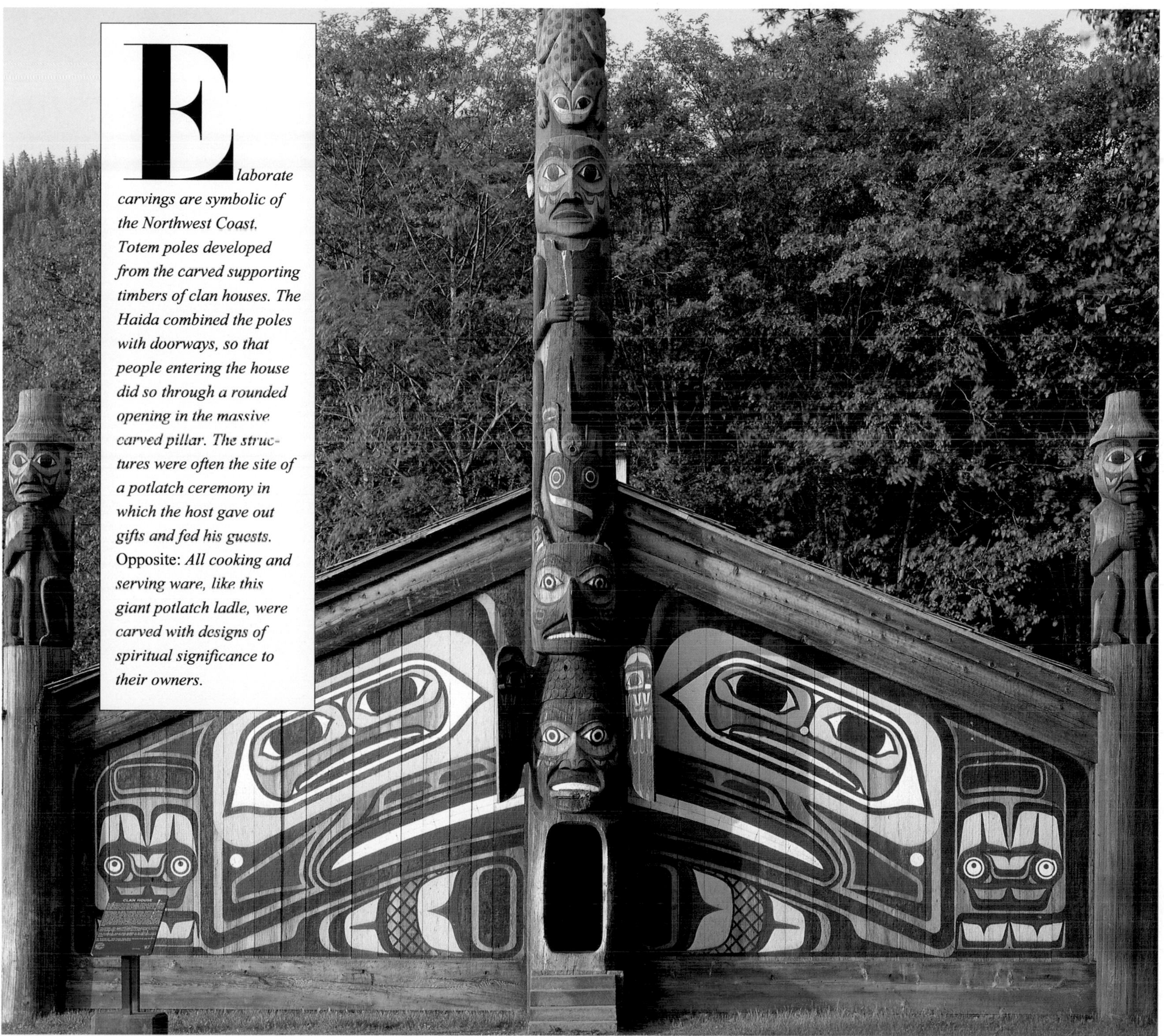

Elaborate carvings are symbolic of the Northwest Coast. Totem poles developed from the carved supporting timbers of clan houses. The Haida combined the poles with doorways, so that people entering the house did so through a rounded opening in the massive carved pillar. The structures were often the site of a potlatch ceremony in which the host gave out gifts and fed his guests. Opposite: *All cooking and serving ware, like this giant potlatch ladle, were carved with designs of spiritual significance to their owners.*

Clan or potlatch house

Among Northwest Coast tribes ceremonial masks represented spirits and mythological creatures. Even if they portrayed the same spirit, no two masks were the same; each carver interpreted a given story his own way. One story tells of a horri-

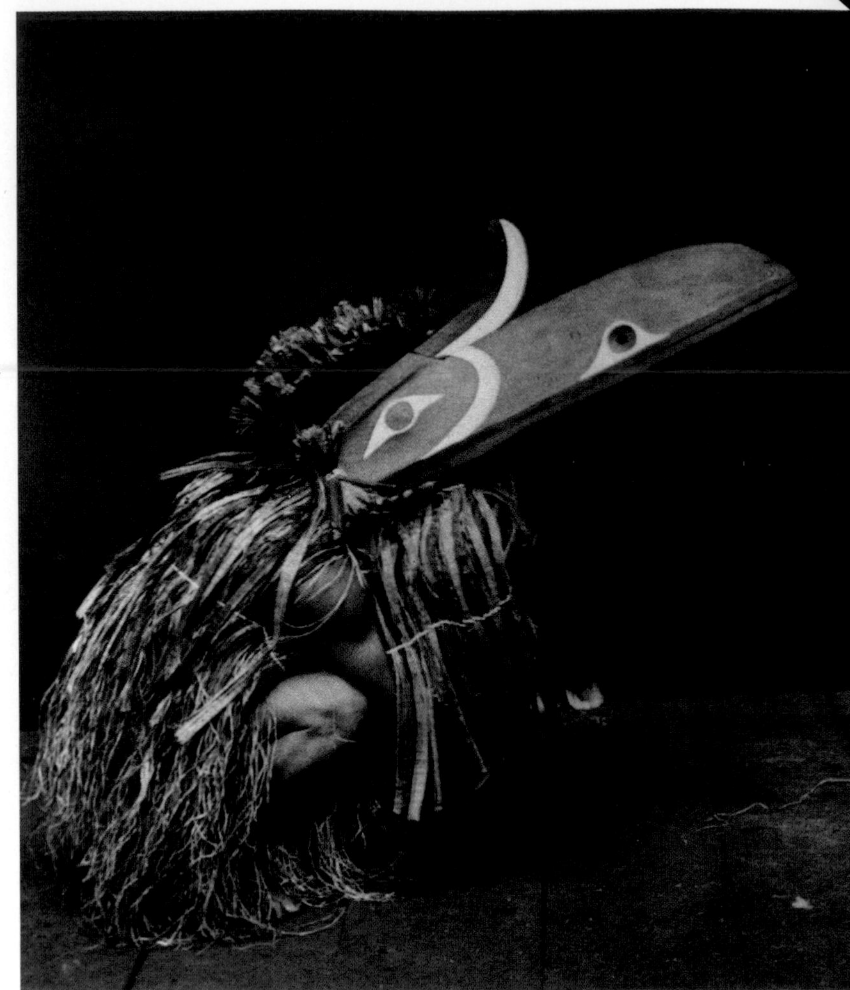

Kwakiutl dancers

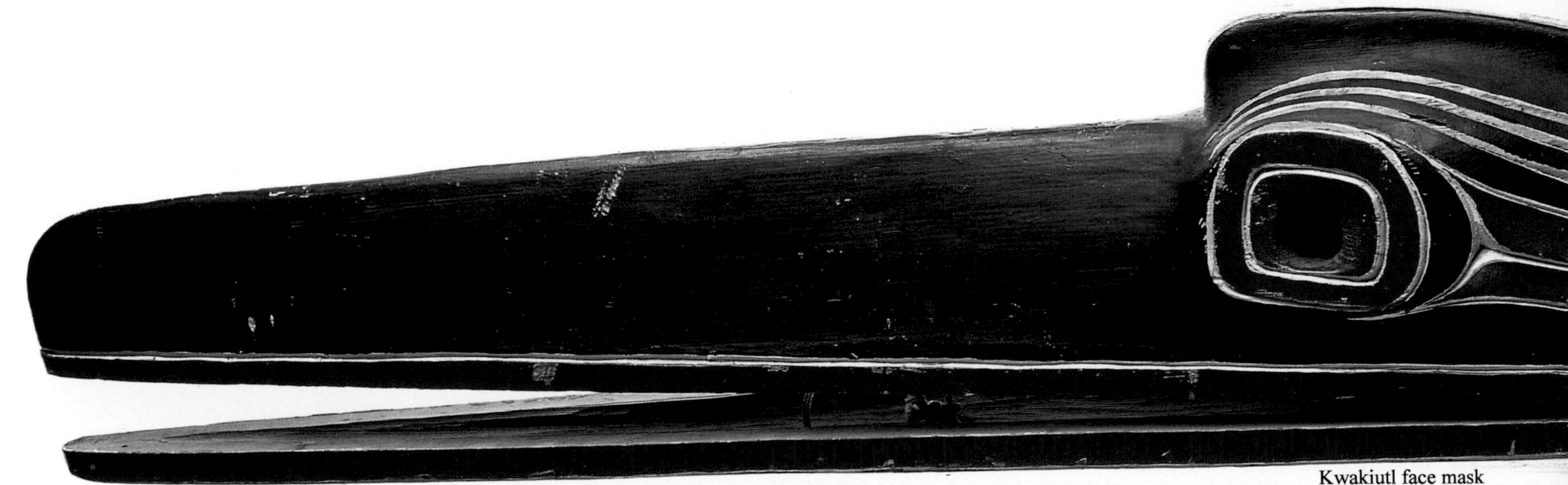

Kwakiutl face mask

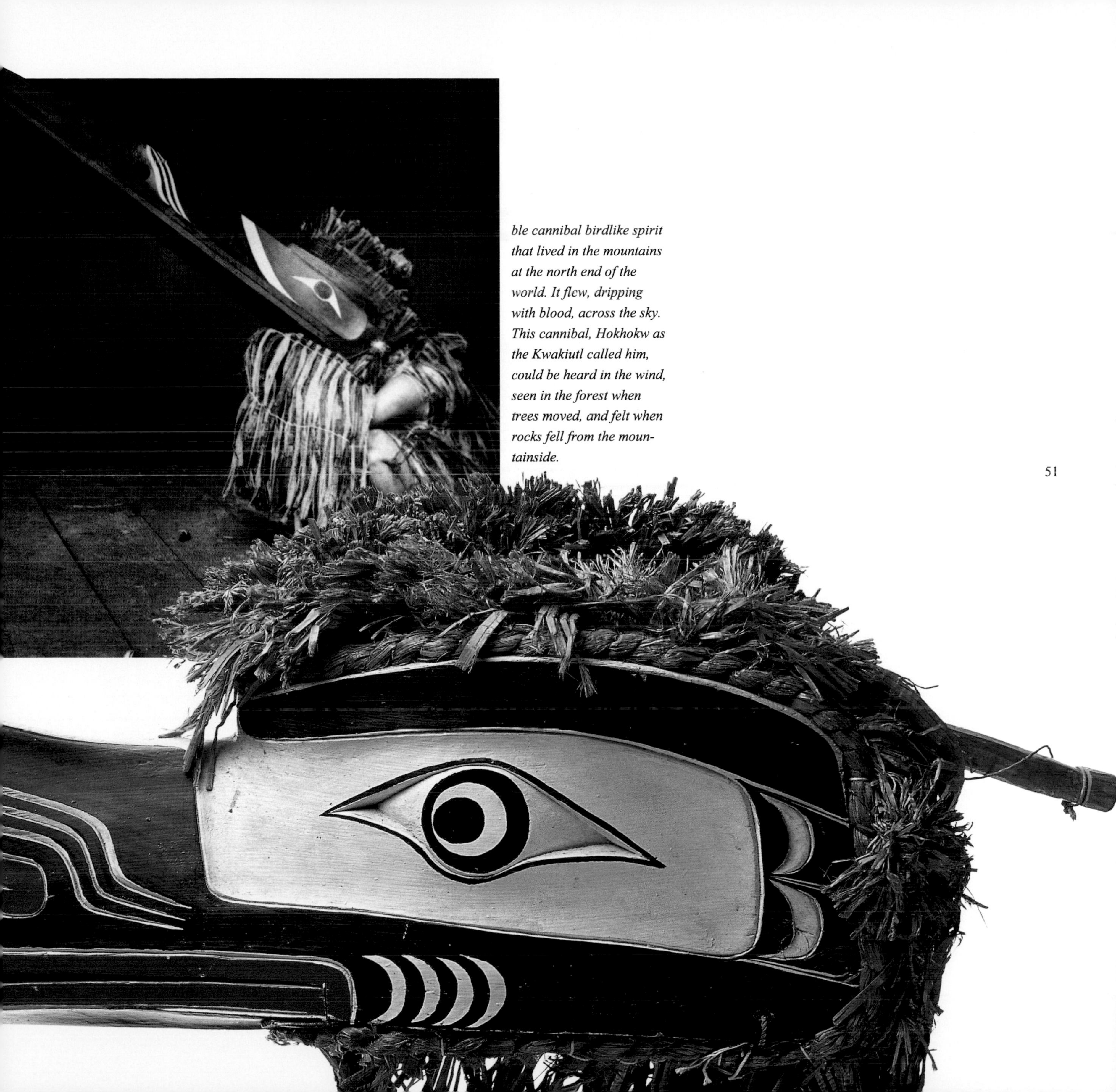

ble cannibal birdlike spirit that lived in the mountains at the north end of the world. It flew, dripping with blood, across the sky. This cannibal, Hokhokw as the Kwakiutl called him, could be heard in the wind, seen in the forest when trees moved, and felt when rocks fell from the mountainside.

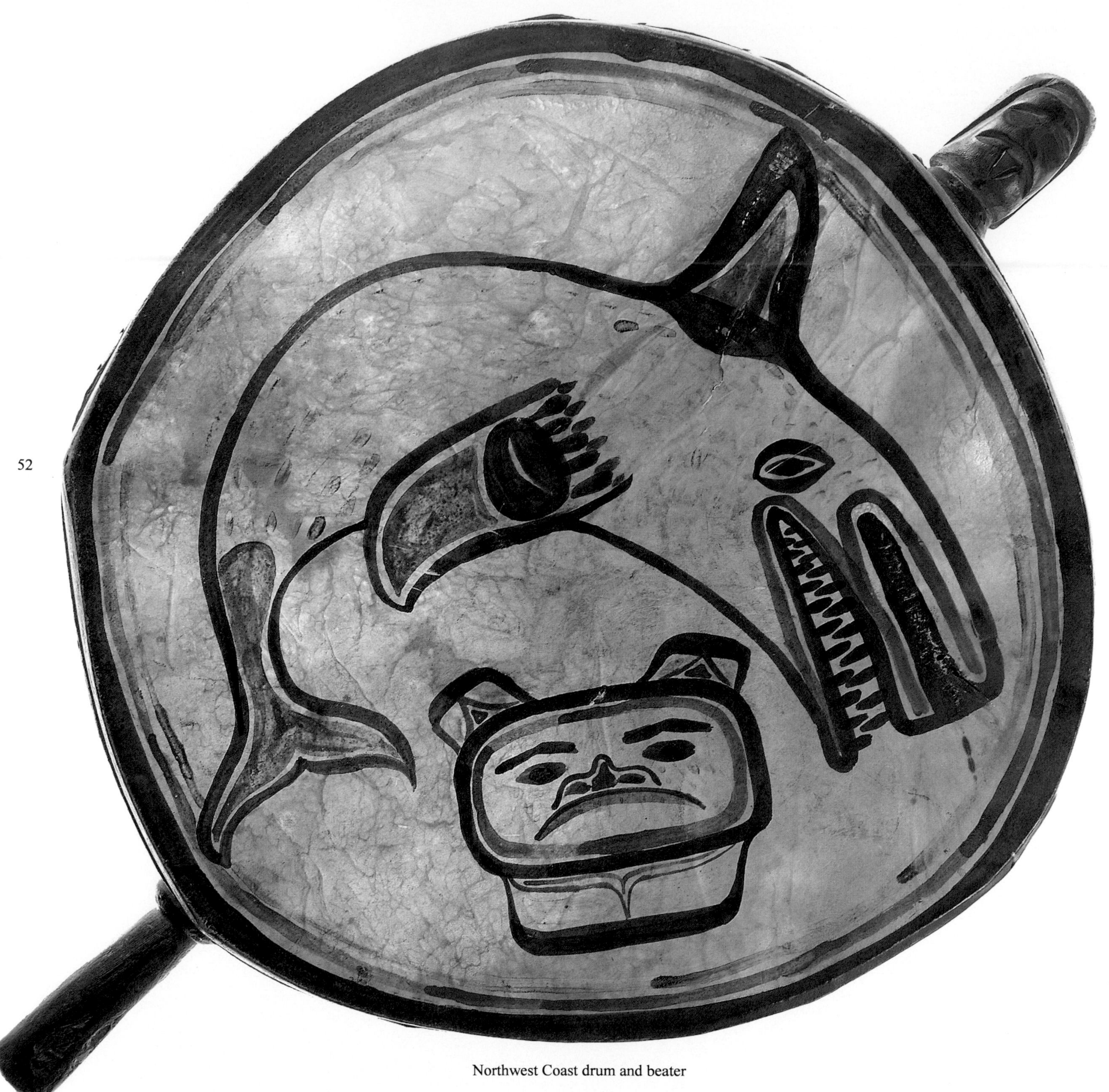

Northwest Coast drum and beater

Large or small, drums were used in social and religious ceremonies. They were symbols of unity. The Northwest Coast tribes decorated them with elaborate paintings from nature. The one at left has a killer whale (orca) and a bear. The one at right has an eagle, the chief of all animals, and a killer whale.

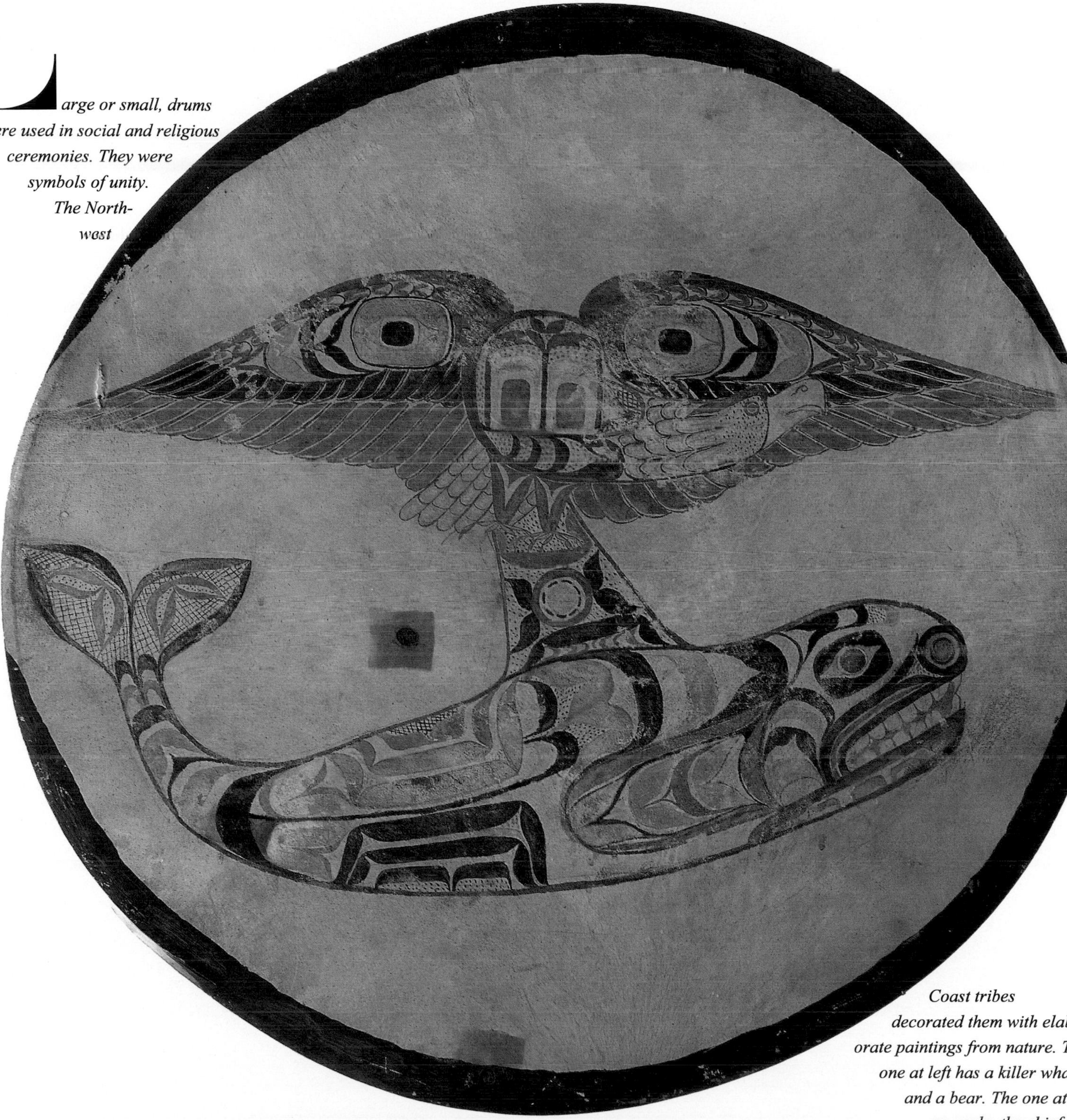

Northwest Coast drum

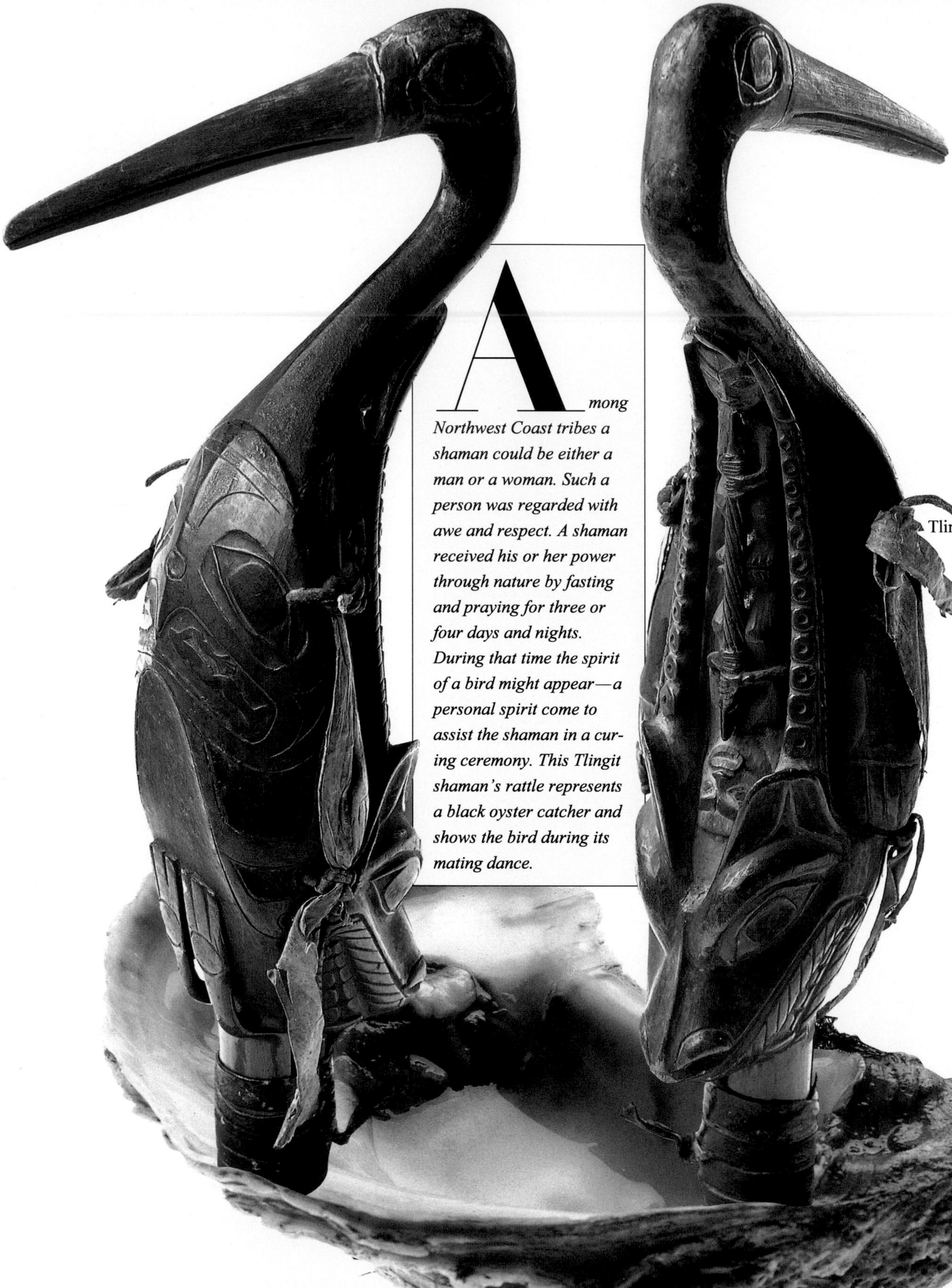

Among Northwest Coast tribes a shaman could be either a man or a woman. Such a person was regarded with awe and respect. A shaman received his or her power through nature by fasting and praying for three or four days and nights. During that time the spirit of a bird might appear—a personal spirit come to assist the shaman in a curing ceremony. This Tlingit shaman's rattle represents a black oyster catcher and shows the bird during its mating dance.

Tlingit rattle

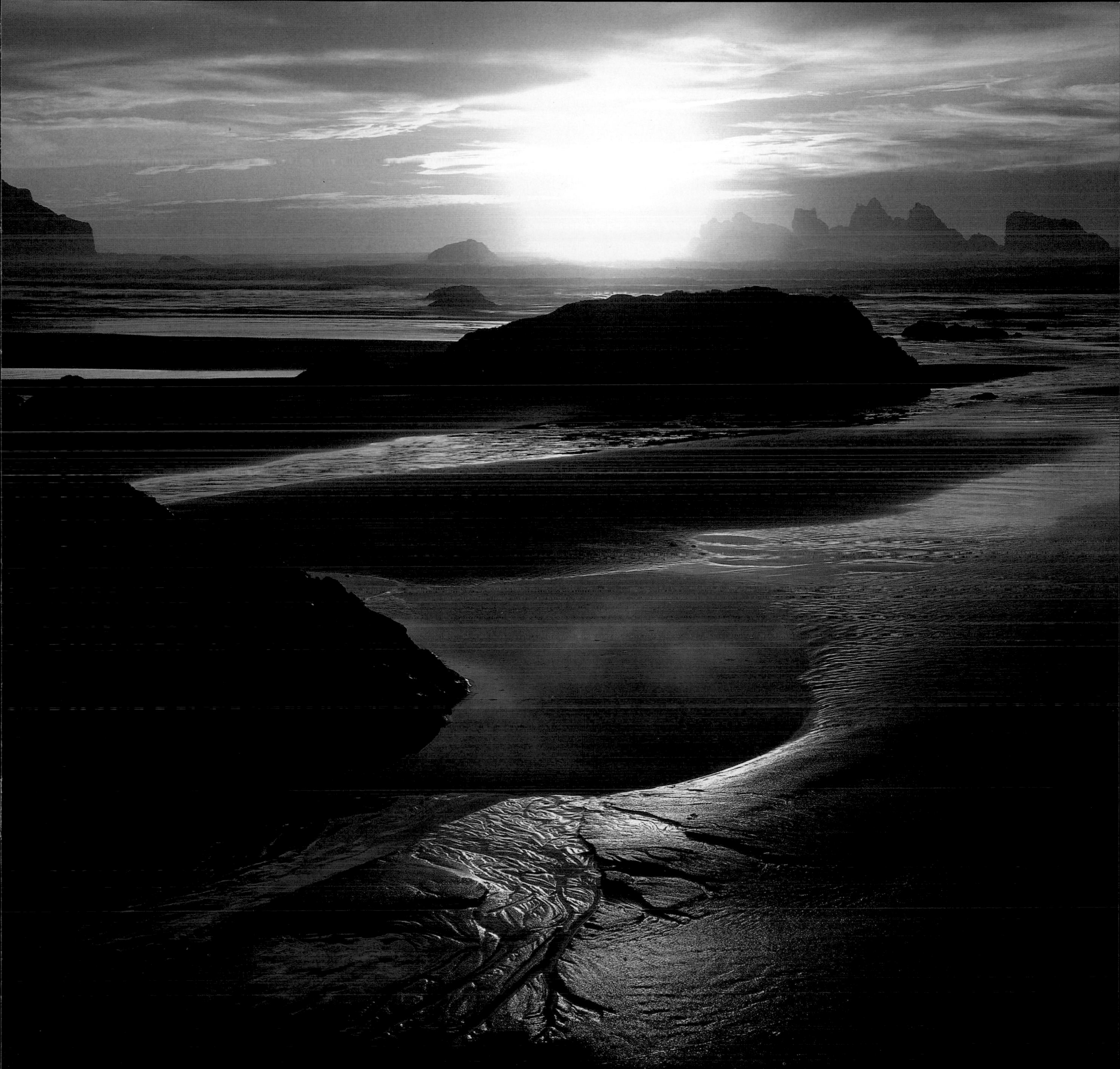

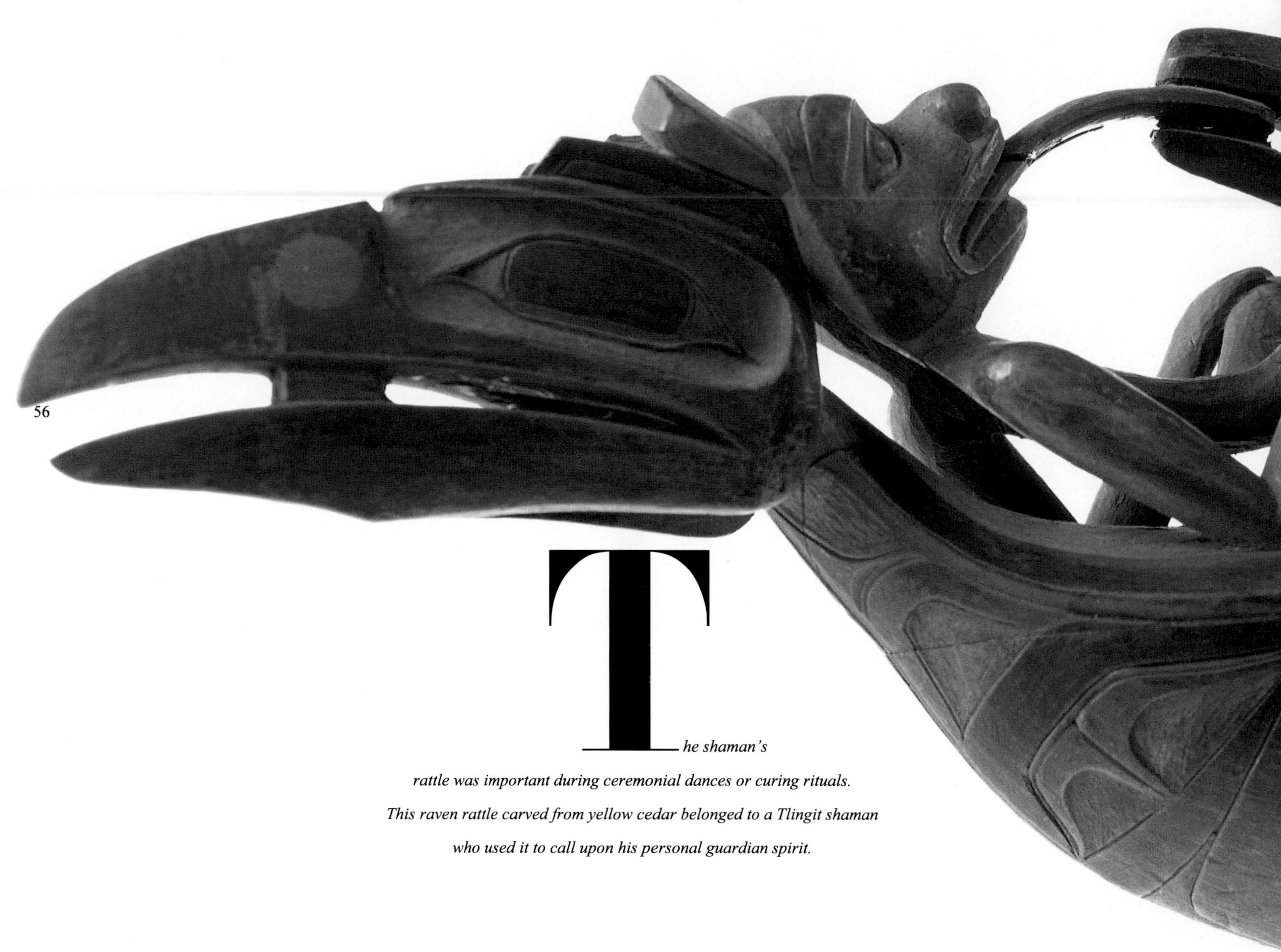

56

The shaman's rattle was important during ceremonial dances or curing rituals. This raven rattle carved from yellow cedar belonged to a Tlingit shaman who used it to call upon his personal guardian spirit.

On the bird's back is a reclining human figure with mask and a bird's head; the human's tongue is held in the bird's beak. This rattle was used during the winter lao laxa dance. Among the Northwest Coast tribes the raven was the one that created the world and put people and animals upon it.

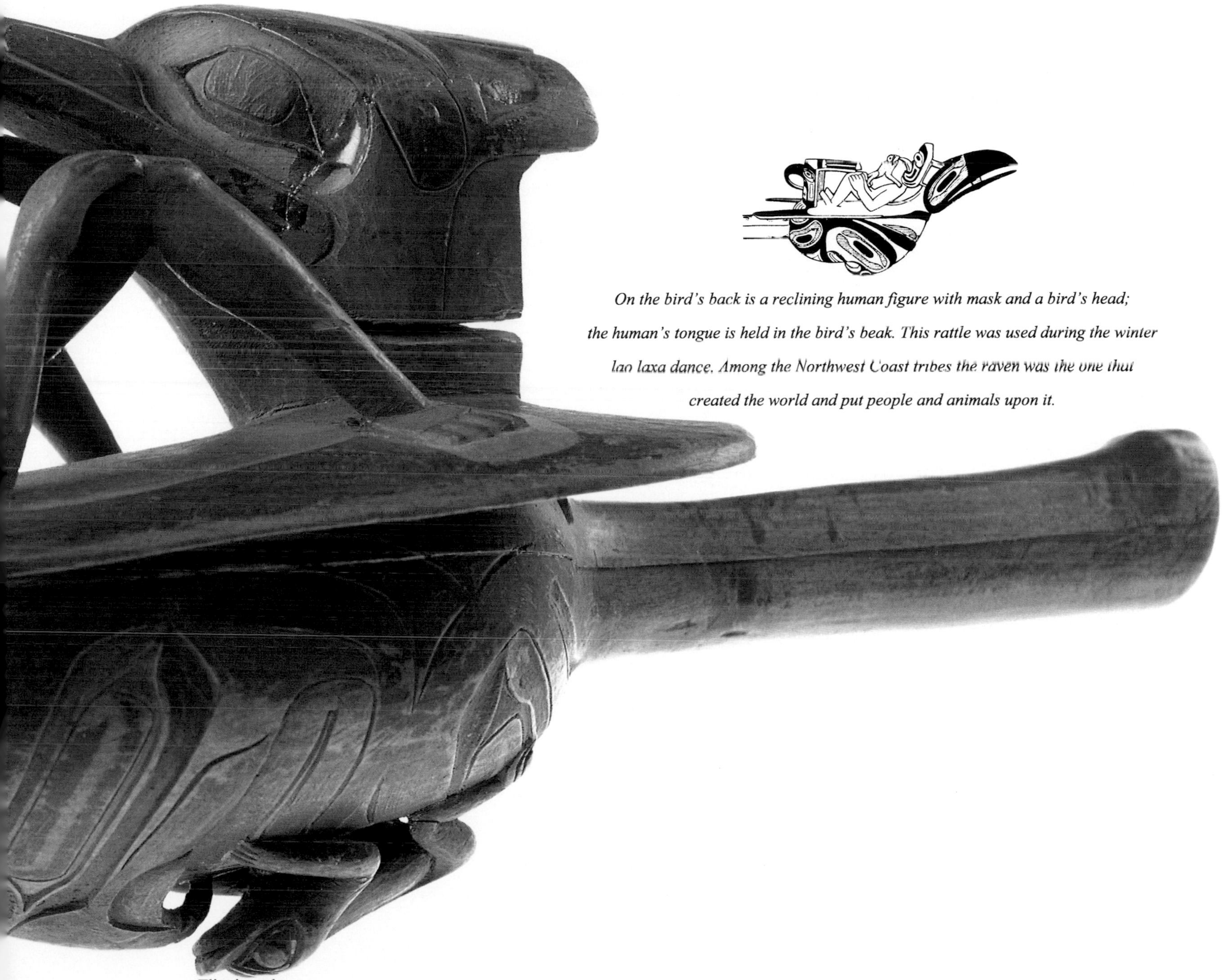

57

Tlingit rattle

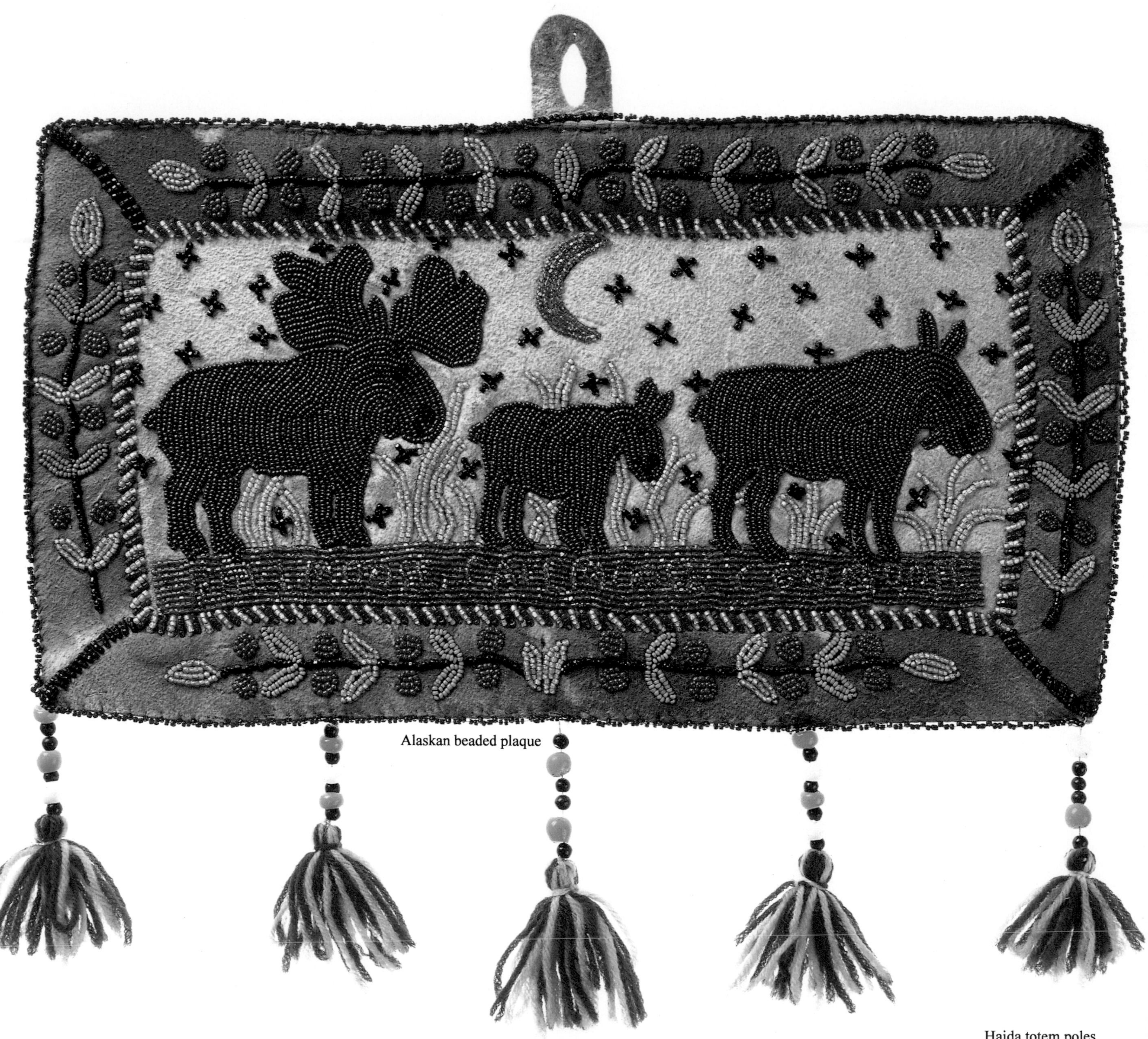

Alaskan beaded plaque

Haida totem poles

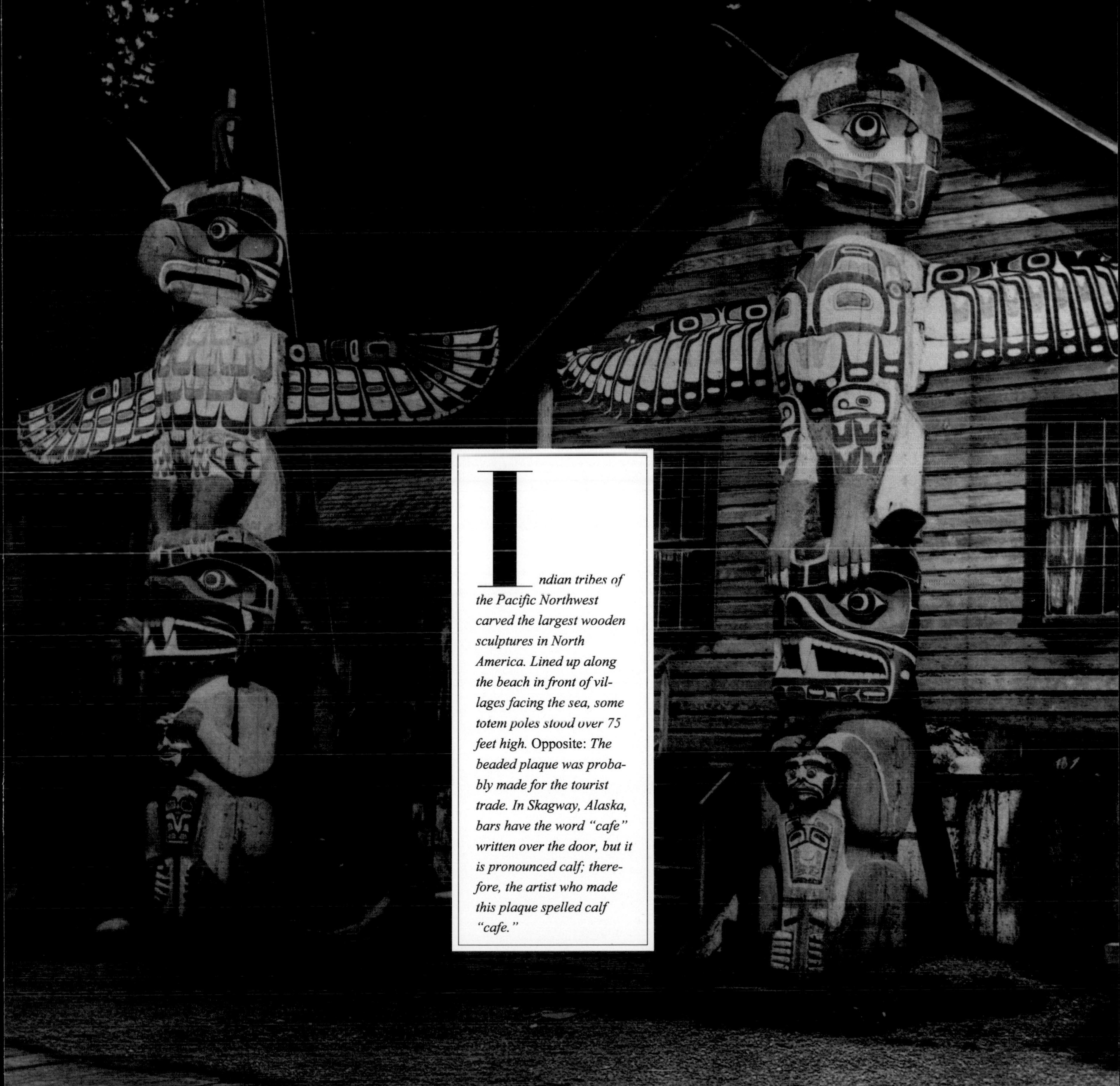

Indian tribes of the Pacific Northwest carved the largest wooden sculptures in North America. Lined up along the beach in front of villages facing the sea, some totem poles stood over 75 feet high. Opposite: *The beaded plaque was probably made for the tourist trade. In Skagway, Alaska, bars have the word "cafe" written over the door, but it is pronounced calf; therefore, the artist who made this plaque spelled calf "cafe."*

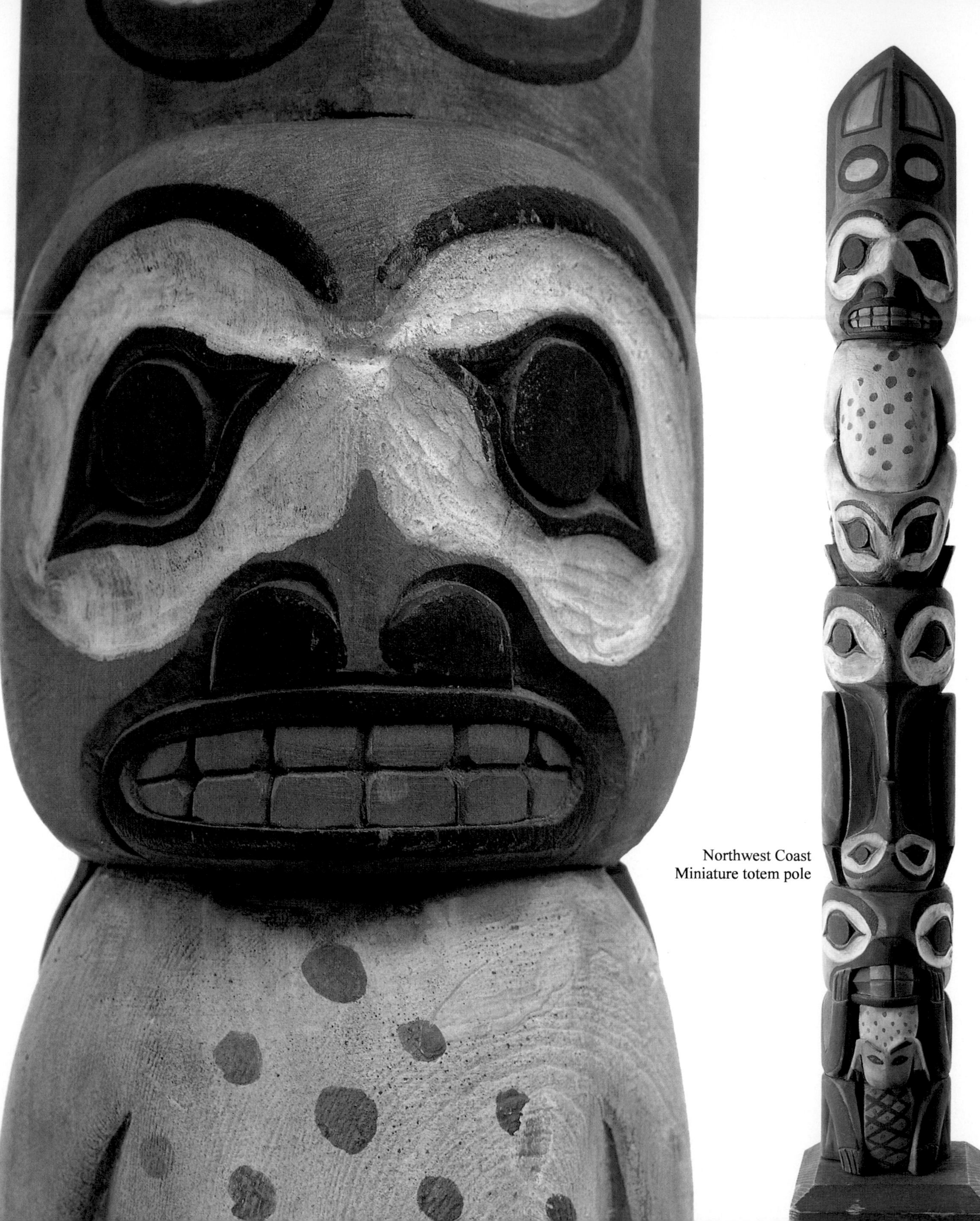

Northwest Coast
Miniature totem pole

In the Pacific Northwest, just about everything the Indians possessed—totem poles, houses, canoes, masks, hats, rattles, ceremonial staffs, and many other objects—was made from red cedar, a sacred material. Prior to carving a full-sized totem pole, a miniature model was made. Poles were three dimensional showing creatures both legendary and real, including wolves, ravens, thunderbirds, bears, and fish.

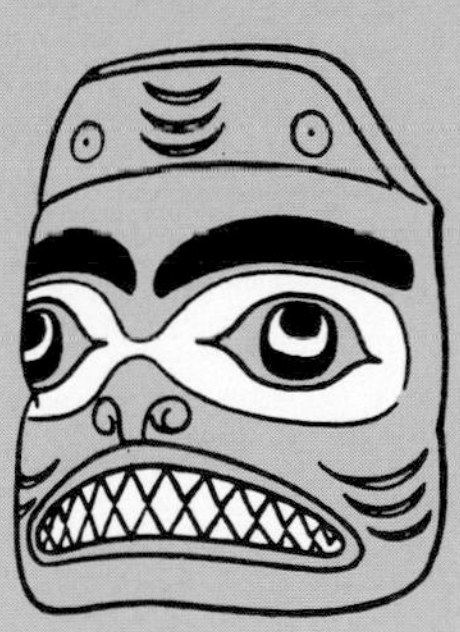

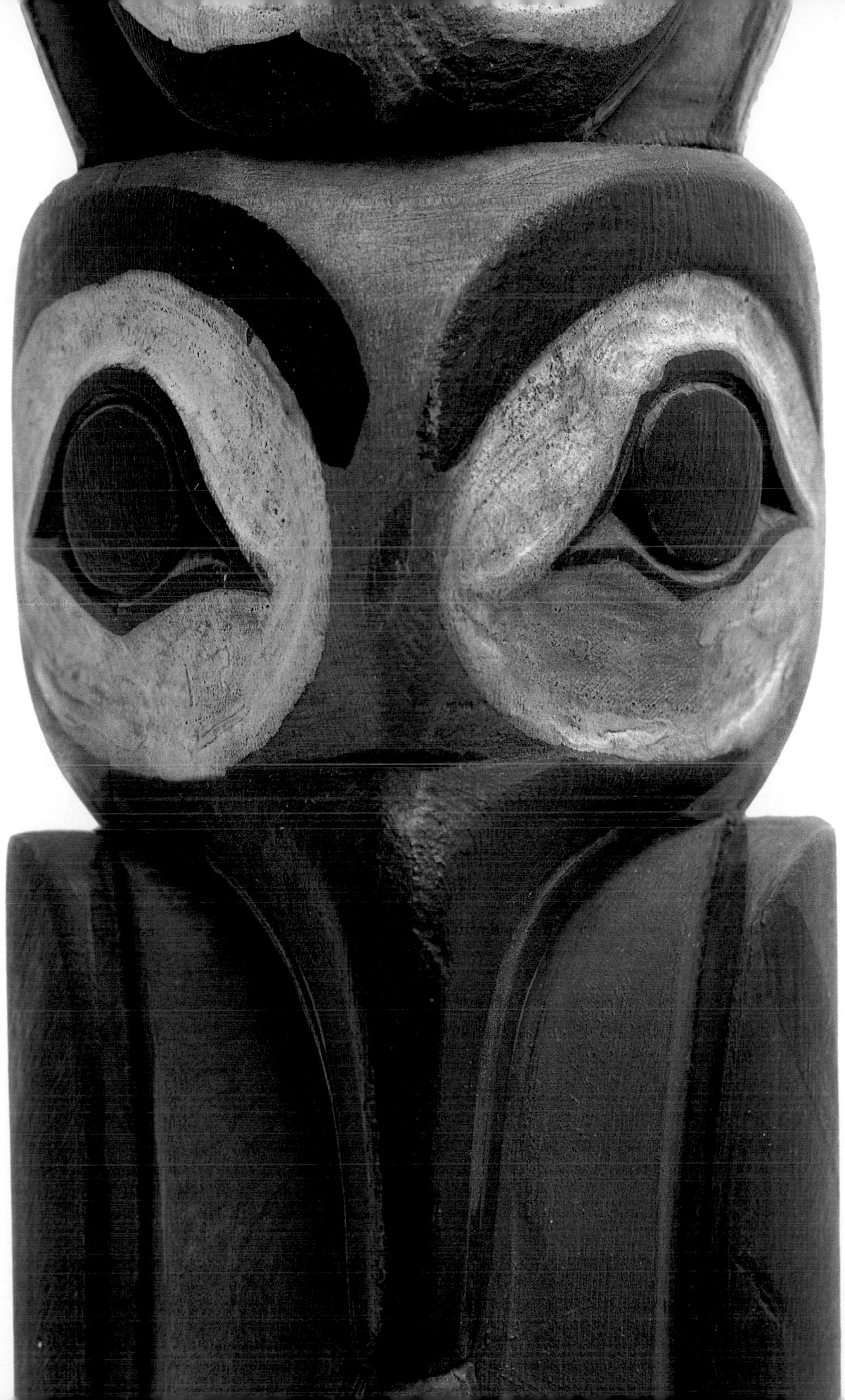

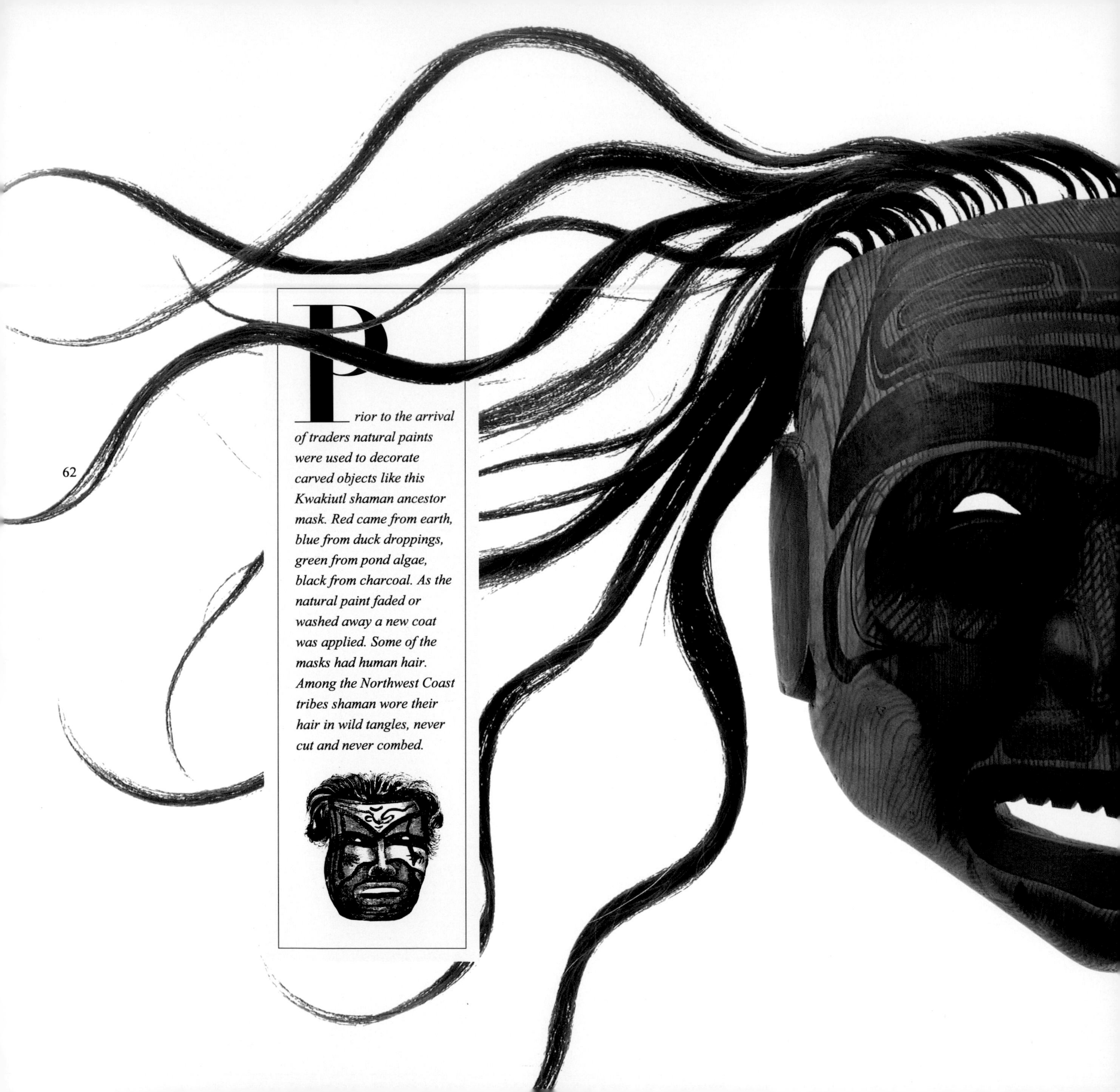

Prior to the arrival of traders natural paints were used to decorate carved objects like this Kwakiutl shaman ancestor mask. Red came from earth, blue from duck droppings, green from pond algae, black from charcoal. As the natural paint faded or washed away a new coat was applied. Some of the masks had human hair. Among the Northwest Coast tribes shaman wore their hair in wild tangles, never cut and never combed.

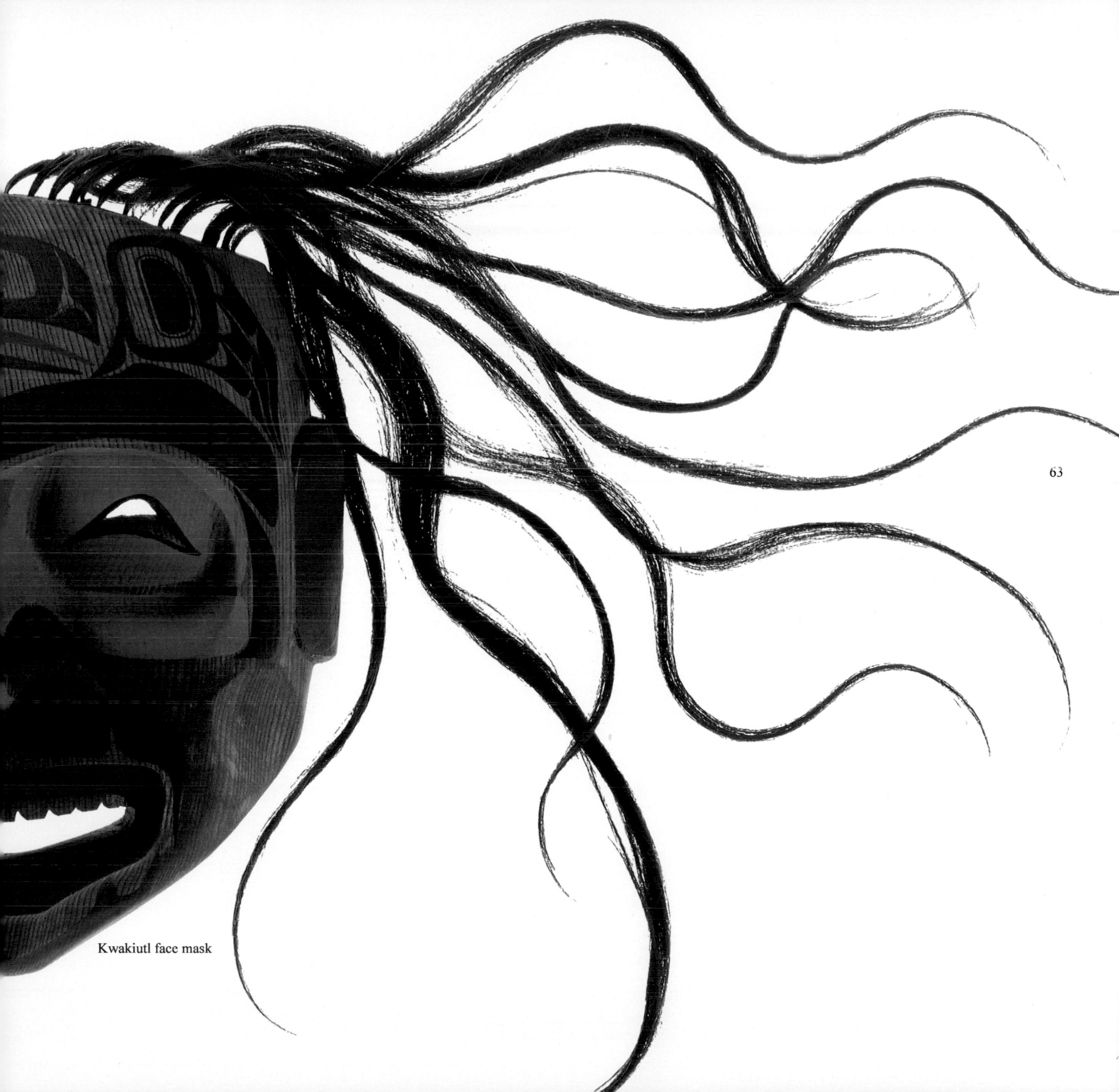

Kwakiutl face mask

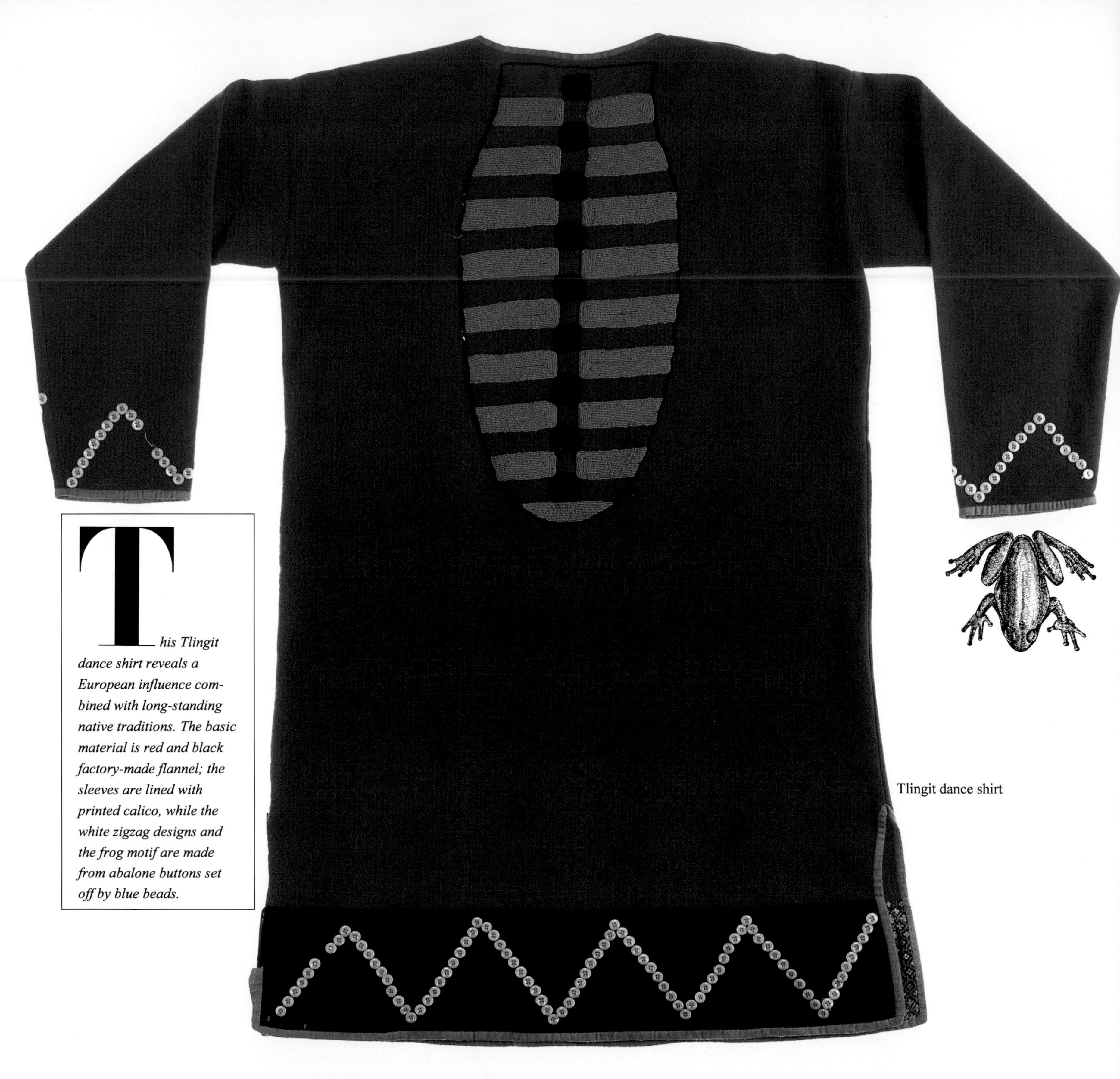

This Tlingit dance shirt reveals a European influence combined with long-standing native traditions. The basic material is red and black factory-made flannel; the sleeves are lined with printed calico, while the white zigzag designs and the frog motif are made from abalone buttons set off by blue beads.

Tlingit dance shirt

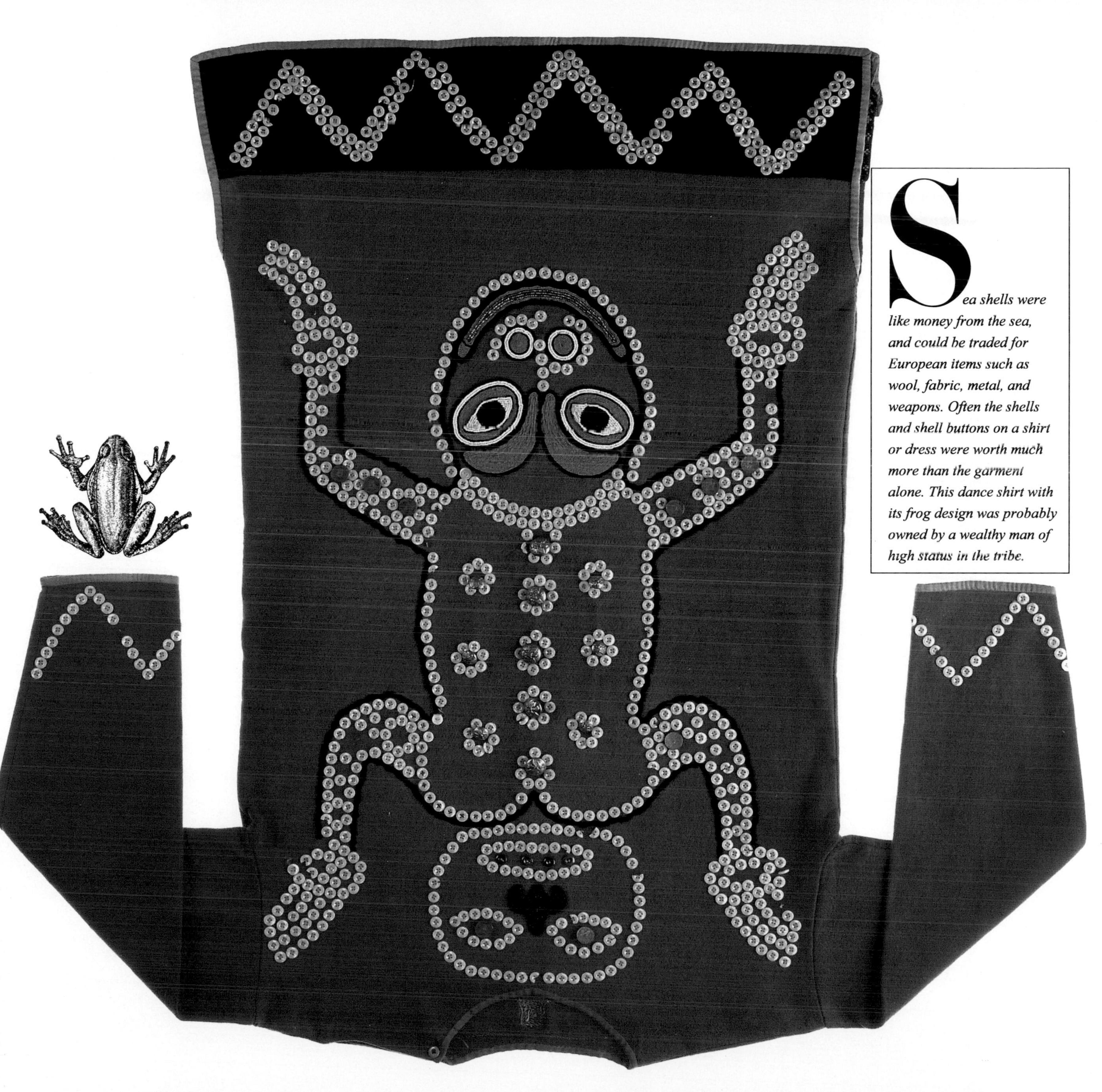

Sea shells were like money from the sea, and could be traded for European items such as wool, fabric, metal, and weapons. Often the shells and shell buttons on a shirt or dress were worth much more than the garment alone. This dance shirt with its frog design was probably owned by a wealthy man of high status in the tribe.

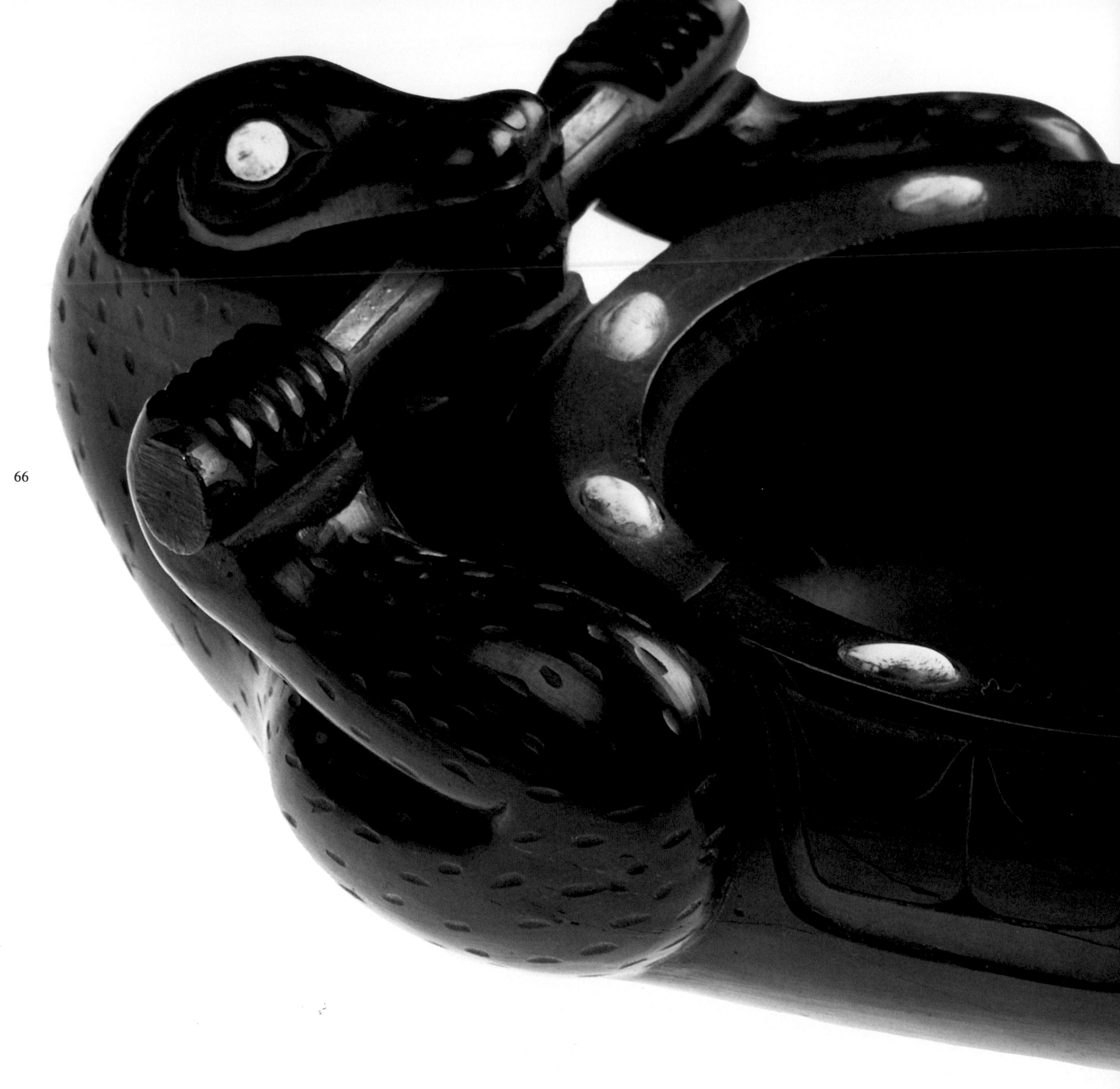

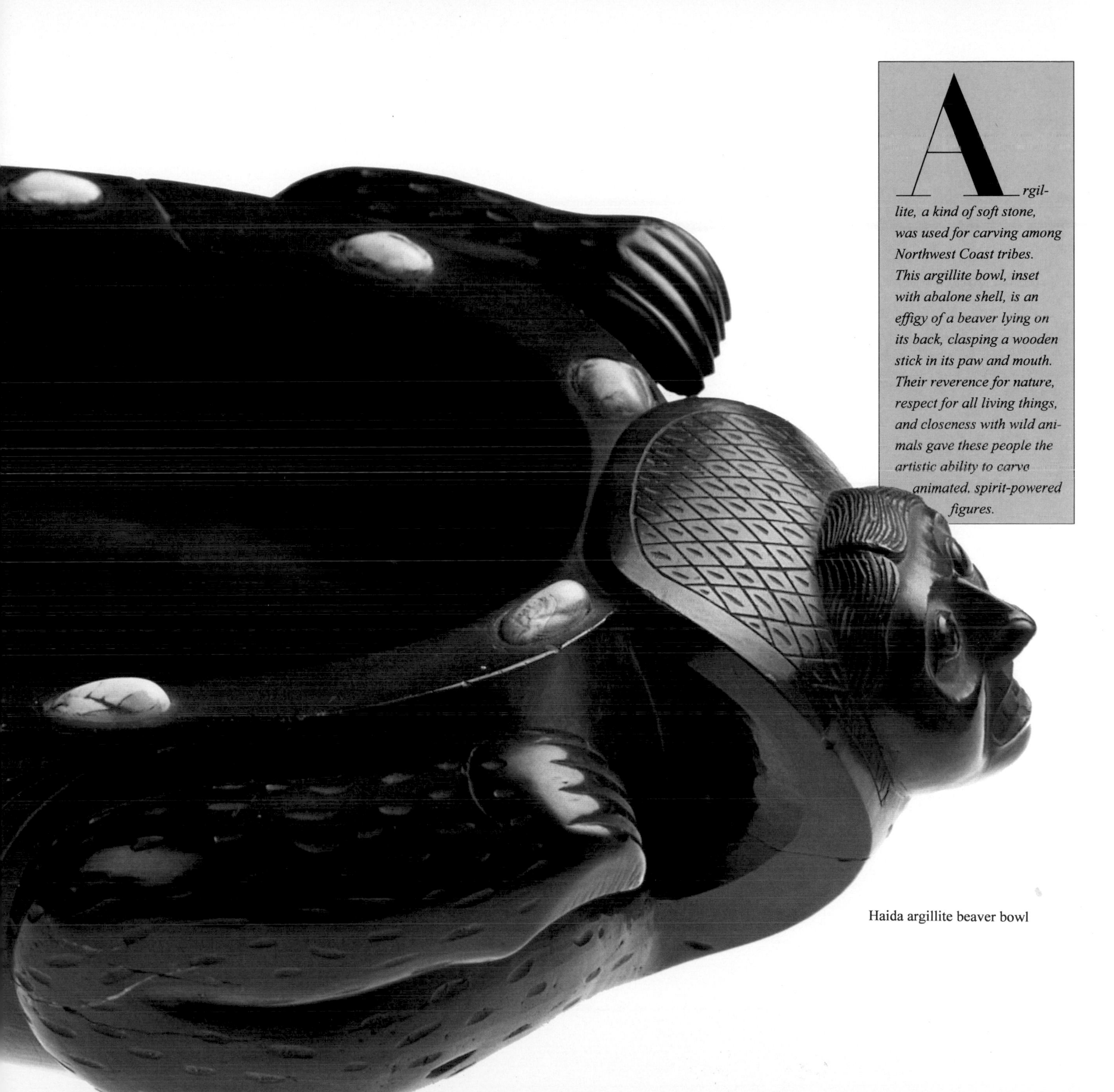

Argillite, a kind of soft stone, was used for carving among Northwest Coast tribes. This argillite bowl, inset with abalone shell, is an effigy of a beaver lying on its back, clasping a wooden stick in its paw and mouth. Their reverence for nature, respect for all living things, and closeness with wild animals gave these people the artistic ability to carve animated, spirit-powered figures.

Haida argillite beaver bowl

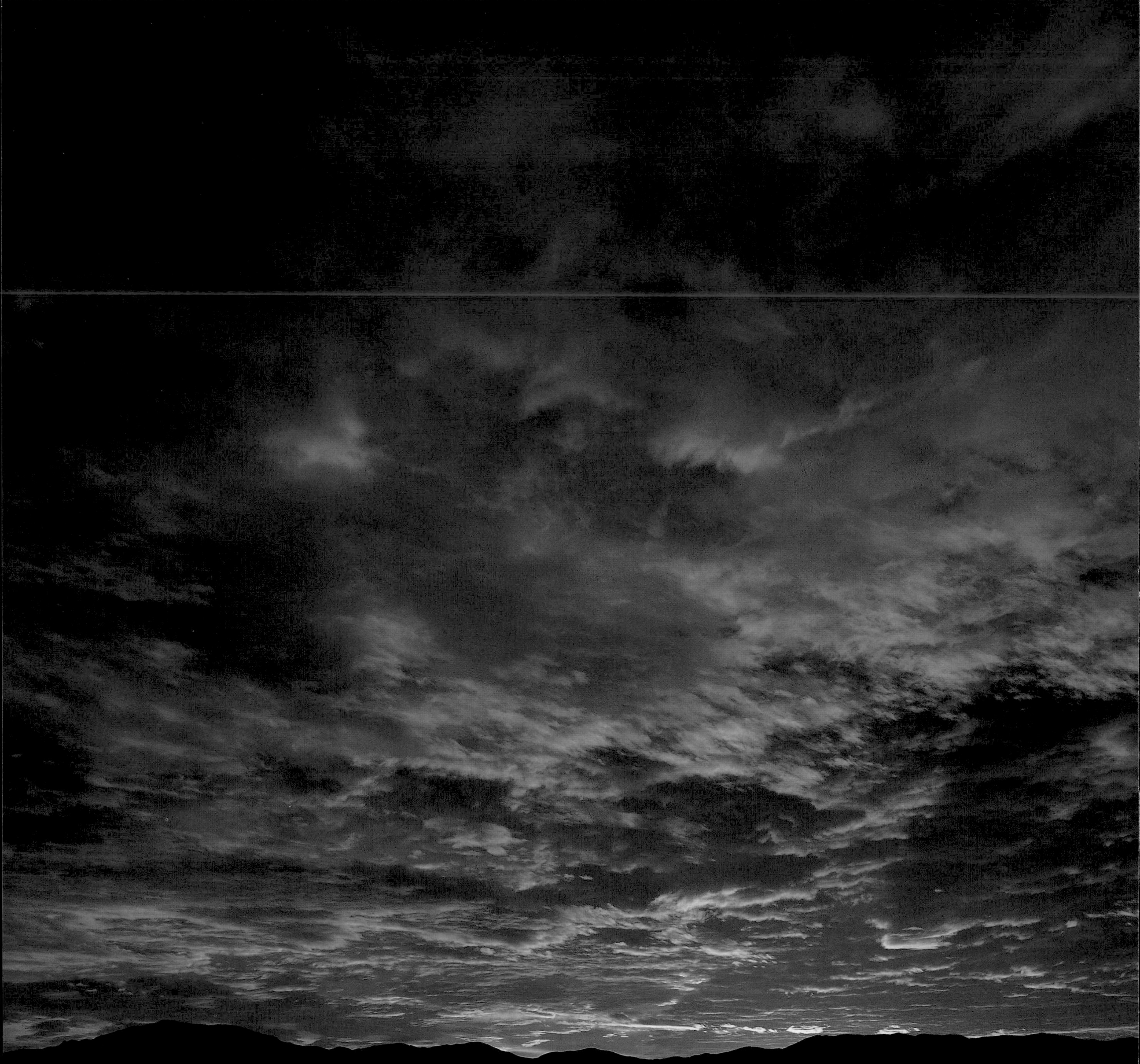

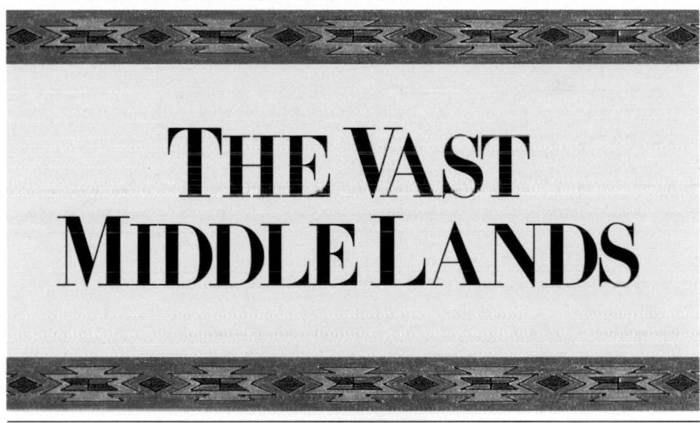
THE VAST
MIDDLE LANDS

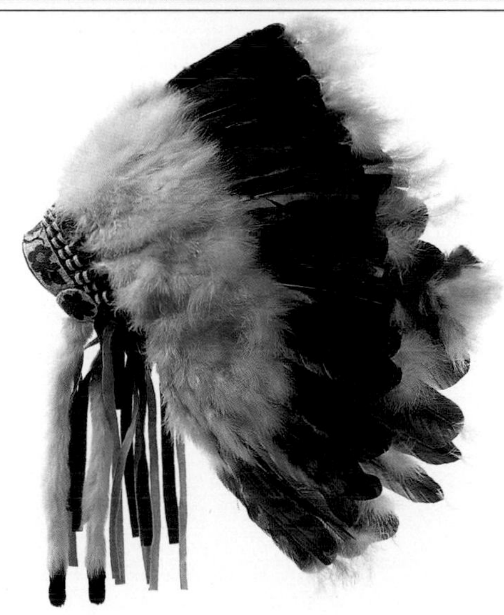

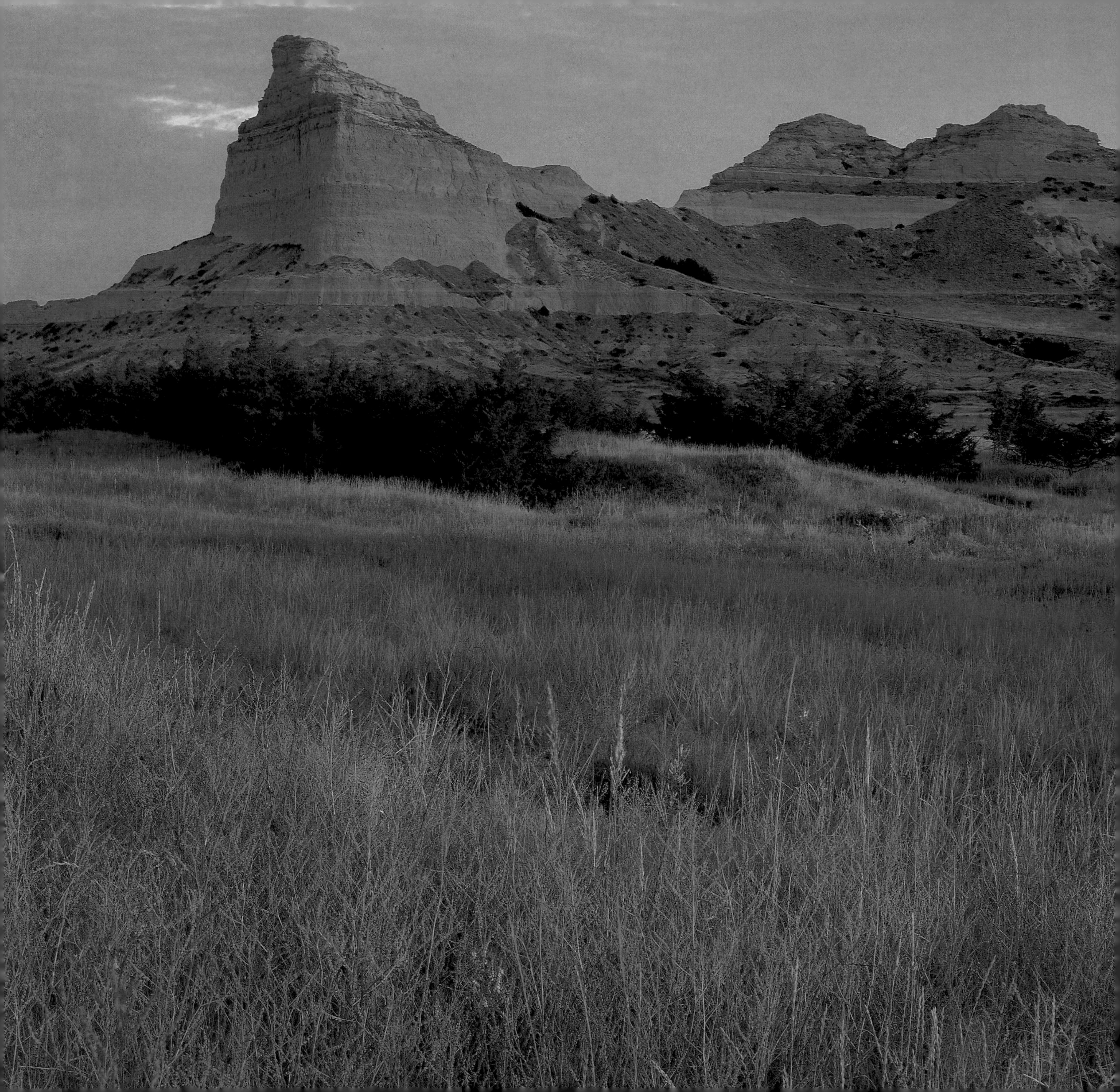

THE VAST MIDDLE LANDS

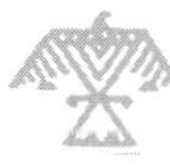
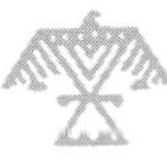
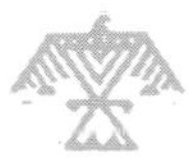

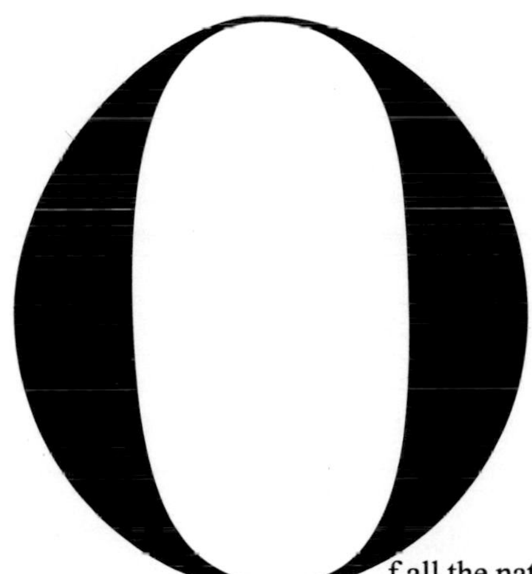

Of all the native cultures that lived and still live in North America, the people of the Great Plains have been the most celebrated. The plains were a sea of grass, scored by rivers and streams all flowing east toward the Mississippi and pounded by millions of buffalo who trailed clouds of dust in the wake of their immense passing. It was a land of sky and air, where the wind moved unbroken and steady, with great strength, sweeping before it storm fronts and thunder clouds.

It was here, from around 1750 to 1850, that Lakota (Sioux), Absaroke, Cheyenne, Arapaho, Comanche, Kiowa, Blackfoot, and other tribes reached the height of their power, riding into prominence on the back of God's Dog, as they called the horse —an animal brought to America by the Spanish, but ideally suited to life on the plains. It is not hard to imagine what a blessing it must have been to acquire horses.

Before then, all travel was by foot. Dogs were the only pack animals. People stayed close to river valleys, where Pawnee and Mandan and other tribes developed agricultural societies around villages of domed, earth-sheltered houses. In the summer, they

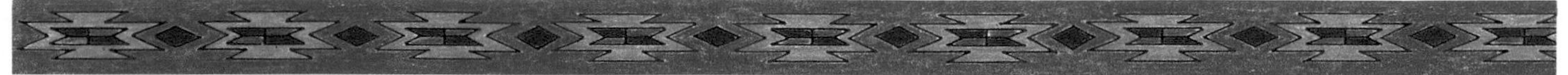

ventured out on foot for short hunts during which they would drive the buffalo over cliffs or into temporary corrals. But they always returned to their homes by the river.

Then came horses. For the first time, people could roam long distances. They could chase the great herds for miles into open country and bring them down with arrows, spears, and when they acquired them through trade, firearms.

So developed a nomadic hunting life based on horses for transport and buffalo for just about everything else. As the source of food, shelter, clothing, utensils, and more, the buffalo occupied a position of enormous spiritual as well as physical significance. Their importance is impossible to overstate. A single tipi required between six to twenty-eight skins, depending on their size. Sewn together in a half circle, the skin cover was stretched over a cone of wooden lodgepoles and often painted with bright decorations of symbolic importance to the owner. Tipis withstood powerful prairie winds and provided snug shelter in the worst of winter weather, yet they were easily collapsed and rolled up for traveling and light enough to be dragged behind a horse on a travois (itself made from two lodgepoles).

Yet even with horses to bear the load, a nomadic life required efficiency. During summer, camps might be moved several times a month, and any extraneous items were soon left behind. The furnishings for life on the plains had to be light, portable, and very carefully thought out.

Rectangular leather bags called parfleches were used to hold everything from spare clothing to dried meat. Medicine bundles, collections of objects sacred to an individual or a tribe, were kept in parfleches superbly decorated with beads, dyed porcupine quills, and paint. Also in the tipi were collapsible backrests made from willow twigs. Cradle boards served as beds and carriers for infants. Bows made of wood were strung with buffalo sinew. Buffalo skins made quivers for arrows, war shields, bedding skins, cooking skins (filled with liquids and heated with hot stones dropped in from a nearby fire), moccasins, leggings, gloves, and of course, tack for horses. Although most men rode bareback, women used saddles patterned after Spanish designs with wooden frames bound in leather.

Among the most important items to be found in any tipi was the smoking pipe, with its long wooden stem and a bowl usually carved from soft stone. Pipes represented a link between the earthly and the spiritual worlds. Many were used for everyday smoking and personal rituals; others, owned not by individuals but by tribes, often highly decorated with feathers and beadwork, were brought out only on special occasions. Such pipes had great power. Their presence solemnized the most important events. To be the keeper of a tribe's sacred pipe was a high honor.

Ironically, the events of a few tragic decades in the latter half of the nineteenth century, during which

Hopi Kachina doll

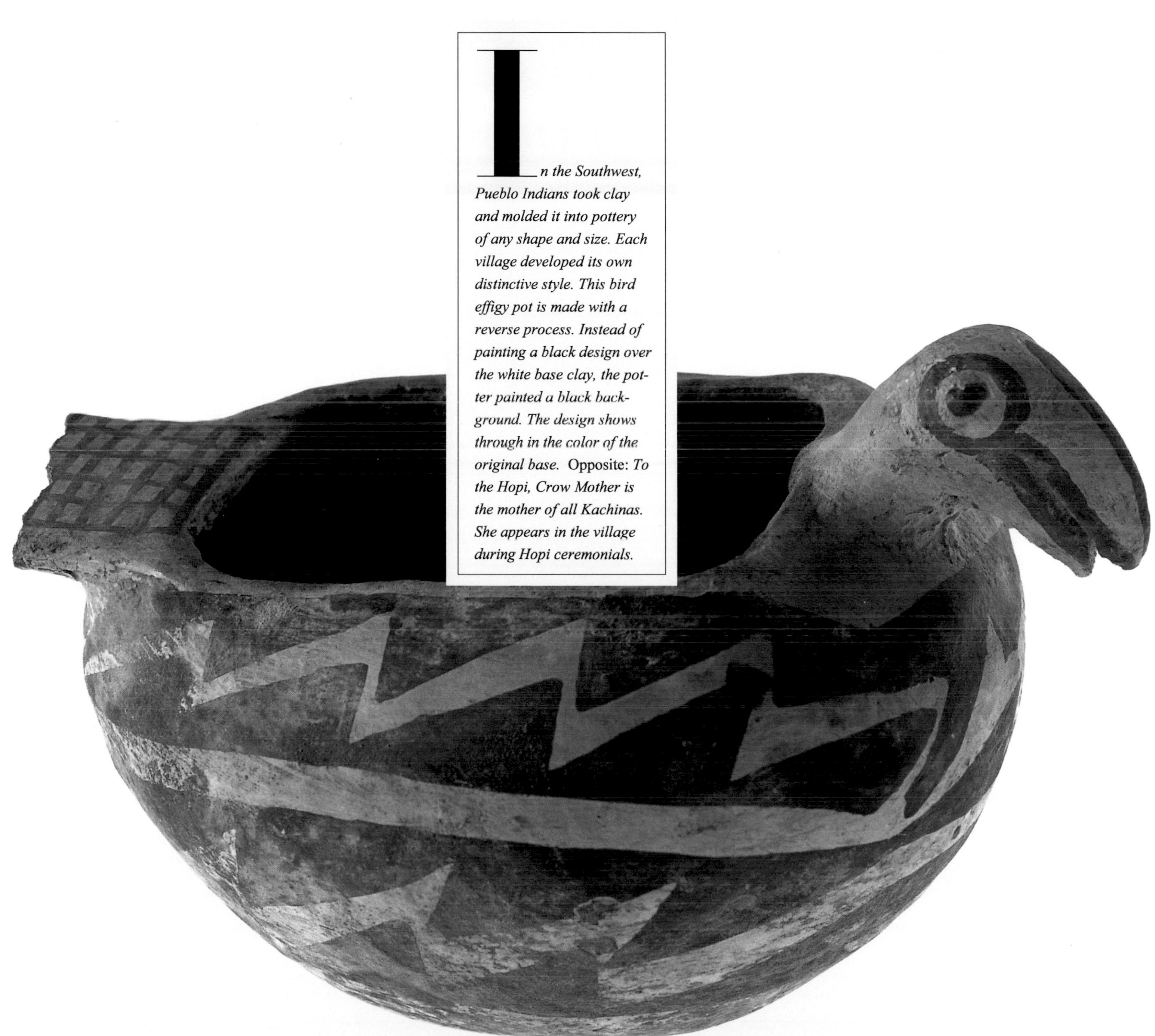

In the Southwest, Pueblo Indians took clay and molded it into pottery of any shape and size. Each village developed its own distinctive style. This bird effigy pot is made with a reverse process. Instead of painting a black design over the white base clay, the potter painted a black background. The design shows through in the color of the original base. Opposite: *To the Hopi, Crow Mother is the mother of all Kachinas. She appears in the village during Hopi ceremonials.*

Pueblo bird effigy pot

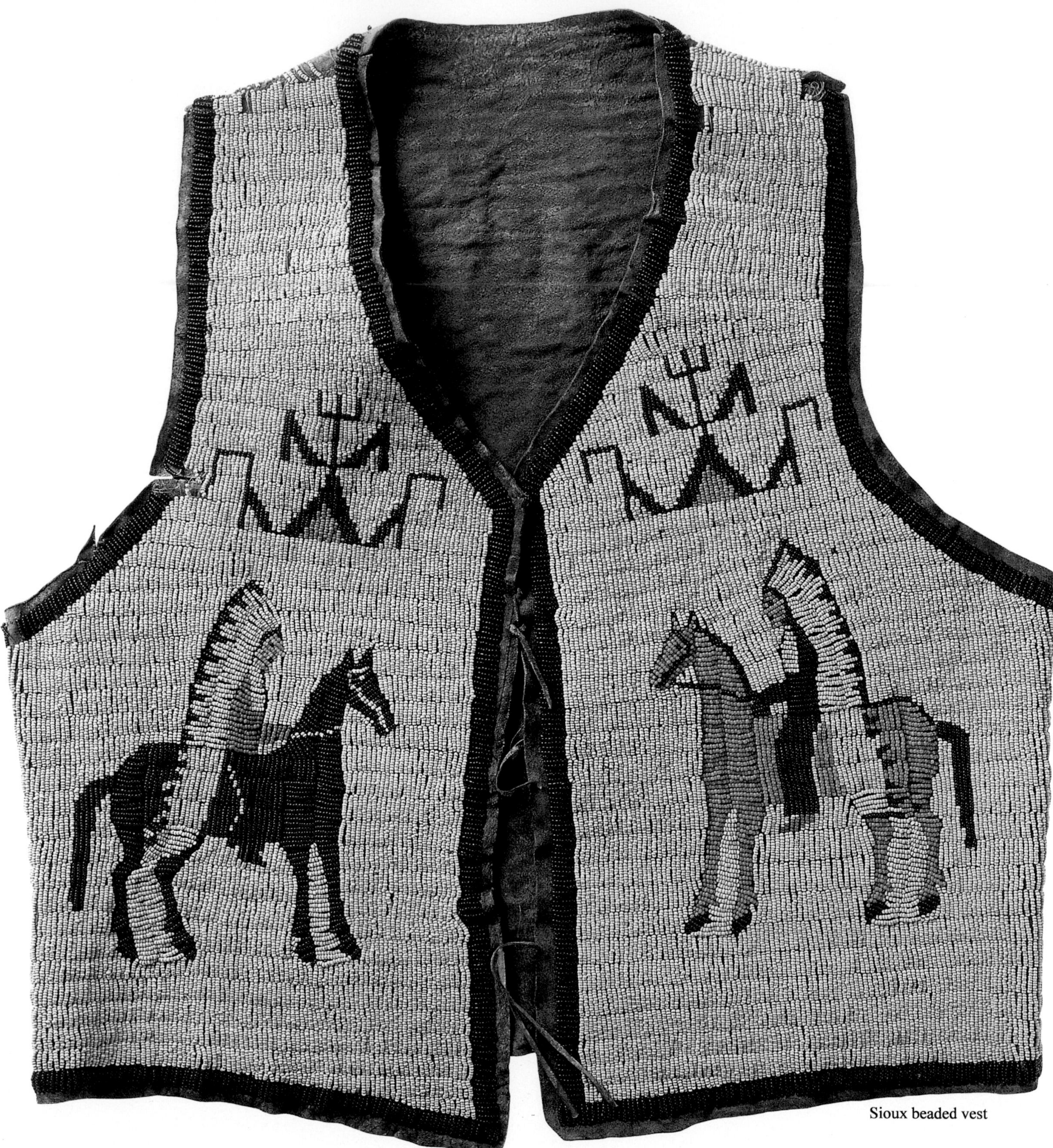

Sioux beaded vest

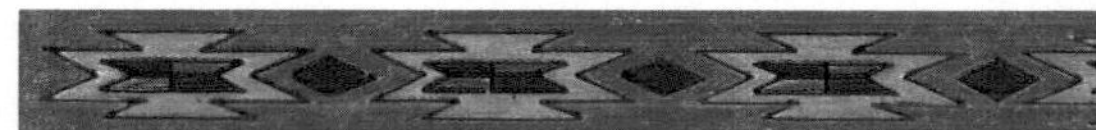

tribes were defeated and the buffalo herds slaughtered, were what firmly established the images of tipis, feathered headdresses, buffalo hunts, sacred pipes, and painted ponies as the symbols of all Native American tribes. In their darkest days, the plains people made a great impression upon the world.

Yet there were many other people and ways of life in the area we call the American West. The plains are only one part of a much larger and marvelously complicated territory—a varied landscape where the climate changes from one mile to the next, and every turn brings a new vista. Wherever they lived, Native Americans found ways to survive and flourish—ways appropriate to the natural conditions of their homelands.

None were more skillful than the people of the Great Basin. Centered in Nevada and including parts of Utah, Idaho, California, and Oregon, this topography is a corrugation of parallel mountain ranges supporting cool green forests above valleys dominated by sagebrush. Rivers flow in from surrounding highlands and off the summits of interior ranges, but none flow out. The water collects in marshes and shallow saline lakes only to evaporate into what can accurately be called thin air.

The Great Basin is a land subject to fast-moving extremes in weather, and almost nowhere rich in food sources like large mammals. It includes such landmarks of austerity as Death Valley and the Great Salt Lake Desert. The people who lived here—the Paiute, Shoshoni, Bannock, Washo, and others—coped with what might be the continent's most challenging living conditions outside of the Arctic. They lived a wandering existence, constantly on the lookout for sources of food, usually small animals, fish, and wild plants.

At times, food was found in abundance, and these were occasions for celebration, feasting, and the gathering of clans; yet in the absence of such bounteous animals as the buffalo and given the near impossibility of growing crops, natural conditions in the Great Basin dictated an astonishingly varied diet. Rabbits and pinyon pine nuts served as staples, yet just about anything encountered and caught would be eaten: waterfowl and other birds that nested in the lowland marshes; fish in the lakes and mountain streams; Mormon crickets, grasshoppers, ants, lizards, roots and bulbs, berries, and the seeds of grasses.

Every season brought new foodstuffs and new challenges. While summer was the time of fat rabbits and bird eggs, winter was the time of scarcity

In the 1800s, small glass seed beads brought by European traders replaced the traditional porcupine quillwork of the Plains and Intermountain tribes. Heavily beaded garments such as the vest on the opposite page were reserved for special occasions. Below: *Parents and grandparents made toys like this miniature beaded cradleboard and doll. The children treasured the toys made for them, then passed them on to younger children.*

Nez Perce doll cradleboard

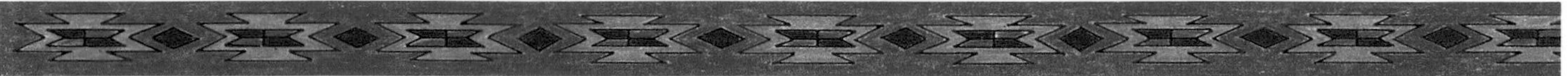

—not only because of snow and cold but because so many animals disappeared then. Ground squirrels and other rodents went into hibernation. Birds migrated to warmer climates. In lakes, fish were protected by an armor of ice. At times like these, food stored during summer became critically important.

The belongings of Great Basin tribes reflected their simple, mobile lifestyle and a philosophy that put little stock in the deeds of war. Their weapons—bows and arrows, spears, and clubs—were used primarily for hunting. They avoided conflict with other people, an inclination that caused white settlers to underestimate their skill and courage. Life was hard, but they made do with an unparalleled economy of possessions. Everything they needed they could carry on their backs or pick up as they went along. Antelope skins were a great luxury when available, but if not, there were rabbits, whose flesh provided a staple food and whose skins, cut in strips and twisted together, made thick, furry yarn that could be woven into capes, blankets, and robes. For load carrying, storage, and even for hats, they made baskets of skillfully tight weave, some lined with pine pitch to hold water. Their duck decoys, some made from real duck skins, were good enough to bring live birds to within reach of bowhunters. For gathering seeds, plants, and pinyon nuts, they devised an array of clever beaters and collectors. At camp, they made fires by spinning a cane stick against a block of sagebrush wood. They carried the most important tools in their heads, and much of that ancient knowledge has disappeared forever.

Conditions were also harsh in the southwestern deserts of Arizona, New Mexico, and parts of neighboring states—a land of colored rock and blue sky unsoftened by the pale of moisture. Included here is the Colorado Plateau, an uplifted block of red rock, deep-shadowed canyons, and mesas sprinkled with a thin forest of juniper and pinyon pine. Southward, the land drops away to the Mojave and Sonoran deserts, where is found the classic American desert of tall cacti, ocotillo, mesquite, joshua trees, and palo verde. Roadrunners dash about in search of rattlesnakes. Venerable mountains stand half-buried in their own rubble because the climate is too dry to carry away the products of erosion.

Yet the overall climate in the Southwest has one advantage over the Great Basin: It is warmer, providing a longer frost-free growing season, making agriculture possible wherever water is available. And although deserts are by definition dry places, there is enough water for those who understand the land. The Navajo, Apache, Pima, Papago, Hopi, Zuni, and other people became expert dry-land farmers. For staples, they grew (and still grow) corn, beans, and squash; in addition, they ran herds of sheep, goats, and cattle and learned to harvest the surprising bounty of native desert plants. Success involved an intimate

Pueblo stirrup jar

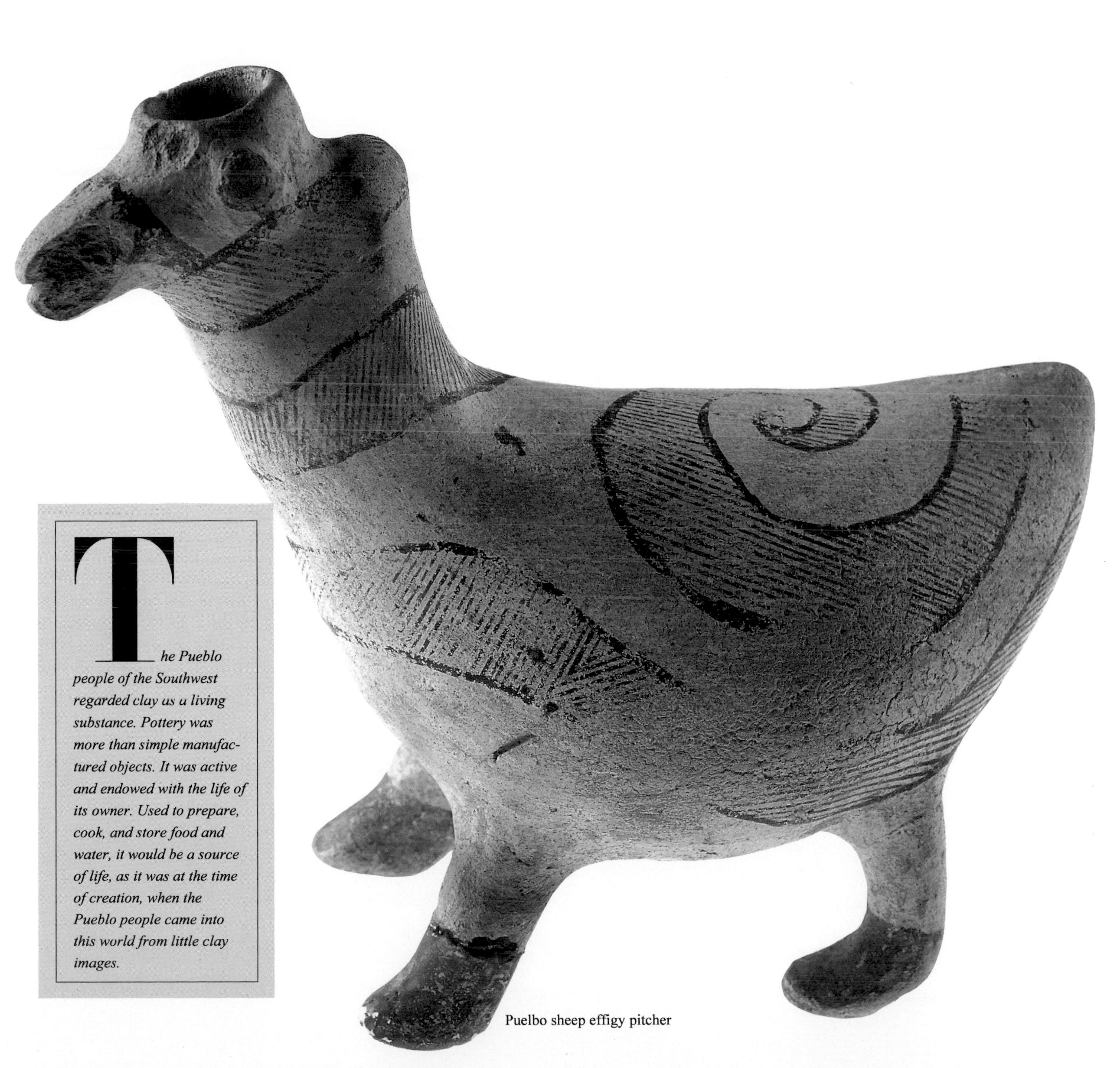

The Pueblo people of the Southwest regarded clay as a living substance. Pottery was more than simple manufactured objects. It was active and endowed with the life of its owner. Used to prepare, cook, and store food and water, it would be a source of life, as it was at the time of creation, when the Pueblo people came into this world from little clay images.

Puelbo sheep effigy pitcher

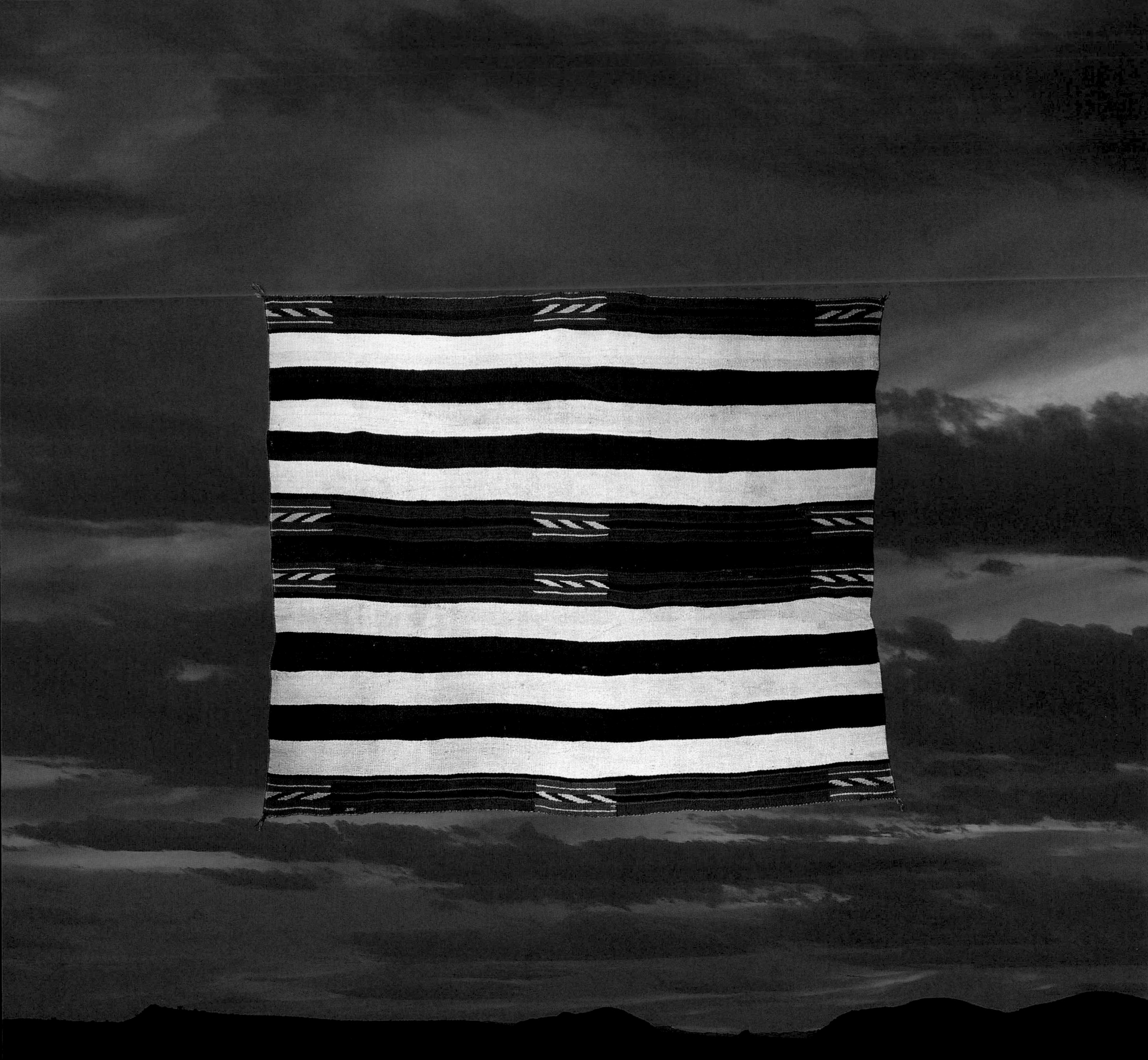

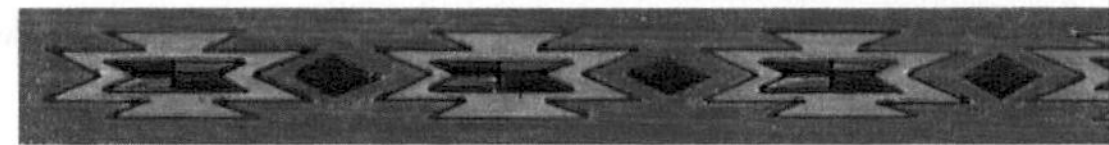

knowledge of the geography of moisture. They knew where to find naturally occurring water. They understood where water would flow when it rained and how to make the best use of it. They also understood the spiritual side of water—how to bring it, through ritual, from the sky when needed.

More than other environments, and largely because of its spiny austerity, the desert is endowed with a sense of timelessness. Things grow slowly; landscapes endure. The same is true of the southwestern cultures whose roots, like those of the native blackbrush, go deep. This is especially true of the pueblo tribes now living on the Hopi Mesas and along the Rio Grande Valley. Their ancestors built the famous cliff dwellings at Mesa Verde and other places—dwellings that still stand after more than a thousand years.

The Southwest is a place of earth tones, of bare soil and rock. It is appropriate, then, that among the chief arts of the region would be pottery made from native clay and weaving that reflects the colors and shapes of the desert. Pueblo tribes are also famous for the accoutrements of ritual—Kachina masks and dolls, Zuni fetishes, dance costumes, songs, stories, and the decorative motifs on virtually everything from pottery to architecture. Every aspect of life has religious significance; every action has some influence on the workings of the world.

The Navajo tell how Spider Woman came down from her high stone pinnacle in Canyon de Chelly and taught the people to weave. Using the wool of their sheep, Navajos wove utilitarian items such as shirts, dresses, belts and blankets for their own use and for trade to other tribes. Early Navajo blankets were used not as rugs; people wore them for protection from the elements. Shown on this page is one of the most celebrated patterns—the chief blanket, a rare and valuable trade item, prized as a symbol of status from the Great Plains to the Great Basin.

In nature there is balance; in balance there is beauty.

Far to the north, the Columbia Plateau is a broad volcanic upland covering western Washington and parts of Idaho and British Columbia—a jumble of mountains and climates, everything from powdery desert along the Snake River to coastal rain forest in its northern reaches, the whole sewn together by two great rivers, the Columbia and the Fraser.

Here lived people whose staple food, despite their inland location, was salmon. The two major rivers, with hundreds of tributaries, provided migration routes for homecoming salmon as far inland as western Montana and eastern Idaho. The fish came every year in enormous numbers, searching out the clear, gravel-bottomed streams and creeks where their lives had begun. They came to breed and lay eggs of their own; they also came to provide food for some thirty distinct tribes, including the Shuswap, Kutenai, Columbia, Flathead, Nez Perce, Umatilla, and Klamath.

Because of their appearance every year in vast numbers at the same places on the same rivers, the salmon made it possible for the people to lead more settled lives than their nomadic neighbors. They built houses not meant to be moved and acquired possessions of the sort that nomads could never afford to carry from place to place. They also engaged in trade,

Navajo wearing blanket

exchanging goods between the coast tribes and the people of the plains. Each autumn there was a grand trading rendezvous at The Dalles, where the Columbia River cuts through the Cascade Mountains.

Among products from the coast came sea shells, notably dentalium, precious to Indians throughout the West. In later years, European goods—metal cooking pots, steel knives and arrowheads, wool blankets and brightly colored cloth, muskets and powder and lead shot—also made their way upriver from trading posts established along the coast. To acquire these things, inland tribes brought elk antlers, furs, bear claws, the dried, sweet bulbs of the camas plant, and other roots and herbs. The Nez Perce, who by arrangements with friendly plains tribes made annual hunting trips east of the Rockies, brought buffalo robes, horns, and sinew. They were fine craftsmen, known for such specialties as bows made from mountain sheep horn and large, supple carrying bags made from twisted cornhusk.

In later years, the Nez Perce, along with the Palouse and Cayuse, became renowned horse breeders. Their superb spotted horses, the Appaloosa, gained favor far and wide for strength, size, endurance, and beauty. It was not unusual for a single Nez Perce family to own hundreds of horses. Trading made them relatively wealthy, while contact with other tribes gave them a taste for foreign goods and new ideas. For example, from the plains tribes they adopted skin-covered tipis and many of the material goods that came with the nomadic life. Of all the horse-mounted Indians, none could outshine the Nez Perce for spectacle and panoply. In full regalia, their horses wore elaborate headpieces, painted bridles, beaded collars and stirrups, and saddles with high, decorated pommels and cantles. Sitting astride such an animal, a rider wearing a traditional horned headdress with eagle feathers trailing down his back, an embroidered leather shirt hung with white ermine skins, and high, beaded moccasins must have been a wonderful sight.

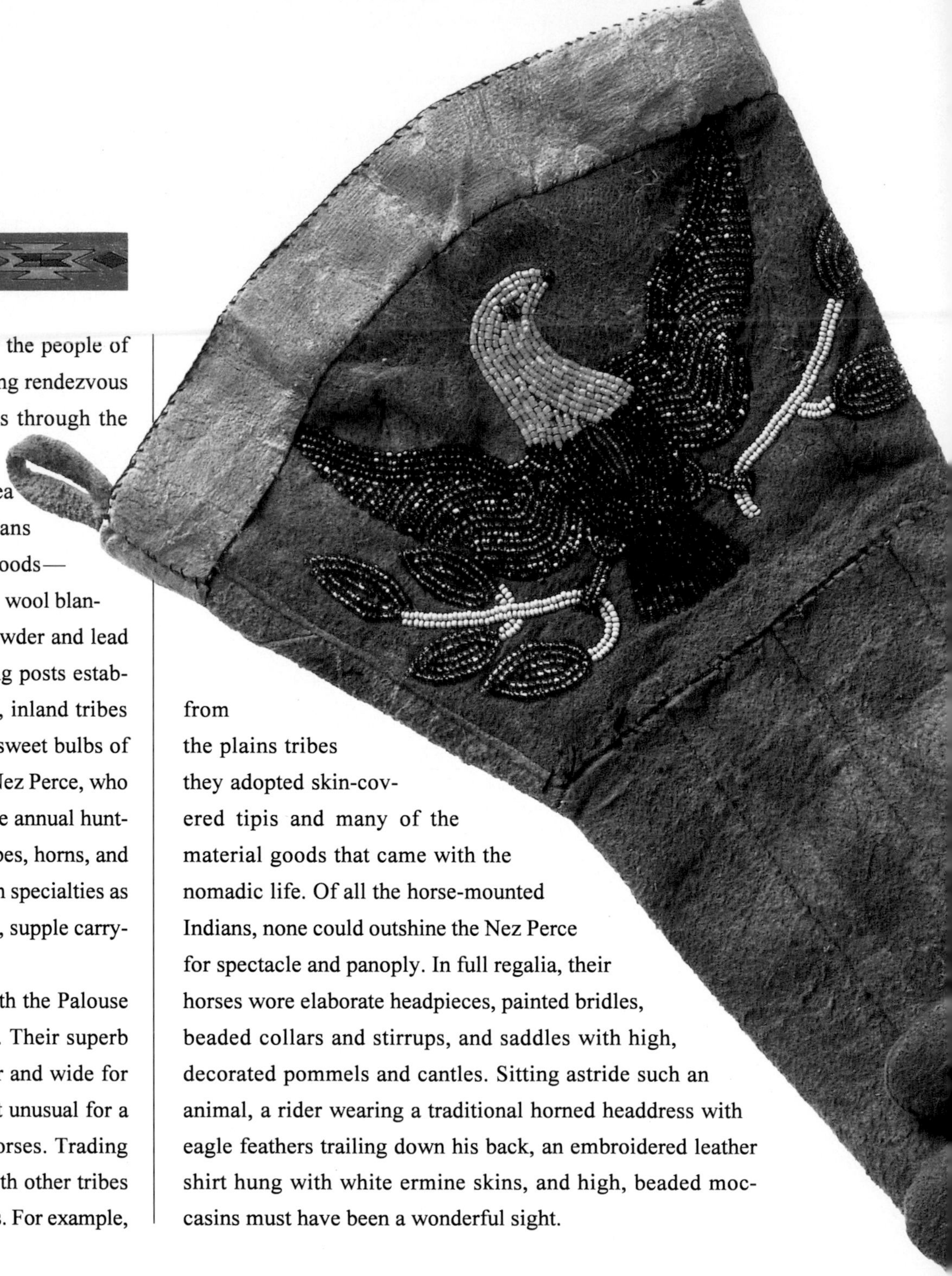

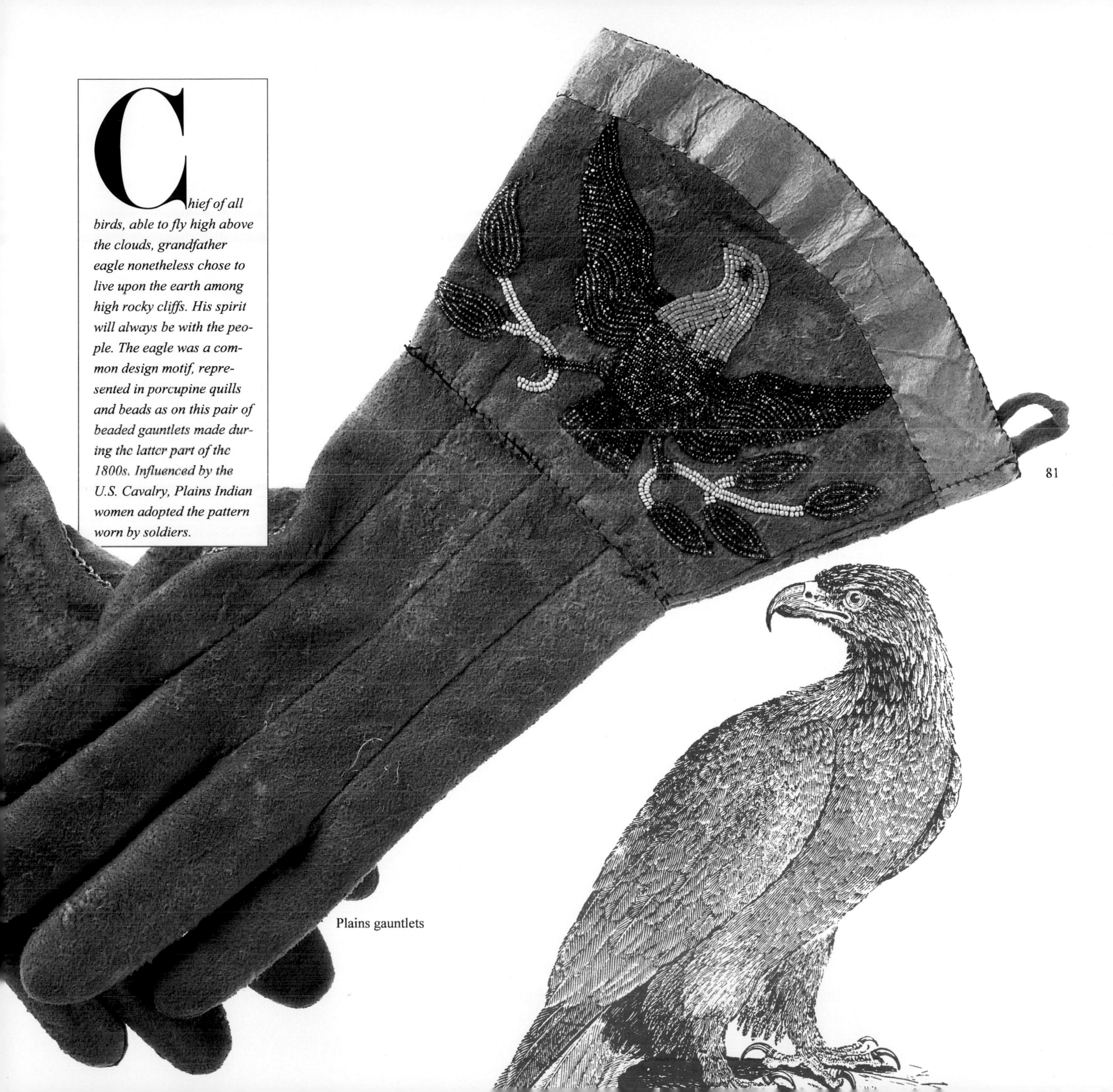

Chief of all birds, able to fly high above the clouds, grandfather eagle nonetheless chose to live upon the earth among high rocky cliffs. His spirit will always be with the people. The eagle was a common design motif, represented in porcupine quills and beads as on this pair of beaded gauntlets made during the latter part of the 1800s. Influenced by the U.S. Cavalry, Plains Indian women adopted the pattern worn by soldiers.

Plains gauntlets

82

N*avajo weavers work on looms of ancient design derived from Pueblo prototypes. After the Spaniards introduced sheep's wool, the Navajo adopted the white man's shear for clipping and the toothcomb for carding the wool. They still spin with the traditional spindle—a disk on a wooden shaft with which they twist and pull the strands of fiber. The eight-point star design on this saddle blanket is borrowed from Hispanic weavers of the mountain villages in northern New Mexico and is typical of the Four Corners area.* Opposite: *A beautifully beaded cradleboard with tribal geometric or stylized floral designs was one of the most highly esteemed beadworks of the Plateau Indian woman. Cradleboards were often made by a close female relative after the baby was born. In return for her labor she might receive a horse or trade goods. The decorative piece on this page is a partial beaded cradleboard cover.*

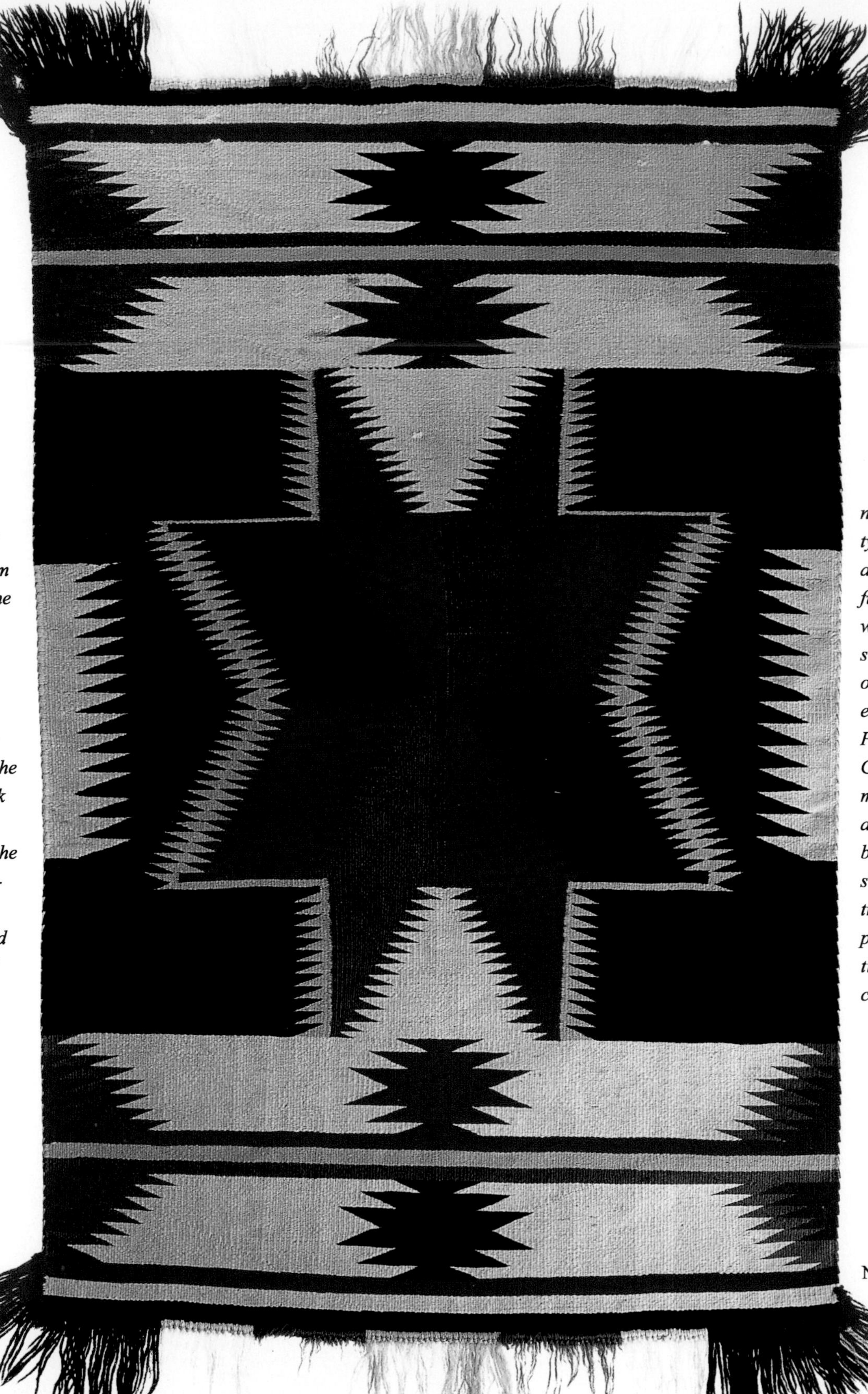

Navajo saddle cover

Plateau cradleboard cover

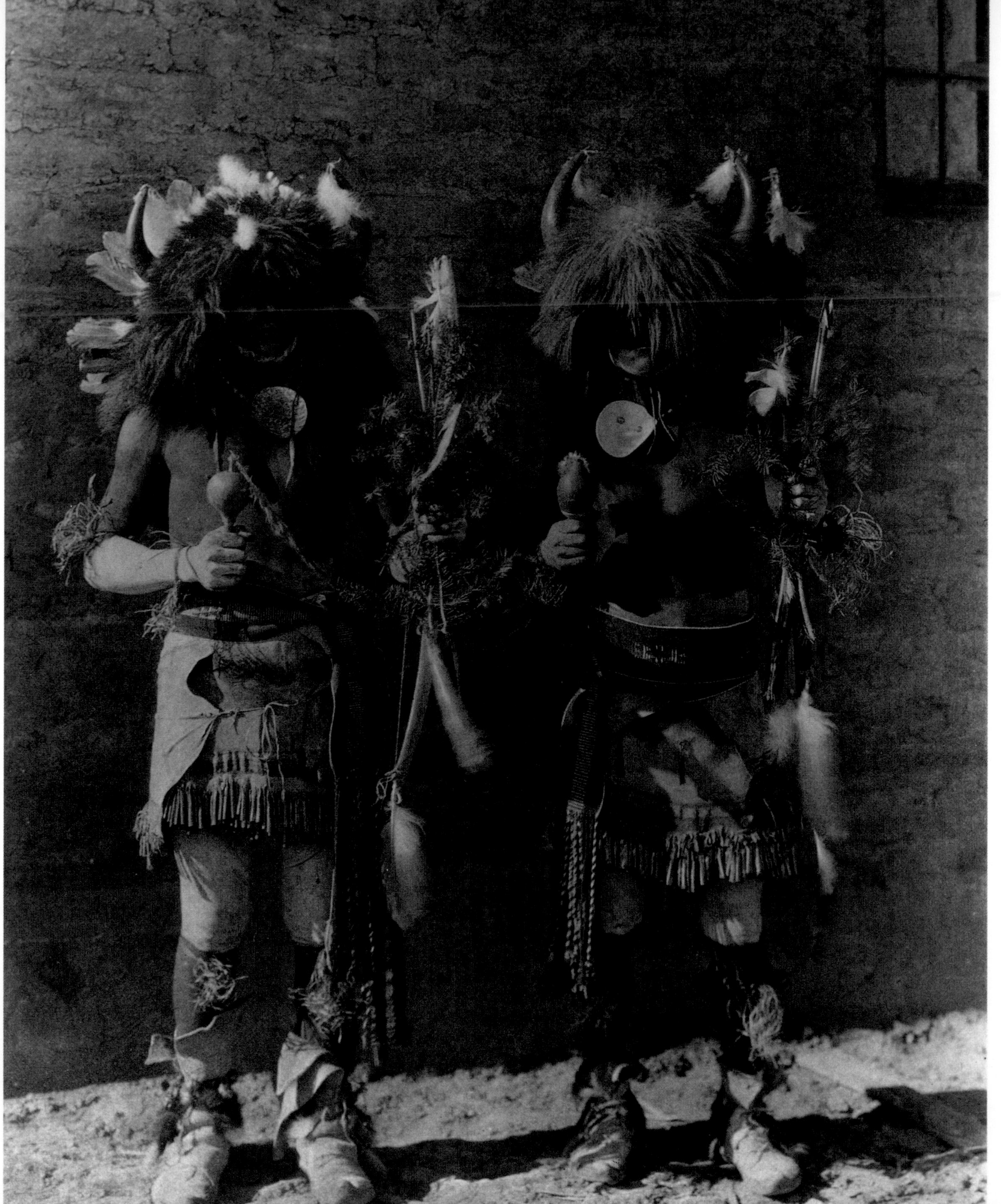

Hopi buffalo Kachina dancers

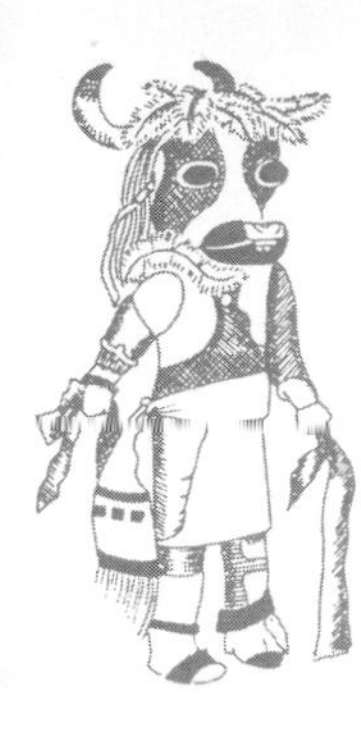

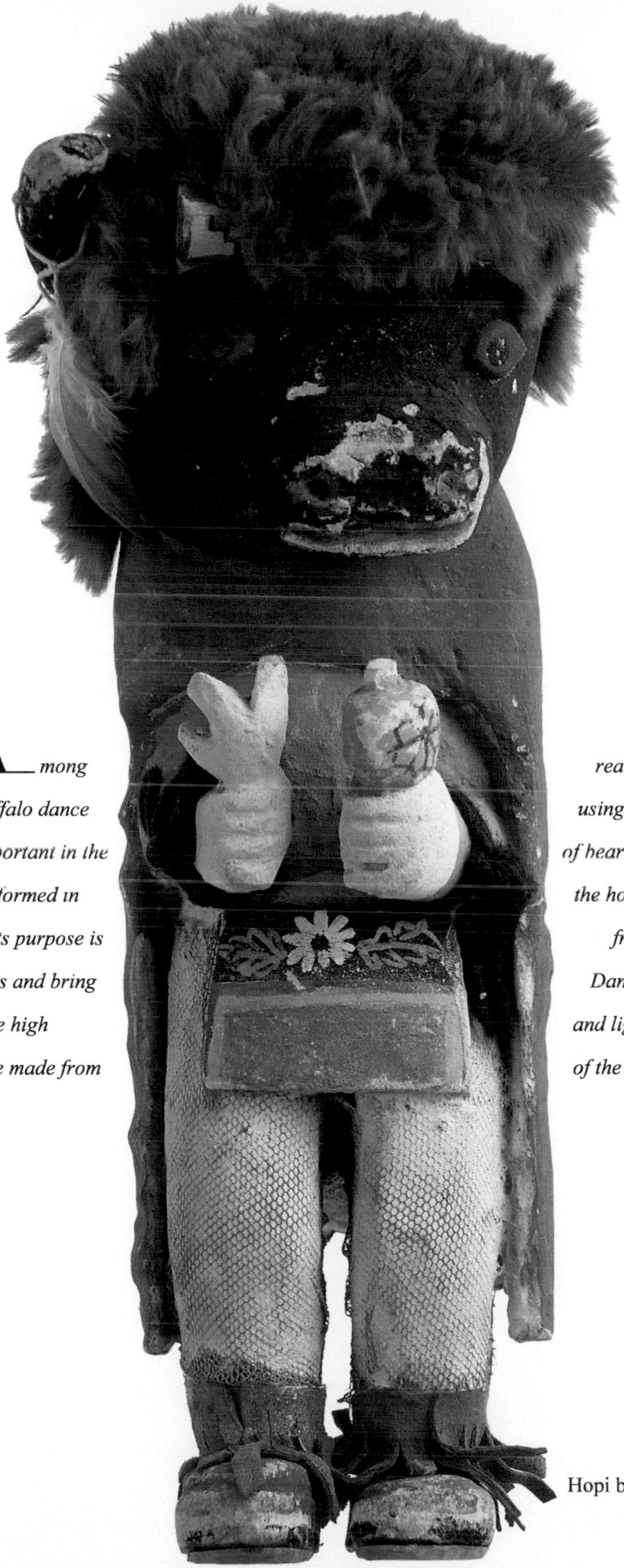

*A*mong Pueblo tribes, the buffalo dance is one of the most important in the ceremonial year. Performed in late fall and winter, its purpose is to drive away sickness and bring purifying snows to the high mountains. Masks are made from real buffalo heads or imitated using cow's horns and the skins of bear or sheep. Eagle down tips the horns; eagle feathers dangle from the dancers' left arms. Dancers carry arrows, rattles, and lightning sticks in evocation of the spiritual power of buffalo.

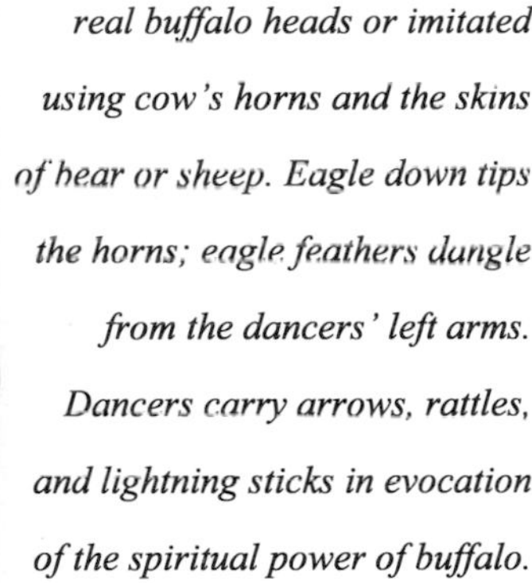

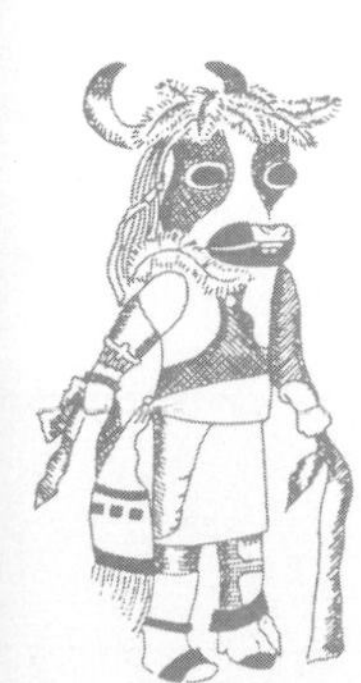

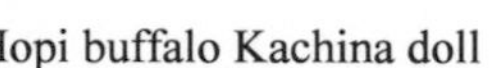

Hopi buffalo Kachina doll

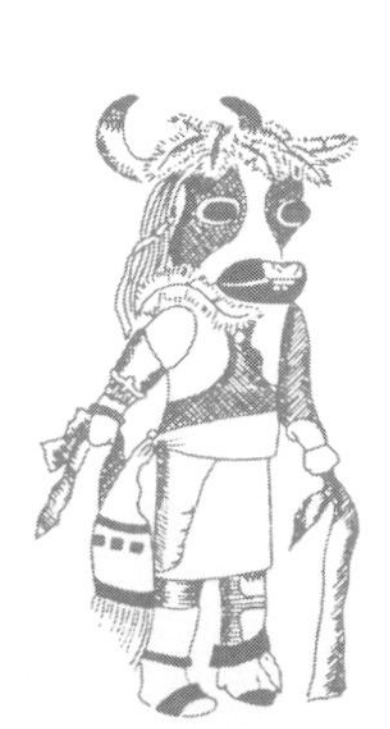

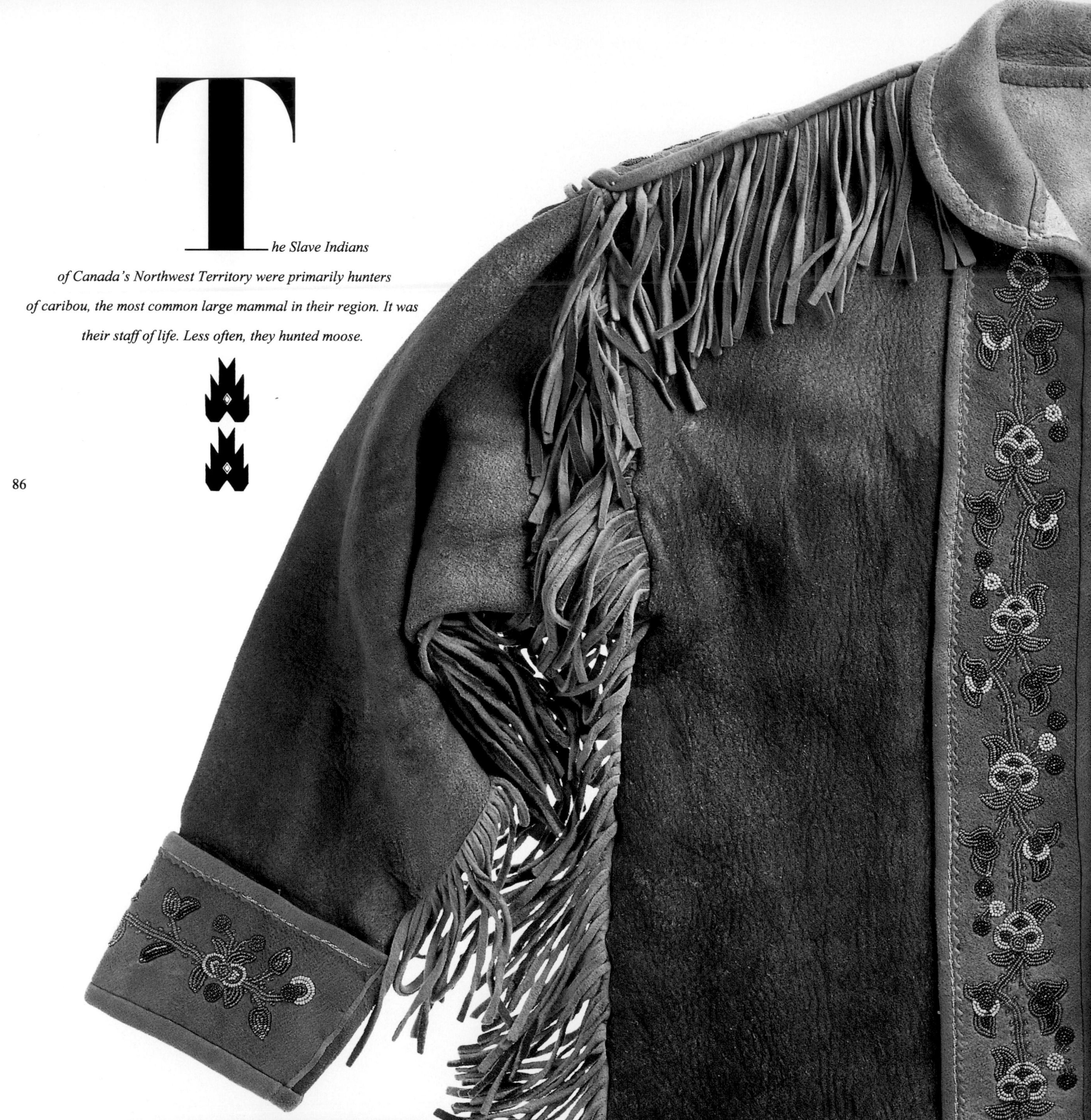

The Slave Indians of Canada's Northwest Territory were primarily hunters of caribou, the most common large mammal in their region. It was their staff of life. Less often, they hunted moose.

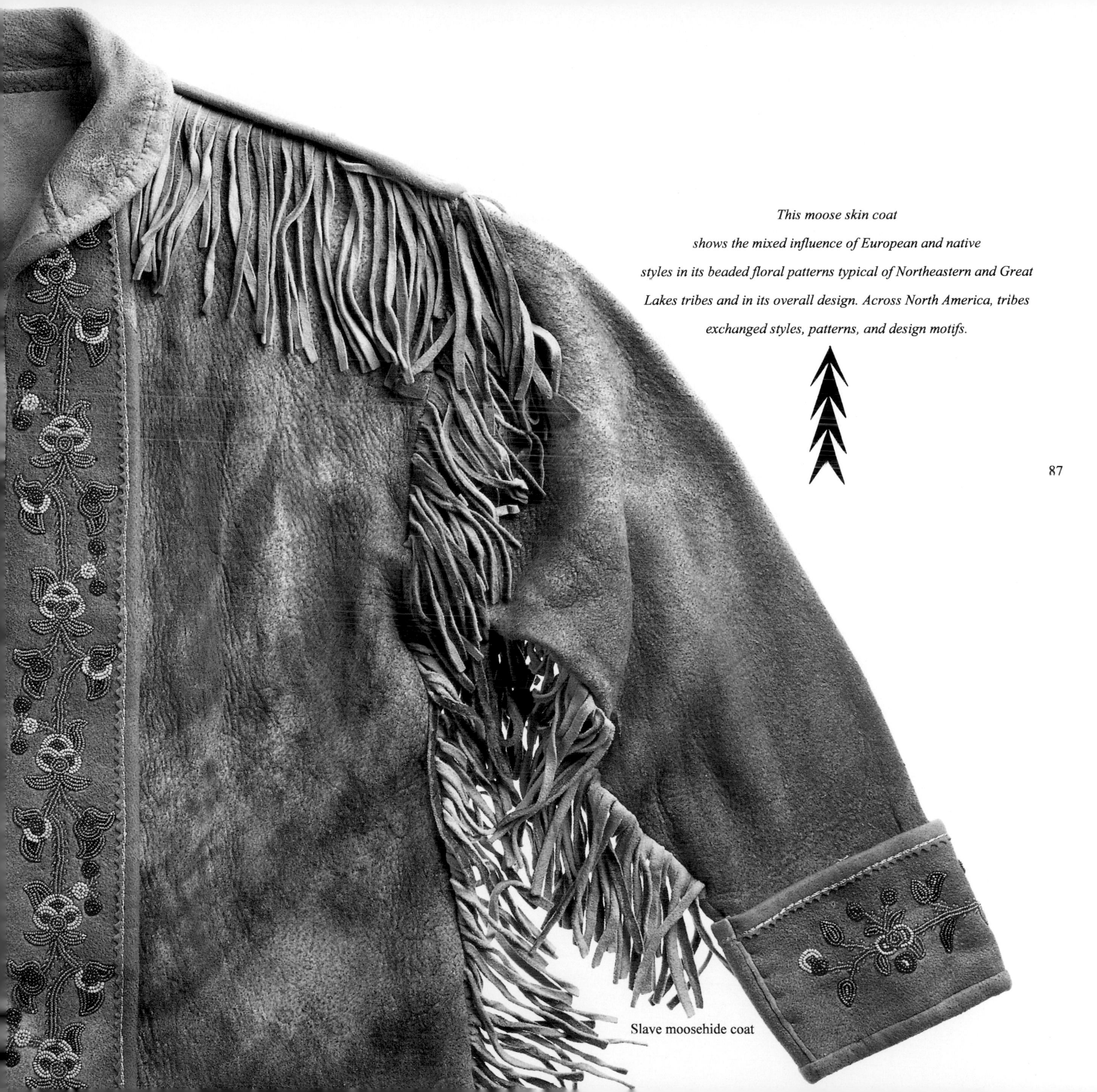

This moose skin coat shows the mixed influence of European and native styles in its beaded floral patterns typical of Northeastern and Great Lakes tribes and in its overall design. Across North America, tribes exchanged styles, patterns, and design motifs.

Slave moosehide coat

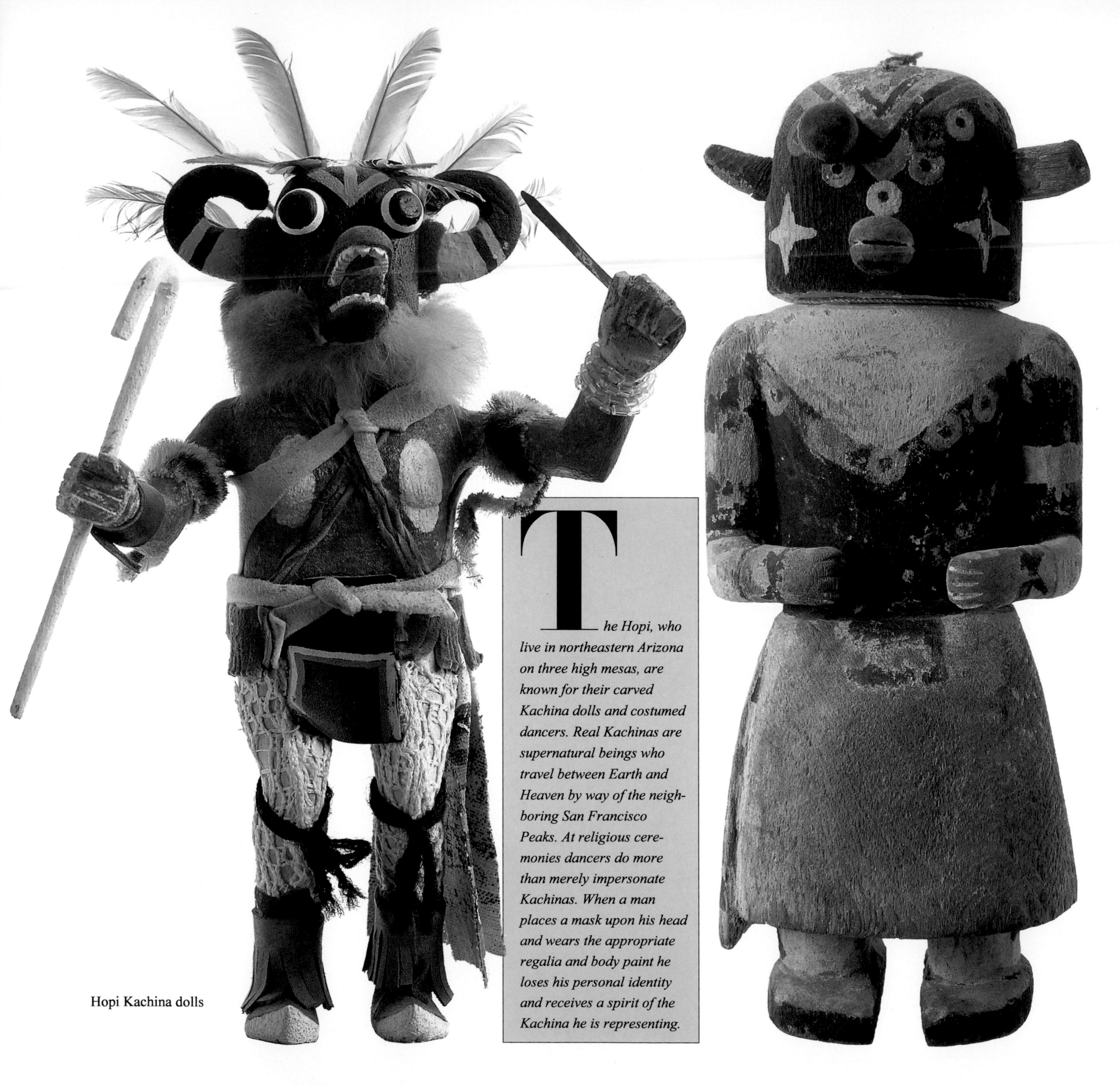

Hopi Kachina dolls

The Hopi, who live in northeastern Arizona on three high mesas, are known for their carved Kachina dolls and costumed dancers. Real Kachinas are supernatural beings who travel between Earth and Heaven by way of the neighboring San Francisco Peaks. At religious ceremonies dancers do more than merely impersonate Kachinas. When a man places a mask upon his head and wears the appropriate regalia and body paint he loses his personal identity and receives a spirit of the Kachina he is representing.

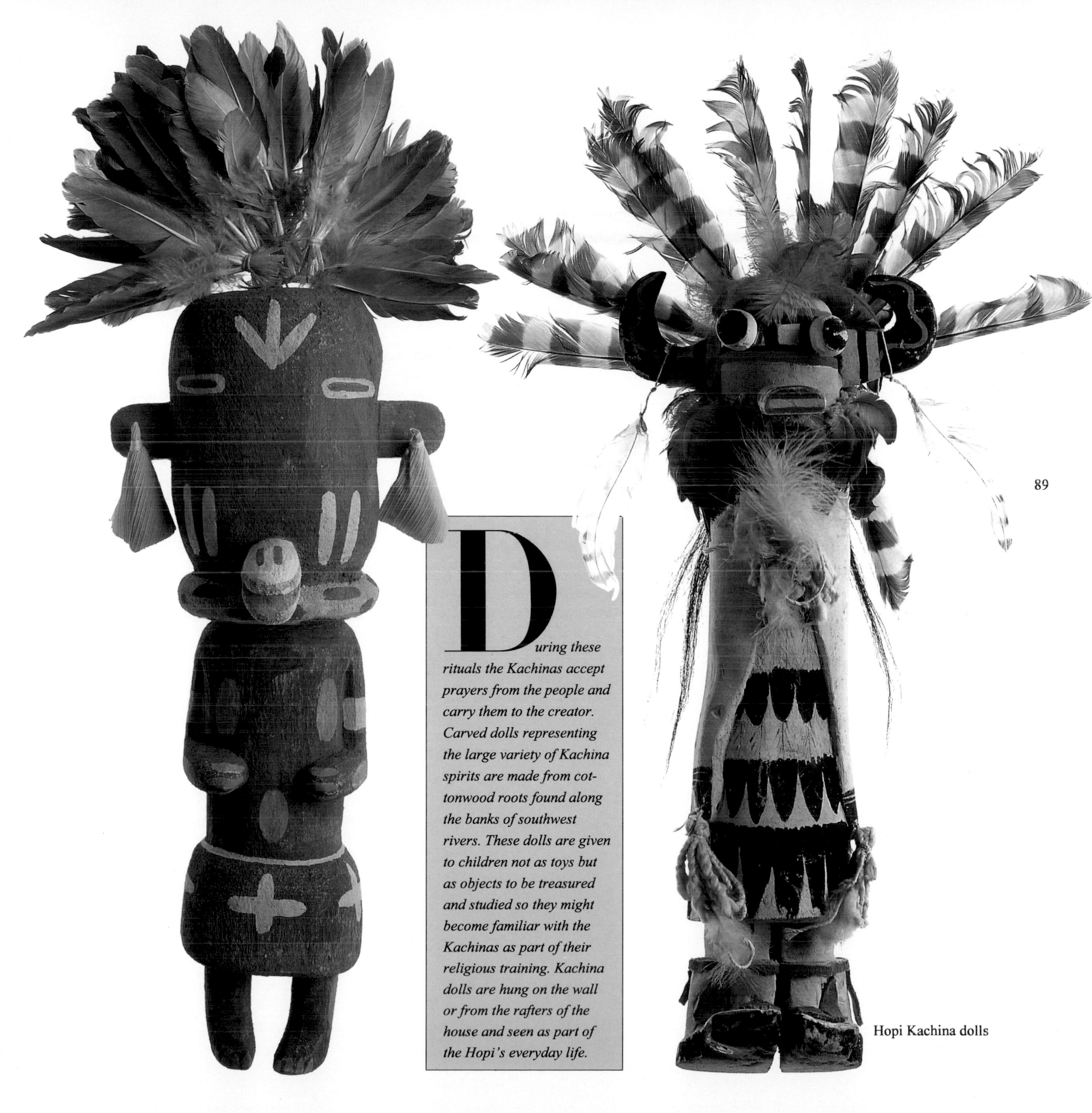

During these rituals the Kachinas accept prayers from the people and carry them to the creator. Carved dolls representing the large variety of Kachina spirits are made from cottonwood roots found along the banks of southwest rivers. These dolls are given to children not as toys but as objects to be treasured and studied so they might become familiar with the Kachinas as part of their religious training. Kachina dolls are hung on the wall or from the rafters of the house and seen as part of the Hopi's everyday life.

Hopi Kachina dolls

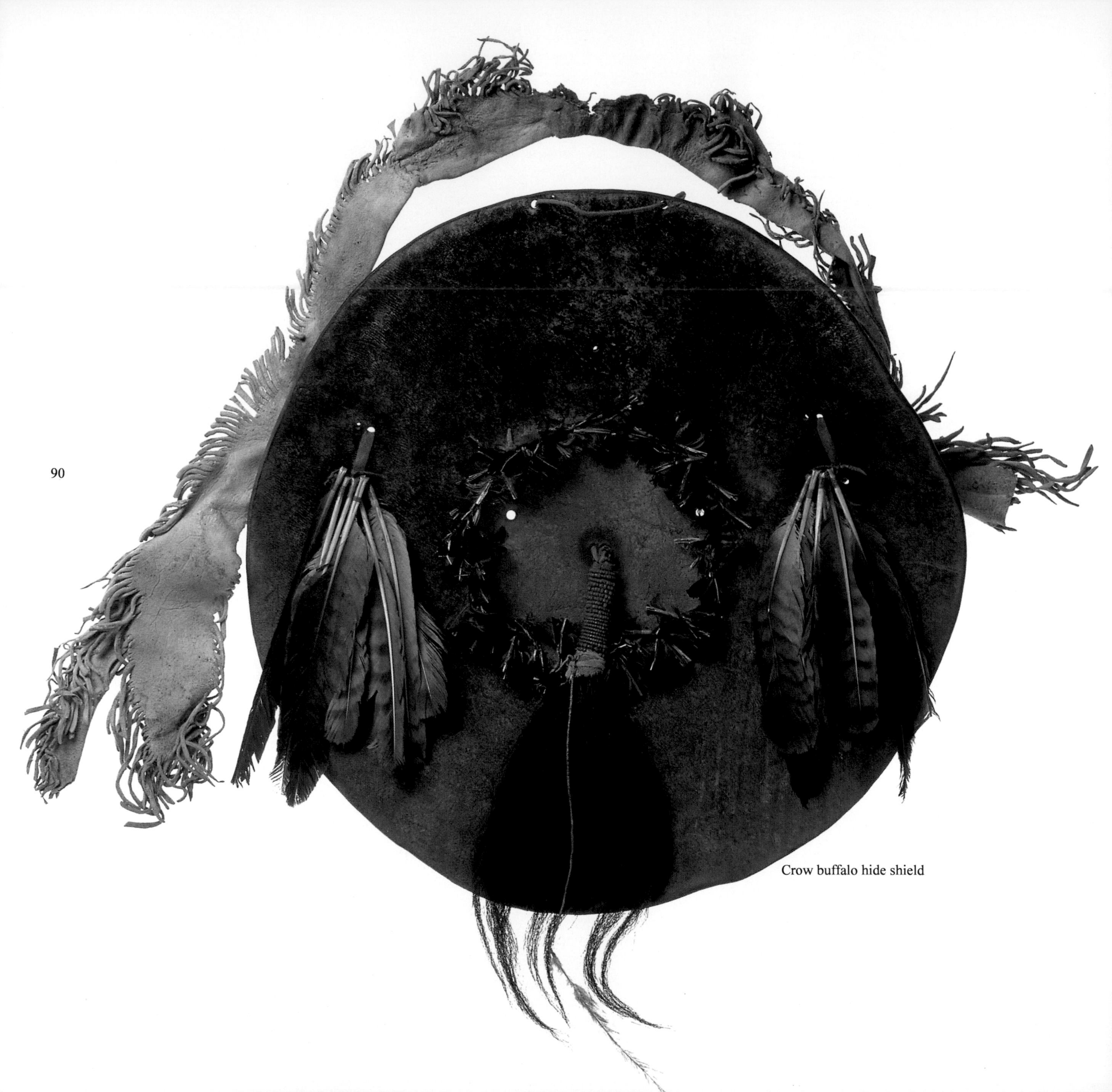

Crow buffalo hide shield

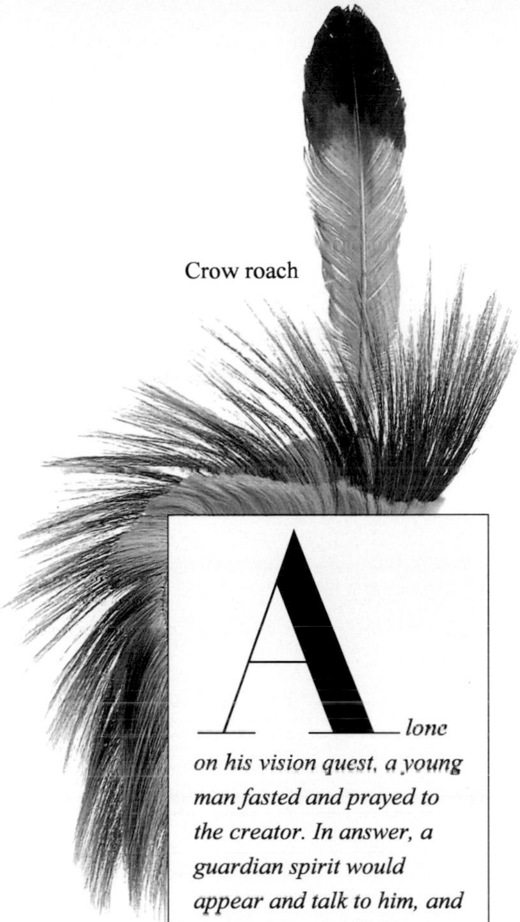

Crow roach

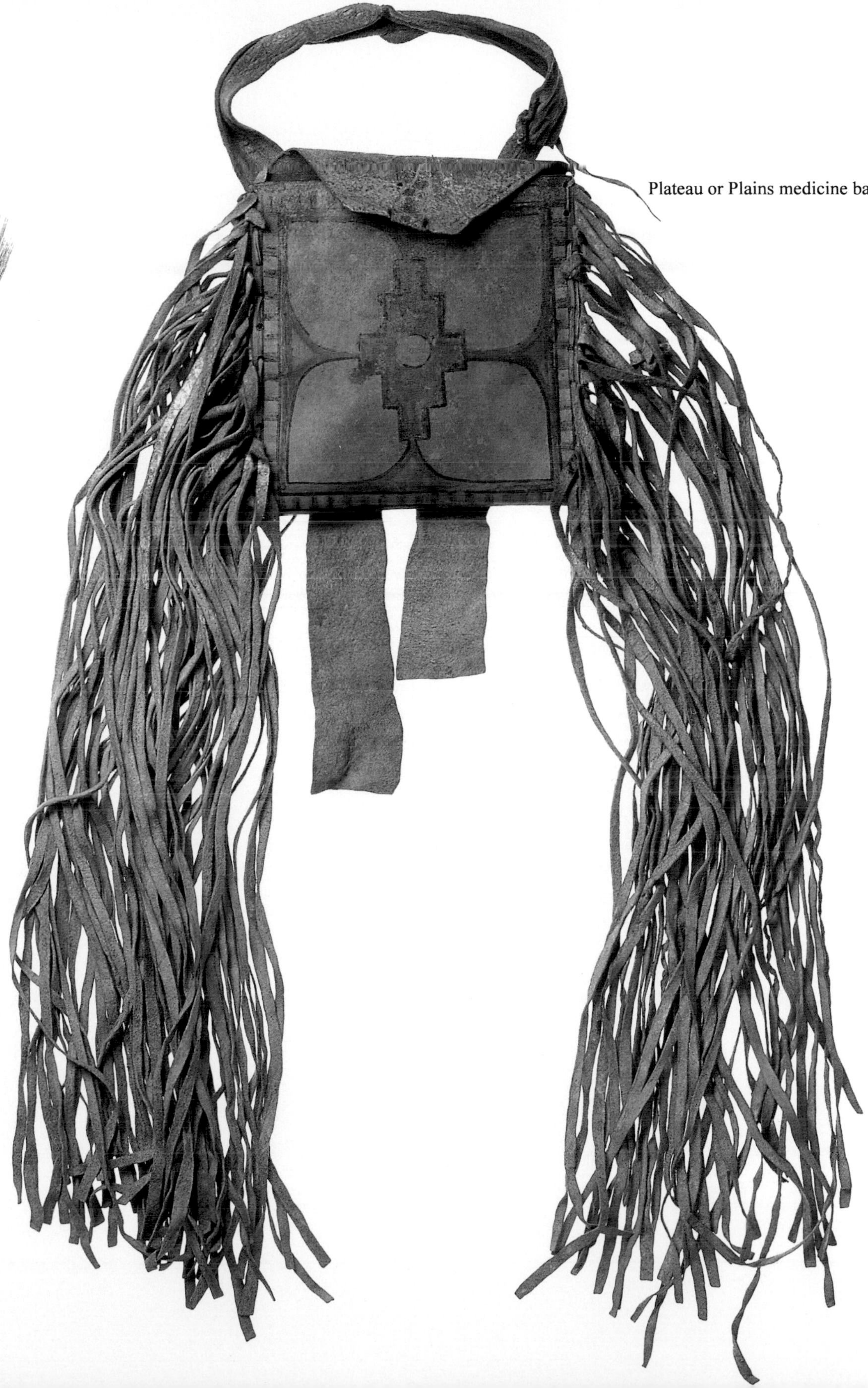

Plateau or Plains medicine bag

A*lone on his vision quest, a young man fasted and prayed to the creator. In answer, a guardian spirit would appear and talk to him, and instruct him in putting together his personal medicine bundle. The bundle might contain animal parts or pebbles with magical powers to heal the sick or to be successful in war. This painted rawhide bag was used to store such sacred materials.* Above: *The headdress called a roach is made from long guard hairs of porcupine worn with one or two eagle feathers for ceremonial or social dancing.* Opposite: *A war shield made from the skin of a bull buffalo's neck was decorated with paint and animal parts symbolizing the owner's guardian spirit.*

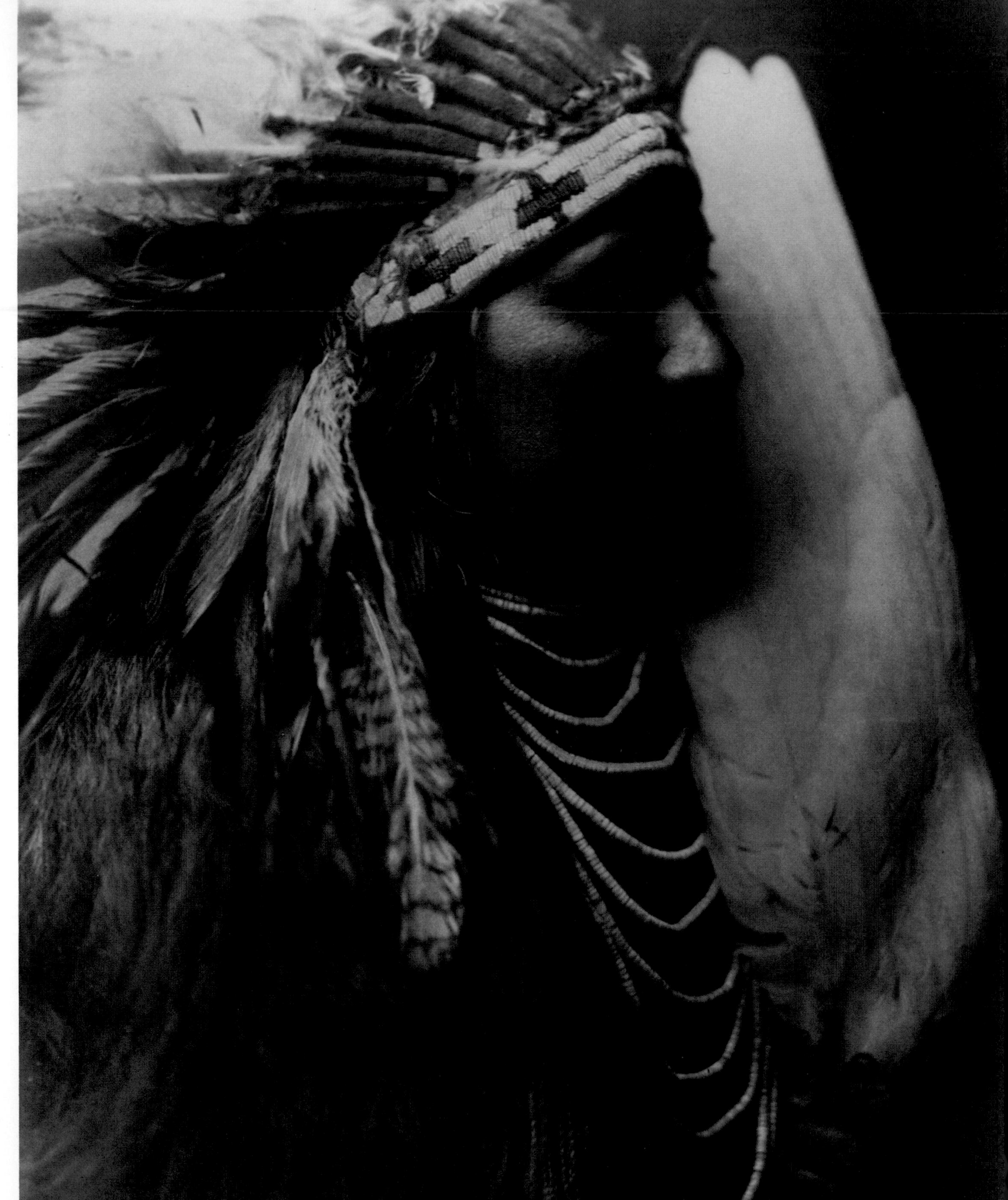

Nez Perce brave

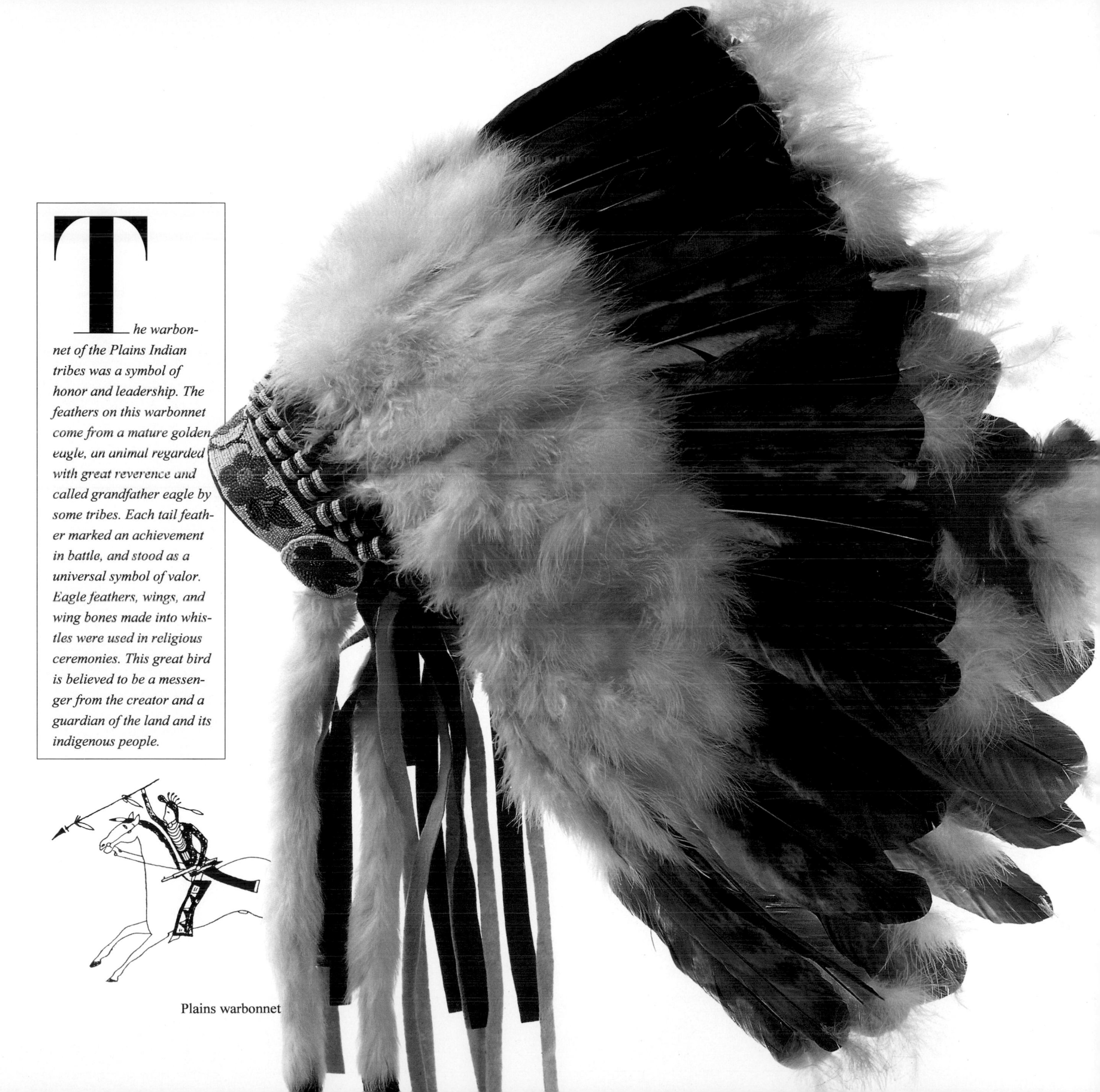

The warbonnet of the Plains Indian tribes was a symbol of honor and leadership. The feathers on this warbonnet come from a mature golden eagle, an animal regarded with great reverence and called grandfather eagle by some tribes. Each tail feather marked an achievement in battle, and stood as a universal symbol of valor. Eagle feathers, wings, and wing bones made into whistles were used in religious ceremonies. This great bird is believed to be a messenger from the creator and a guardian of the land and its indigenous people.

Plains warbonnet

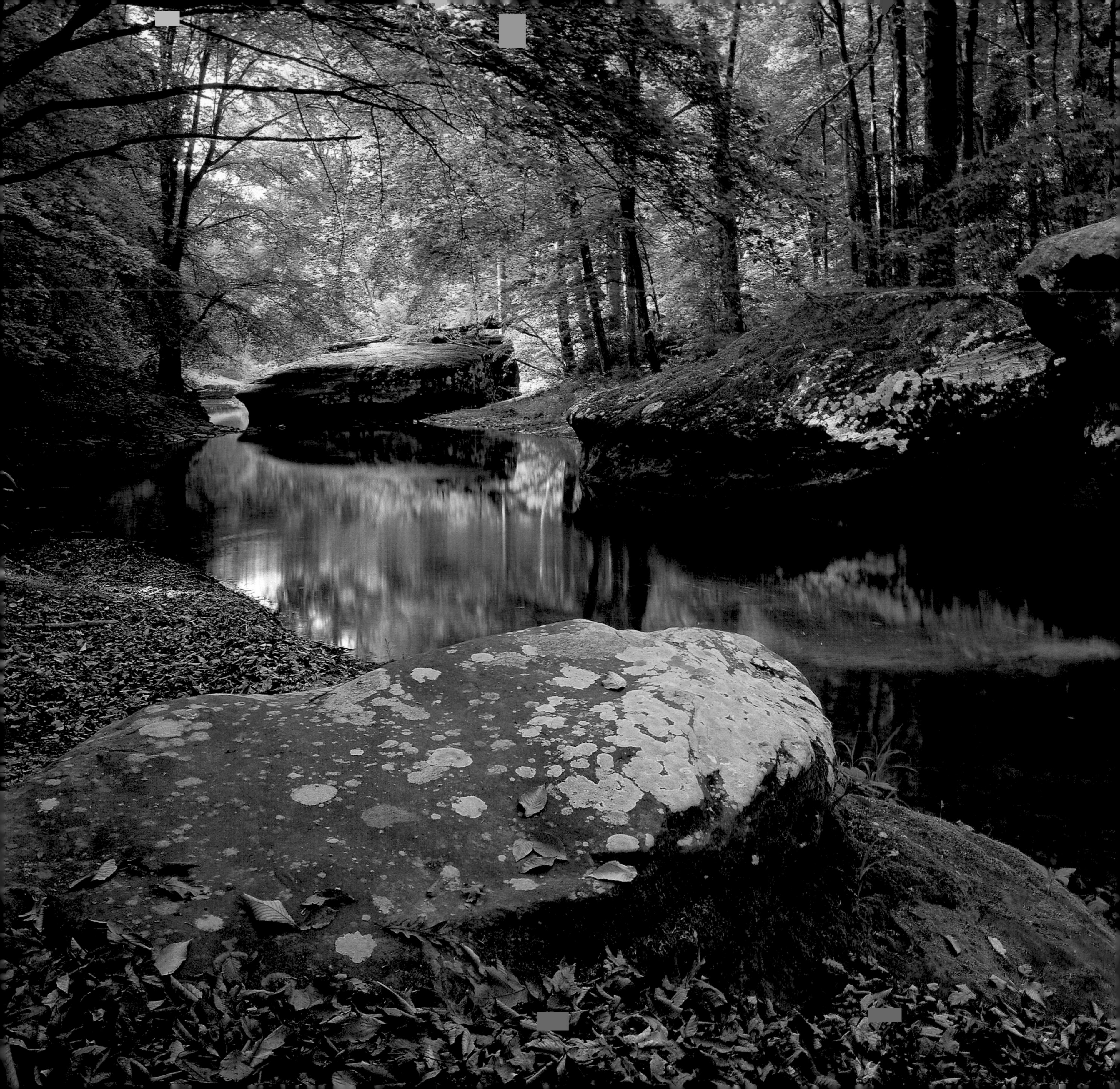

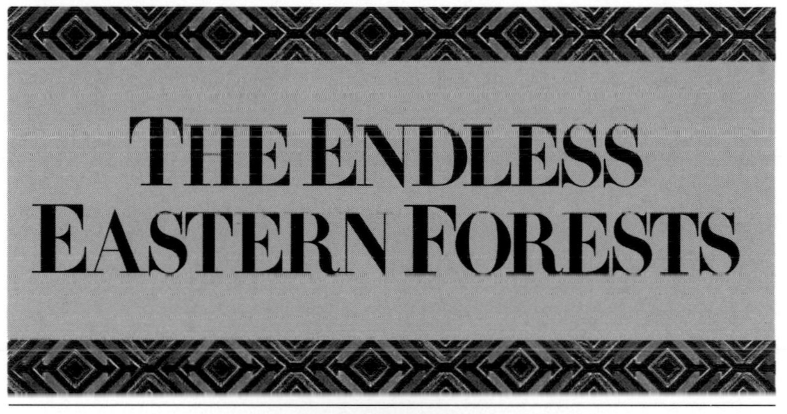

THE ENDLESS EASTERN FORESTS

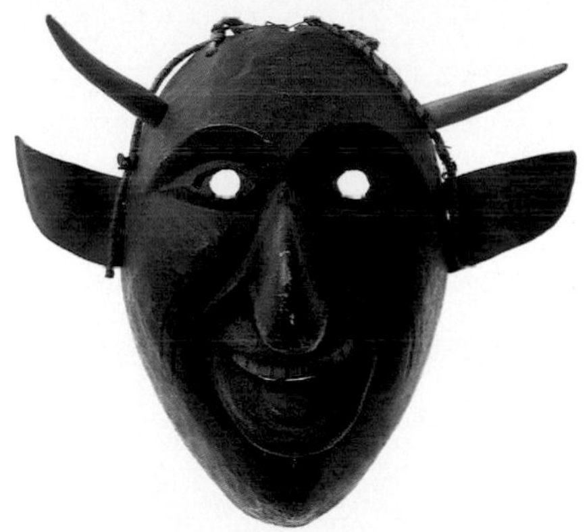

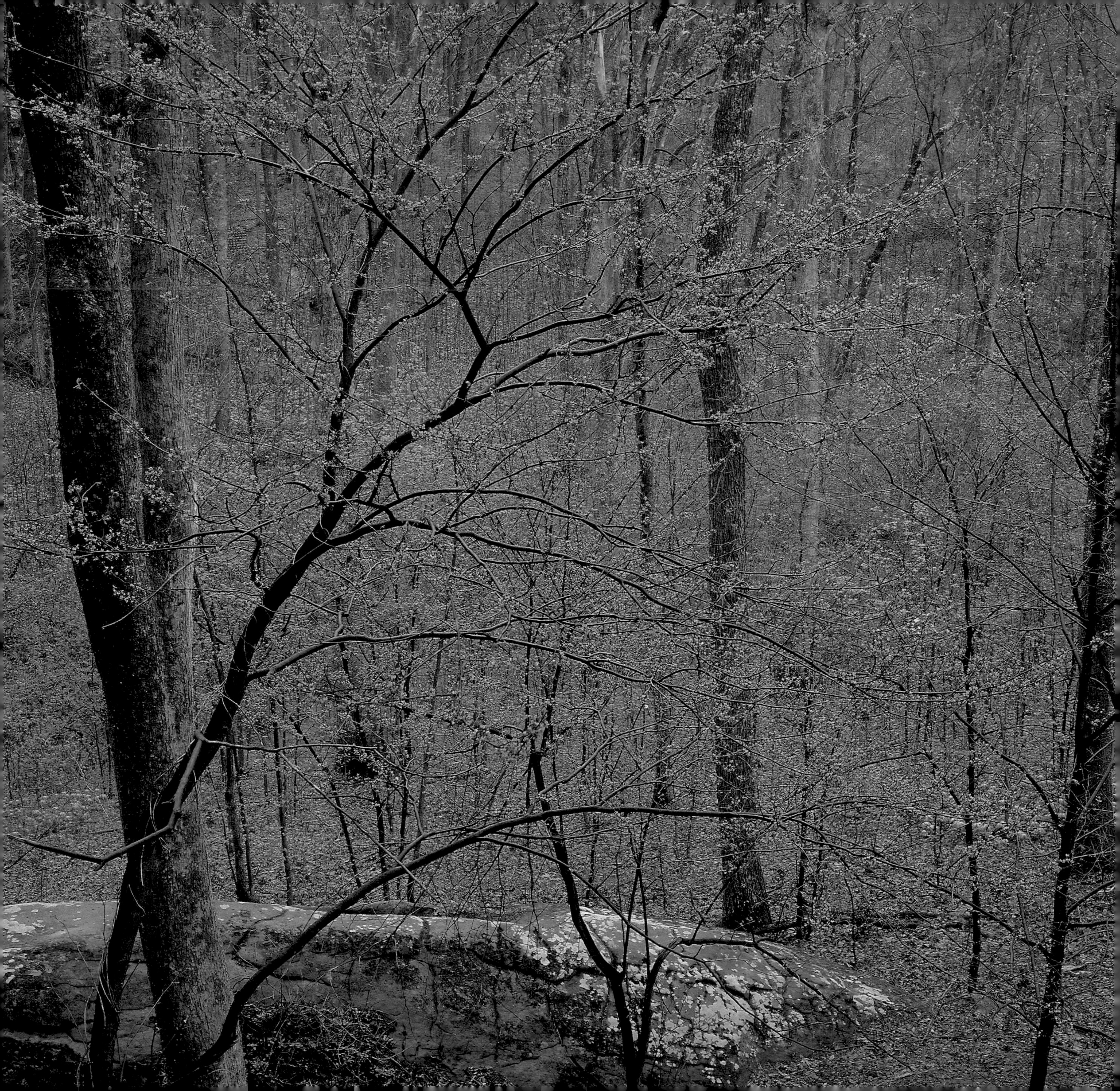

THE ENDLESS EASTERN FORESTS

The eastern forest of two hundred years ago has vanished. Replaced by farms and cities, it has disappeared in the fog of history, and is not easily reconstructed. We know this: Along a ragged line somewhere west of the Mississippi River, the Great Plains slid beneath a leafy canopy, and from that point, across rivers and shadowed valleys and green mountains, there were trees—a great blanket of trees.

It was by no means uniform. There were hundreds of species of trees and thousands of shrubs, wildflowers, and other plants. They grew in a mosaic of biologic communities that varied from north to south, from valley bottoms to the tops of hills. In the north, the vast subarctic forest of black spruce, jackpine, and birch stretched across a land of cold bogs and shallow, rock-rimmed lakes. On its southern margin, this cold forest merged with white pines, birch, ash, elm, basswood, maple, and others. Moving south to warmer lands, the number of species increased dramatically, until in the deep south there were cypress swamps, magnolias, sugar pines, and live oaks with their great muscled spreading limbs.

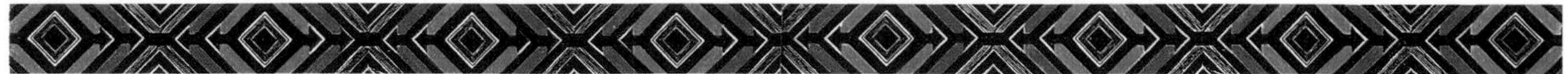

Going from east to west, there were fewer variations in species, but enormous geographical differences. Beginning on broad coastal plains and rocky headlands along the Atlantic coast, the forest climbed to its high point on the Appalachian crest, then swept down the Ohio River Valley and across the Mississippi. It reached north to embrace the Great Lakes with birch and pine and south to lose itself in the bayou country, where Spanish moss hung from the limbs of vast oak trees. Finally the woodland broke into fragments—islands and peninsulas of forest extending into the arid west, its last tendrils marching up the courses of rivers, pushing deep into the sea of tall grass. Yet the plains themselves were treeless.

It is hard to imagine the ancient forests as they stood so long ago. When trees are allowed to live out their natural lives, they—and the resulting forest—acquire characters only hinted at in their youth. Could we walk in such a forest today, we would be struck by the great height of the trees, the thickness of their trunks, and the depth of shade on the damp, leaf-covered earth.

Yet even in its primeval state, the eastern forest was always changing. Lightning-caused wildfires were common. When conditions were particularly dry, great conflagrations could sweep across thousands—perhaps millions—of acres. Tornadoes and hurricanes also took their toll, tearing swathes in the dense canopy, bringing light to the forest floor, and allowing different species to get a foothold.

The degree to which human activities affected the forest is a matter of conjecture. In some places the forest was extensively managed. Indians carved out farm fields by burning the underbrush and felling trees. The Cherokee called themselves the People of Fire, and they used controlled burns near their villages to reduce the risk of destruction from big natural fires. Centuries ago they understood a concept still regarded as controversial among modern forest managers—occasional fire can actually improve the health of a forest.

No one knows how many Native Americans lived in the East before white settlement began to take its toll. Indeed, whole tribes might have vanished beyond the reckoning of history, lost to war and disease and displacement. By current estimates, however, 1.5 to 2 million people called the eastern forest home. They included northern tribes like the Micmac, the Abenaki, the Iroquois, the Chippewa, and the Ojibwa. Along the Atlantic coast, their names remain part of the landscape—the Massachuset, the Delaware, the Chesapeake, the Roanoke, and others; southern tribes included the Cherokee, Natchez, Choctaw, Muskogee, and Pensacola.

For all these people, trees were as important as buffalo were to the plains tribes. Almost every tree gave something good. Maples yielded sweet sap for sugar and syrup. Nuts fell from walnut, hickory, chestnut, and beech trees, among others. The Iroquois used elm bark for the roofs and walls of their homes, or longhouses. The Huron preferred cedar bark for the same purpose. Ash could be split and bent and bound with rawhide to make snowshoe frames.

All across the north country, birch was common. If taken in summer (without killing the tree), it was thin and eas-

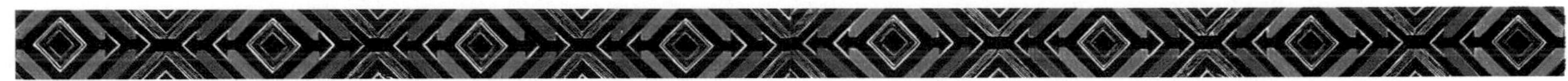

ily worked—ideal for storage containers, quivers, cradleboards, moose calls, maple syrup buckets, and roofing materials for summer wigwams. Bark removed at the end of winter was heavier and thicker, and it was used primarily for building that most efficient and graceful of native inventions, the bark canoe. No other product of the north woods surpassed the craftsmanship and elegance of this superb lightweight boat, nor was any other object a better symbol for life in the forest. To make one properly involved at least four separate trees—white cedar for the frames and ribs, maple for the thwarts and paddles, birchbark for the skin, and black spruce for the roots that sewed together the seams and for sticky pitch to seal them.

The result was a craft capable of hauling heavy loads; yet upon reaching a portage, a single paddler could flip the boat upside down and carry it over his or her head with little effort. Where lakes and rivers were abundant the canoe was an ideal means of travel and transport. Its basic design has never been improved.

Trees provided more than handy building materials. They had spirits and spiritual power. For example, the Iroquois False Face societies—men who used wooden masks in healing ceremonies—tapped the natural power of trees. For each society member, a dream would inspire a mask. The man would locate a living basswood tree and, after saying prayers and asking the tree to share its healing power, carve the face of his dream into the standing trunk. Finally, he would cut it away without killing the tree and then finish the mask with paint, hair, rawhide, metal, and other ornaments.

One common mask style had a bent nose and mouth, recalling the ancient story of two brothers, Great Spirit and Evil Spirit, who created all the things on earth. While one made good things like mountains and valleys and forests, the other brought malady and danger. Having finished their apparently incompatible toils, they held a contest to see who was the stronger. Which one could move that mountain over there? The bad brother went first. Concentrating all his power, he succeeded in shifting it slightly and proudly turned to see his brother's reaction. But in that moment, Great Spirit slid the mountain so close, and so quietly, that when his evil-minded brother turned back, he smashed his face on the rock, disfiguring his nose. Humiliated, he decided to attempt to heal the maladies for which he was also the cause; yet all those undesirable things he made continue troubling the earth to this day, an expression of the duality inherent in all aspects of life.

The healing ritual (still practiced today) was performed when requested by a person suffering a specific and usually minor malady. Members of the society donned their spirit-empowered masks, entered the sick person's longhouse, and made a circle around him. Some carried turtle-shell rattles that they shook while dancing; others took embers from the fire and blew ashes at the sick man. Yet the healing itself was done by the power of the masks—the power of the trees, the power of nature. The person so healed was duty-bound to join the society and help others in need. Thus was the self-renewing strength of nature incorporated into the community.

Continued on page 102

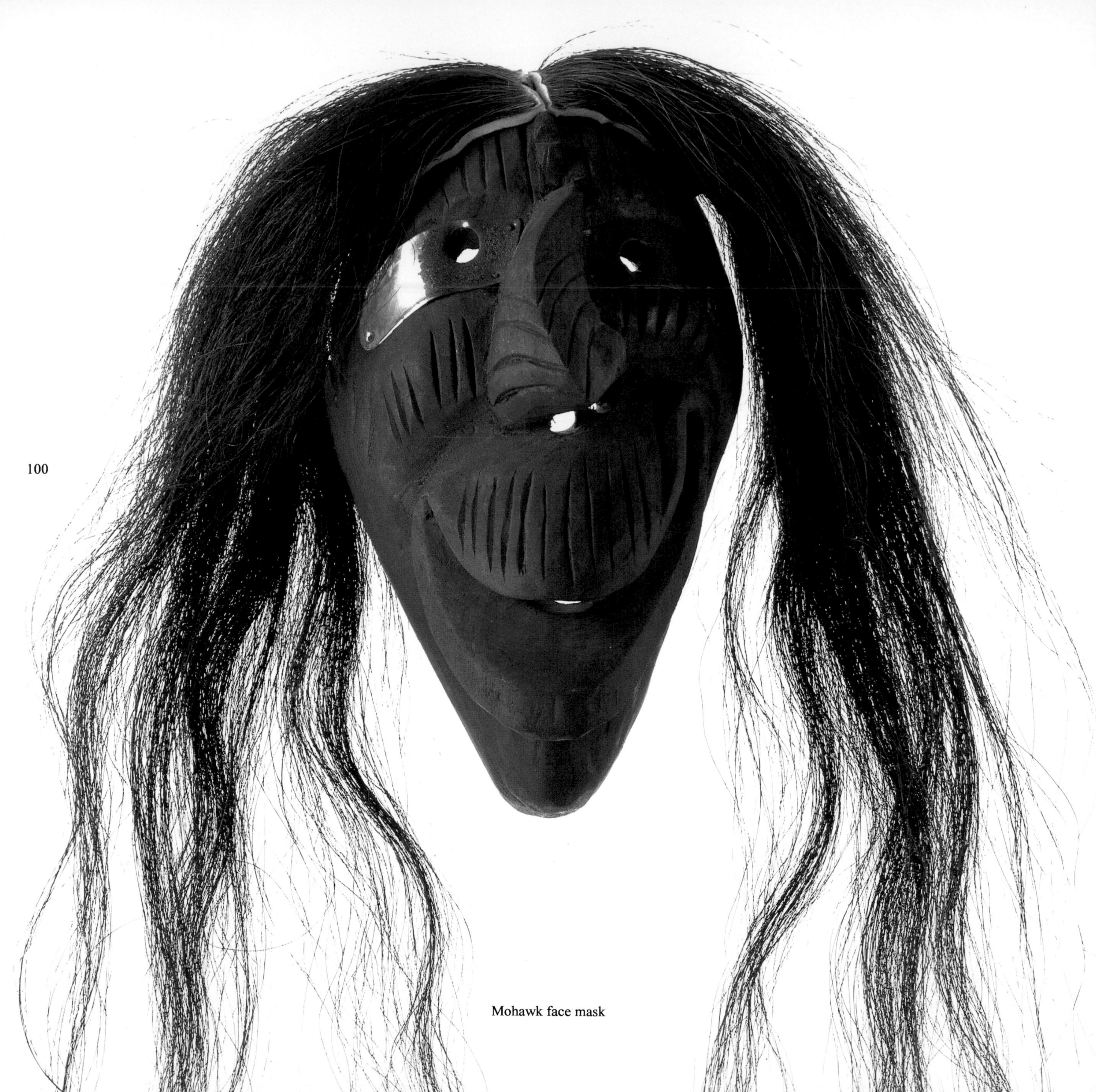

Mohawk face mask

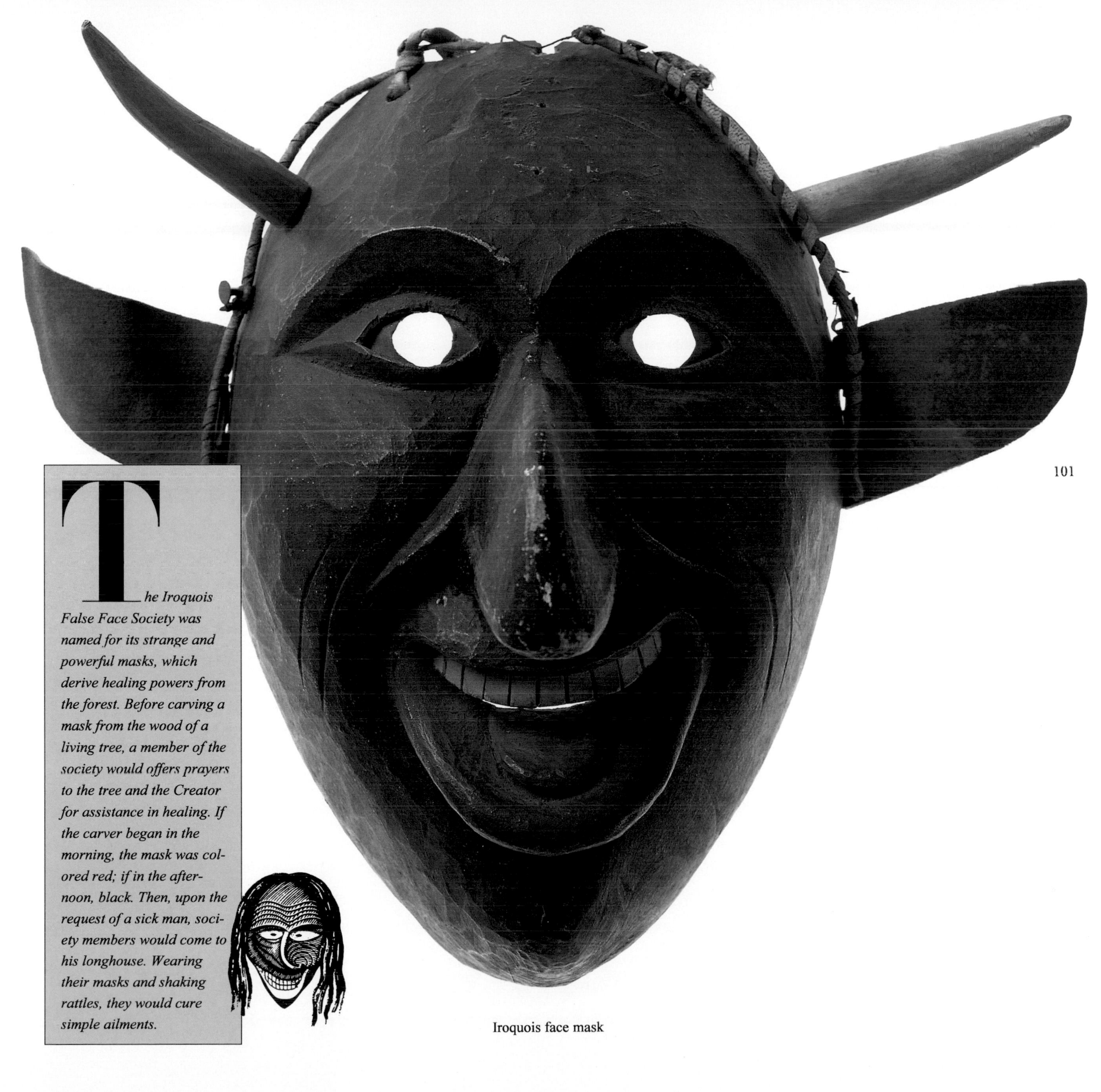

Iroquois face mask

The Iroquois False Face Society was named for its strange and powerful masks, which derive healing powers from the forest. Before carving a mask from the wood of a living tree, a member of the society would offers prayers to the tree and the Creator for assistance in healing. If the carver began in the morning, the mask was colored red; if in the afternoon, black. Then, upon the request of a sick man, society members would come to his longhouse. Wearing their masks and shaking rattles, they would cure simple ailments.

Agriculture was an important aspect of forest life, especially in the south where two crops could be grown in a single season. However, farming was impossible in the subarctic, and in marginal places like northern New England, the Micmac, Penobscot, and Passamaquoddy people regarded planting as one of many subsistence activities. If their crops did poorly, as happened all too often, they could fall back on hunting or gathering. A diversity of food options made this possible, but it also required that they keep on the move.

For these northern people the usual pattern of life was to come together during summer when food was abundant and life relatively easy. Fields might be planted with corn and other crops, but the majority of people occupied themselves with hunting and fishing. Northern rivers were jammed with migrating salmon, sturgeon, smelt, and alewives. Along the seacoast, there were clams, lobster, oysters, and ocean fish. Among plant foods they collected fiddlehead ferns, asparagus, strawberries, blueberries, blackberries, chestnuts, hickory nuts, walnuts, and more. Summer was a big time for socializing and eating.

Native Americans used what was abundant in their natural surroundings. From birch bark northeastern tribes made wigwams, canoes, cradleboards, and a variety of containers, often decorated with porcupine quills to reflect patterns from nature. The quills might be used in their natural colors—white with black tips—or colored with plant dyes. One of their favorites, Indigo blue, was introduced to Woodland tribes by colonists in the 1600s.

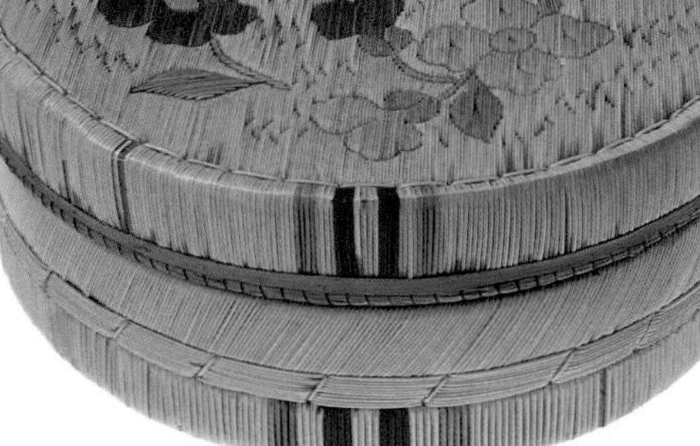

Ojibwa birch bark basket

Winter, in contrast, was a time for solitude. When the leaves turned yellow and the days grew short, northern people split into family groups and scattered to traditional hunting territories. There they would spend the winter in bark-roofed wigwams hunting caribou, deer, wolf, mink, otter, and most important of all, moose. A moose was the equivalent of a buffalo in its size and value, providing everything from meat to antlers to sinew. While deer skins made light, supple clothing for summer, moose hide, thick and durable, was preferred for winter garb. A clever jacket could be made by removing the skin of the forequarters without slitting the forelegs, which could then become one-piece sleeves.

In the warmer climate from the Great Lakes south, farming had a dominant influence. Many tribes replaced hunting with agriculture as the main source of food. Despite tribal differences, the techniques of farming along with many other aspects of culture were similar throughout the entire region. The Iroquois provide a good example.

The people of the longhouse, as the Iroquois called themselves, lived

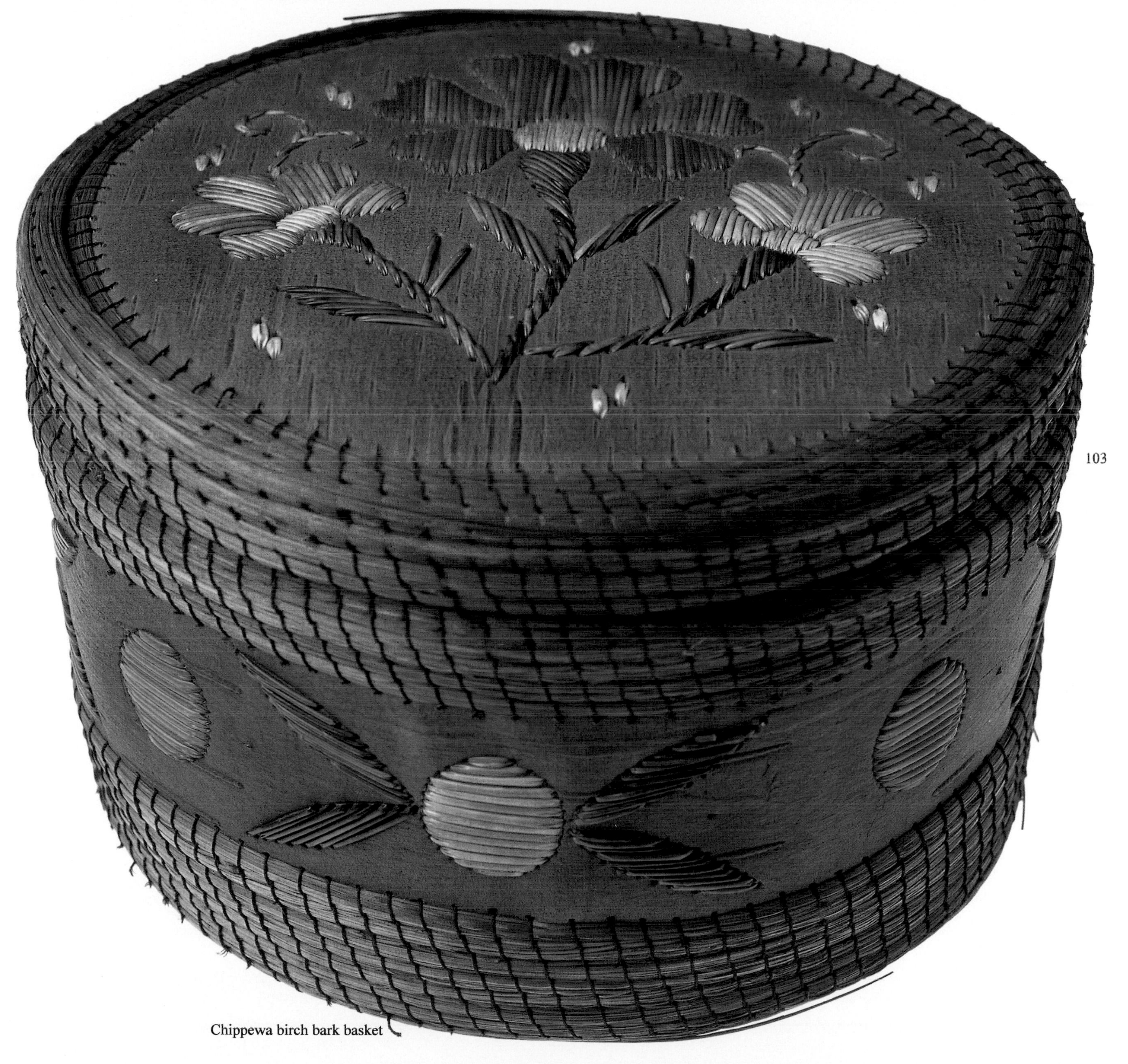

Chippewa birch bark basket

year round in villages, often fortified with high timber stockades. Their longhouses were communal structures made of wooden frames covered with slabs of elm bark. Some were very large, accommodating as many as a dozen families. Outside the village stretched the farm fields, hacked from the forest to grow corn, beans, and squash. So accomplished were they as farmers that a settled life became possible, and villages swelled to as many as two thousand residents. In this setting, the Iroquois developed a sophisticated democratic political structure under the umbrella of the Five Nation Confederacy—an effective military alliance that stood against European encroachment for many years.

The farms of the Iroquois hardly resembled the cornfields of today. They were temporary clearings, expected to produce for a few years; when the soil began to fail, the villages would move far enough to find fresh ground and start over. The first act of preparing a new farm was to cut the small trees, grub out the shrubs, burn them, and scatter the ashes. Unable to fell and remove the large trees, the Iroquois killed them by girdling, lopping off the smaller branches and leaving the naked trunks standing. Among charred stumps and branching roots they planted their corn in widely spaced hills, several kernels to a hill. After the corn sprouted, beans were planted in the same hills, so the beans could use the cornstalks for support. Finally, pumpkin and other kinds of squash trailed along the ground beneath the beans and corn—three crops growing in the same field.

Throughout the eastern woodlands the success and

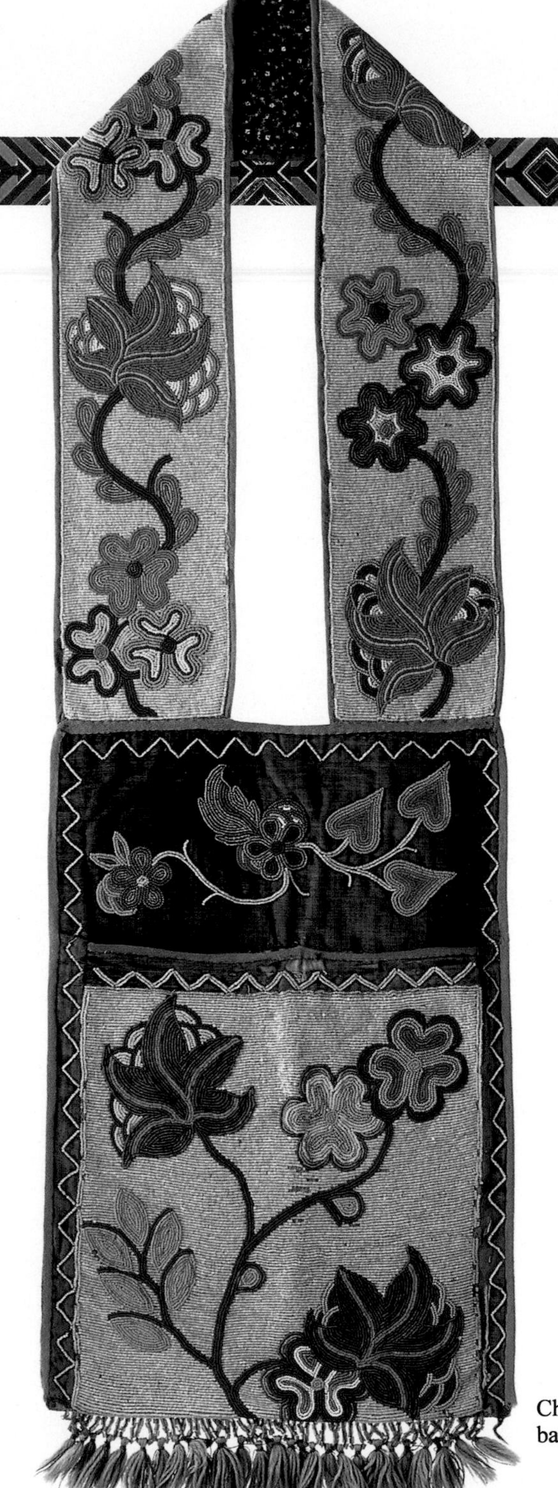

Chippewa or Ojibwa bandolier bag

Before Europeans arrived, women of the eastern woodland and Great Lakes were masters in the decorative use of natural materials including porcupine quills, buffalo wool, and moose hair. In the 1600s French traders introduced glass beads, cloth, and European floral designs. Combining new materials with old techniques, the Iroquois developed a type of lazy-stitch technique in which the arching of the stitch is emphasized by crowding the beads and raising them with padding as in this beaded bag. Opposite: *This bandolier bag was owned by a man of status among the Great Lakes tribes.*

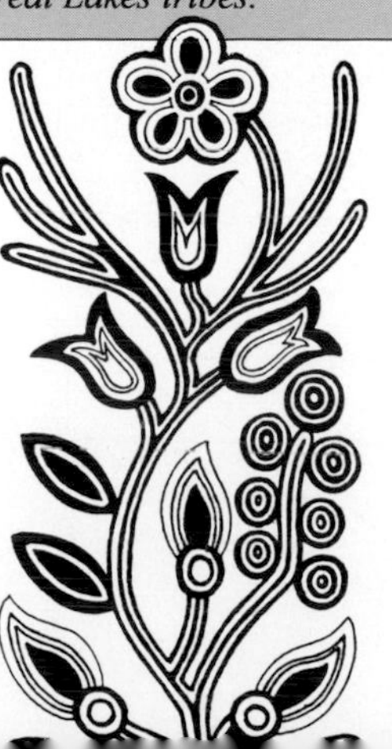

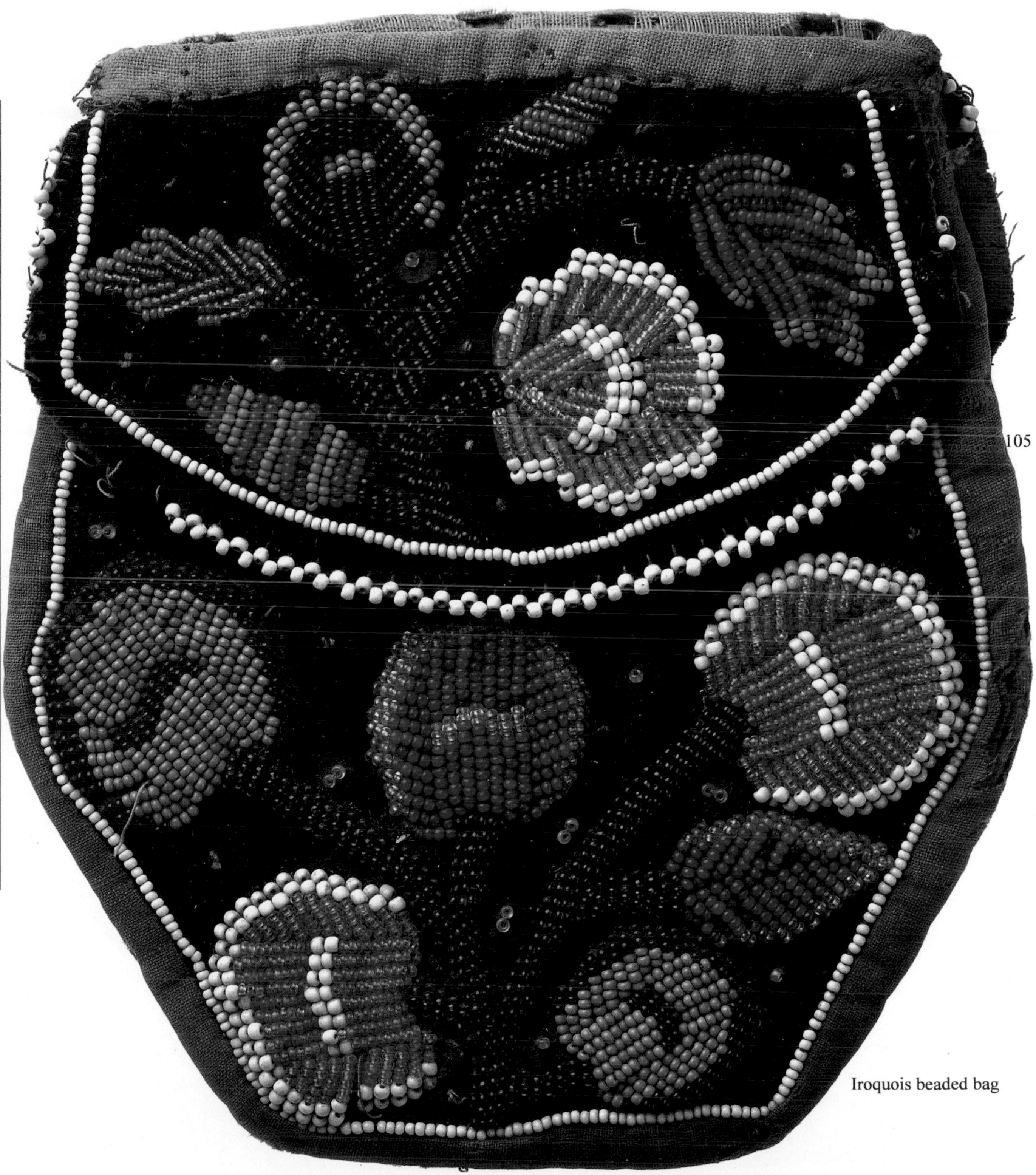

Iroquois beaded bag

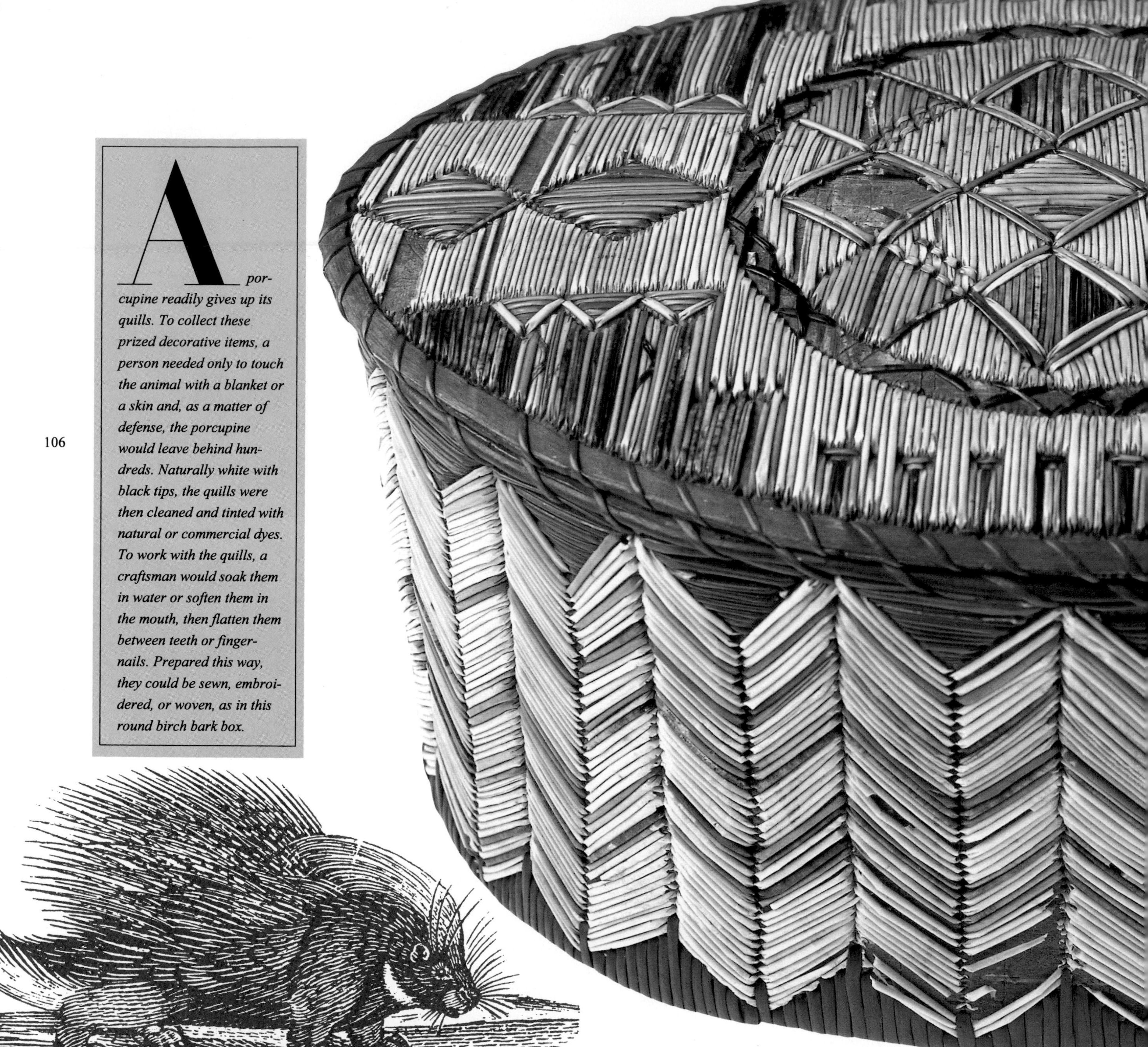

A porcupine readily gives up its quills. To collect these prized decorative items, a person needed only to touch the animal with a blanket or a skin and, as a matter of defense, the porcupine would leave behind hundreds. Naturally white with black tips, the quills were then cleaned and tinted with natural or commercial dyes. To work with the quills, a craftsman would soak them in water or soften them in the mouth, then flatten them between teeth or fingernails. Prepared this way, they could be sewn, embroidered, or woven, as in this round birch bark box.

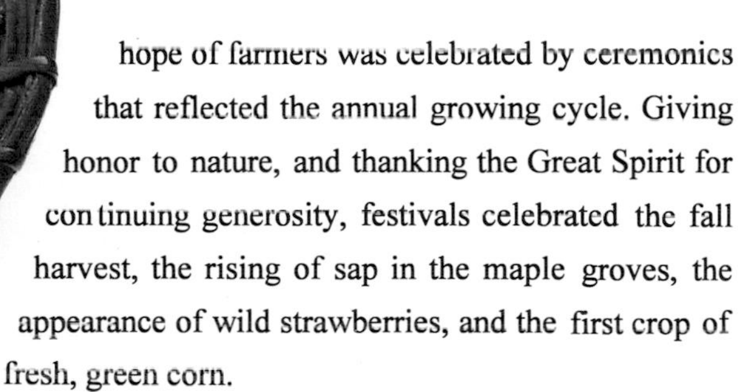

hope of farmers was celebrated by ceremonics that reflected the annual growing cycle. Giving honor to nature, and thanking the Great Spirit for continuing generosity, festivals celebrated the fall harvest, the rising of sap in the maple groves, the appearance of wild strawberries, and the first crop of fresh, green corn.

Summer was also the time for war. It was not war in the modern sense, in which whole societies battle each other for territory or political motives. War among Native Americans involved small groups of men in raiding parties. Each man was independent; he chose to follow a war leader or participate in a given raid as a matter of his own judgement and not because he was ordered to do so. And although a successful raiding party would take captives and seize property and kill foes, the purpose was more to prove courage or fighting prowess than to acquire territory or goods. In keeping with this personal view of war, weaponry was a highly individual matter. There were no uniforms or identical kits among a tribe's fighters. War clubs, bows, quivers, and body paint all reflected an individual warrior's preference, usually as dictated by helper spirits encountered in dreams and visions.

This explains, perhaps, why even the weapons of war, some of which performed terrible deeds, hold such a lasting appeal. As with all the objects pictured in this book, it is their synthesis of personal vision, function, and artistic beauty that speaks to us across the gulf of centuries and cultural differences.

Micmac birch bark basket

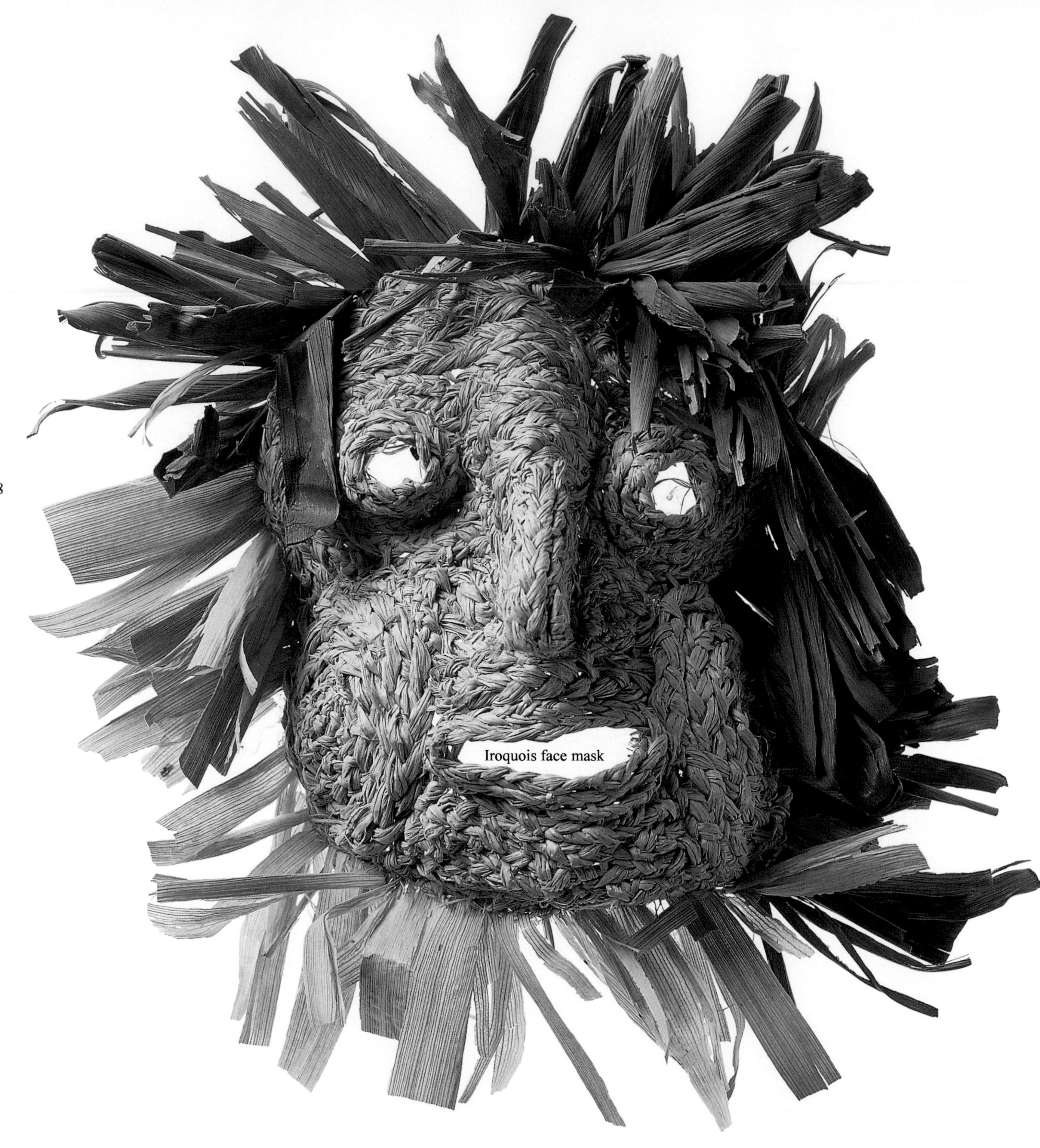

Iroquois face mask

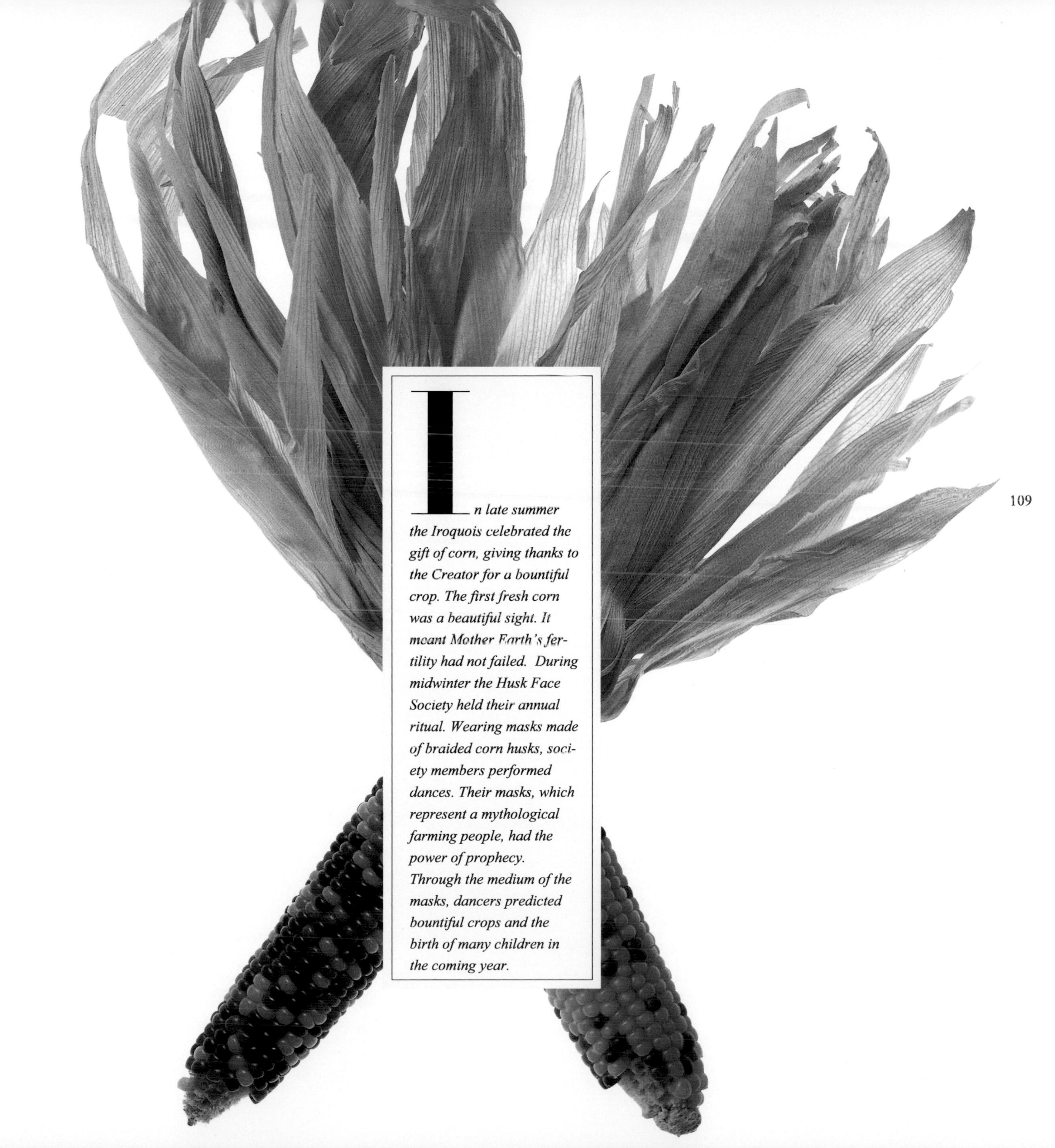

In late summer the Iroquois celebrated the gift of corn, giving thanks to the Creator for a bountiful crop. The first fresh corn was a beautiful sight. It meant Mother Earth's fertility had not failed. During midwinter the Husk Face Society held their annual ritual. Wearing masks made of braided corn husks, society members performed dances. Their masks, which represent a mythological farming people, had the power of prophecy. Through the medium of the masks, dancers predicted bountiful crops and the birth of many children in the coming year.

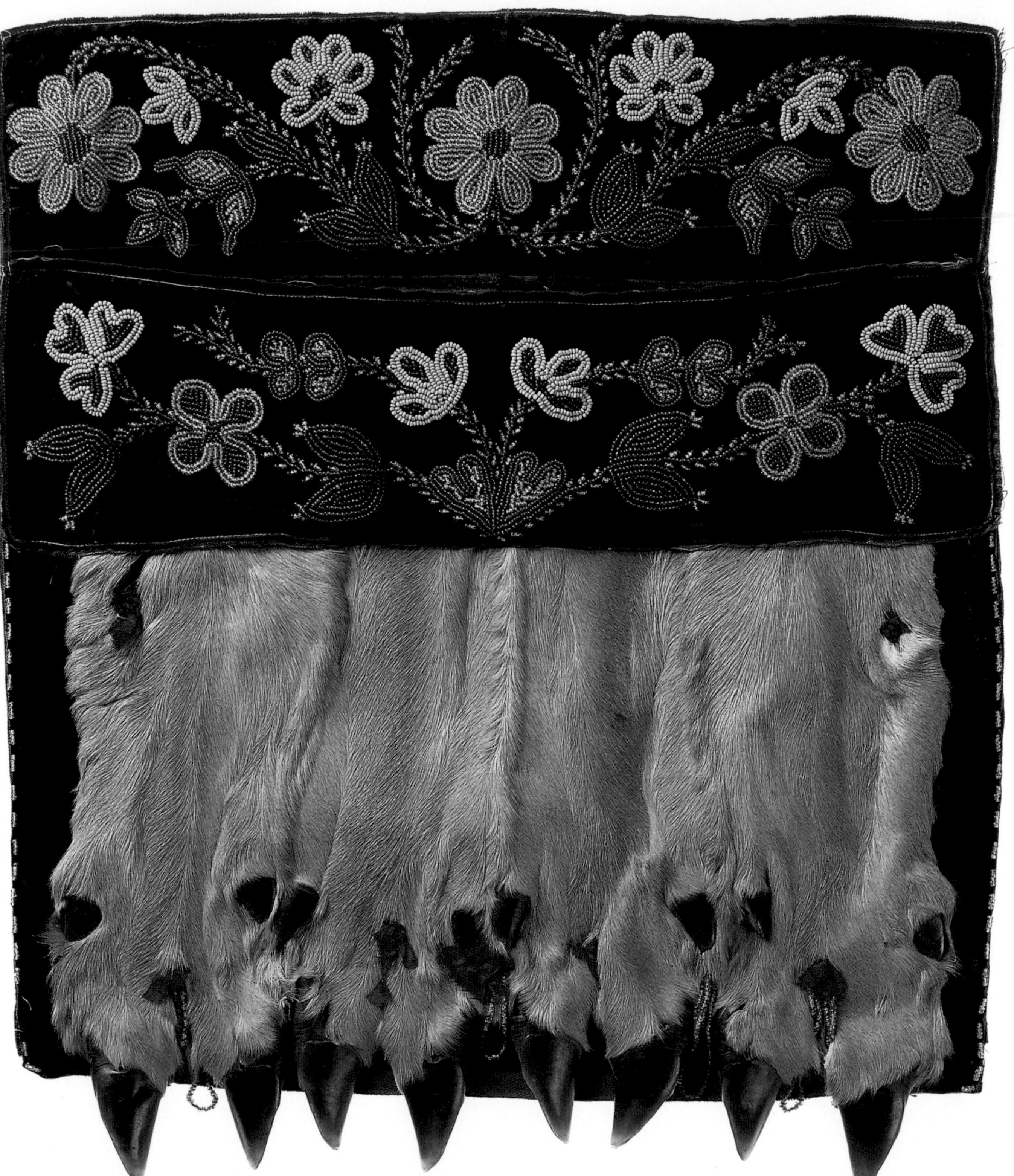

Ornamented bags have always been important to the Great Lakes and Eastern Woodland tribes. A man might own several bags for carrying tobacco, flint and steel, and other supplies. After guns became available, he might also have carried a shot pouch for his shooting accessories. Larger bandolier bags beaded with geometric or floral patterns were worn over one shoulder. These were sometimes called friendship bags because they were given as gifts or traded to the Plains Indian tribes for horses. This beaded bandolier bag is embellished with deer hooves and ribbon.

Ojibwa bandolier bag

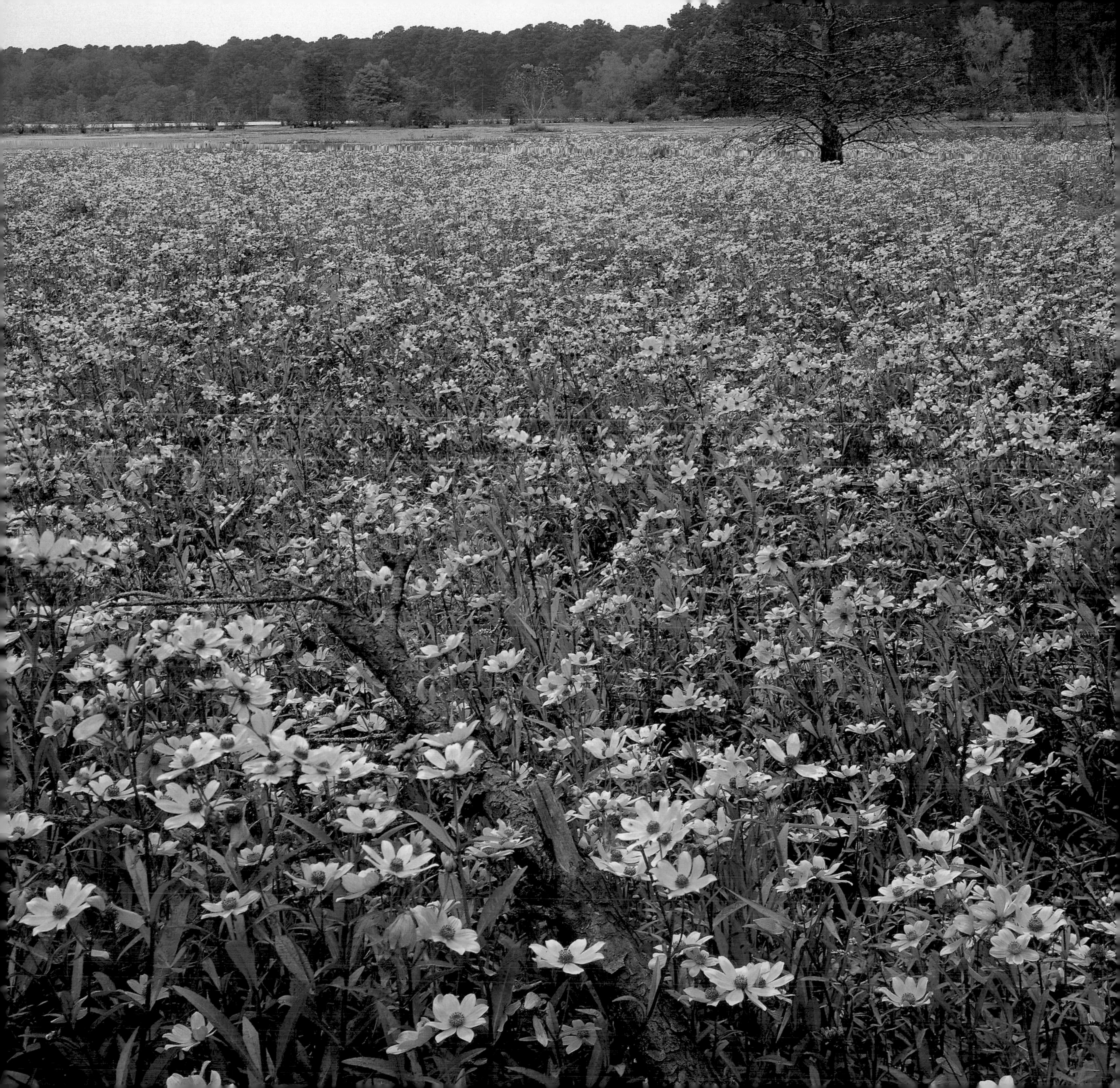

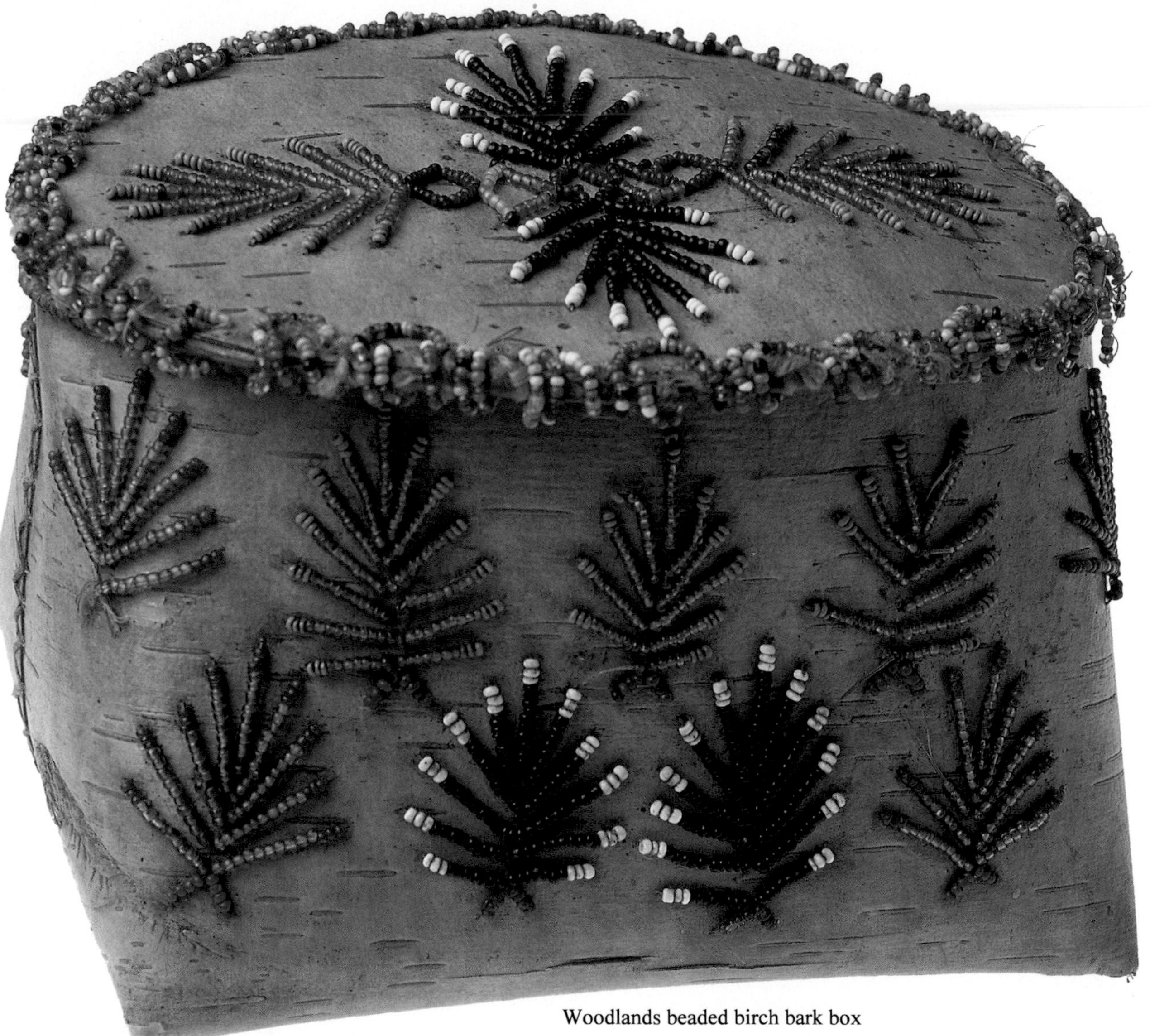

Woodlands beaded birch bark box

Where broad-leafed trees grew tall and thick in the valleys and along shores of lakes lived the Great Lakes and Eastern Woodland tribes—farmers, fishermen, and hunters of the forest. When tree bark was peeled, dried, and flattened, it became the walls of their wigwams. The same bark scraped smooth, curved, stitched, and decorated with porcupine quills or glass beads became containers of various shapes, like this abstract floral box. Most utilitarian objects were decorated with geometric or floral designs.

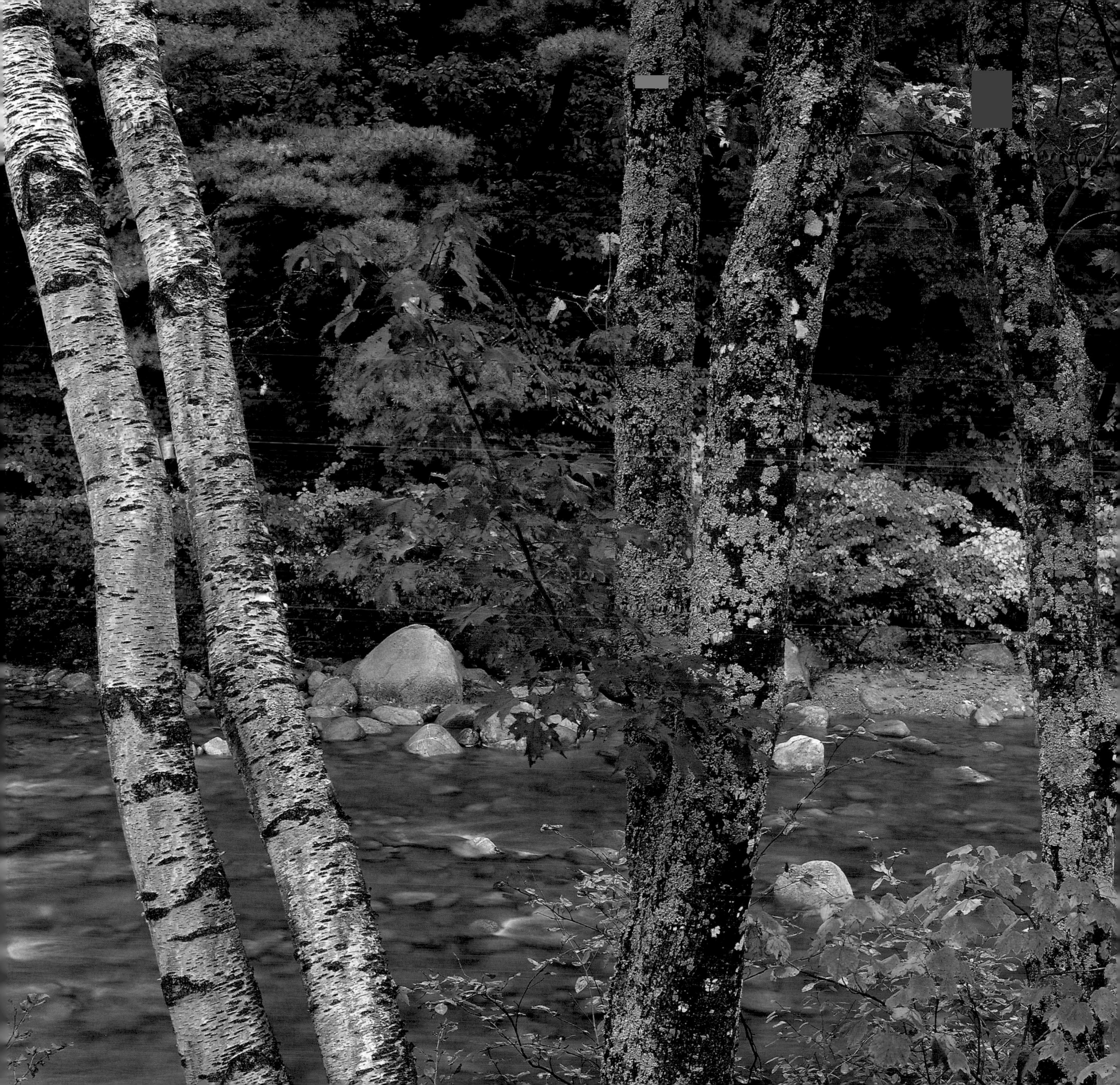

114

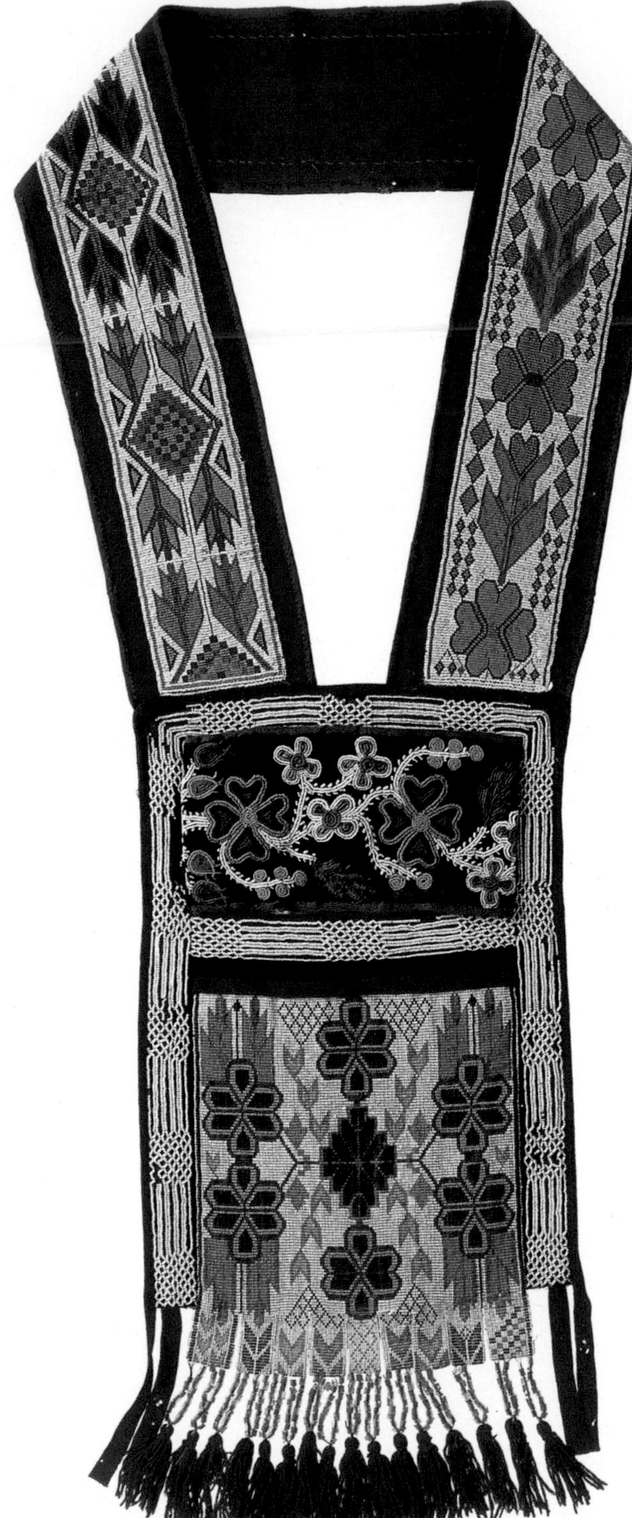

Bandolier bag

These two bandolier or shoulder bags were used by the men of the Great Lakes tribes to carry prized possessions. The design of these stylish carryalls may have been inspired by European shoulder pouches. Tribes of the Great Lakes developed floral designs to a high artistic degree. The bag at the left is from the 1850s and has an abstract floral design. The one on the right is from the late 1800s and has a more traditional realistic pattern.
Opposite: *During the late 1800s women of the northern Great Lakes used silk threads to embroider bags, moccasins, mittens, and gaunlets made from moose and deer hides.At mission schools, nuns taught embroidery to Indian girls as part of their general education in homemaking.*

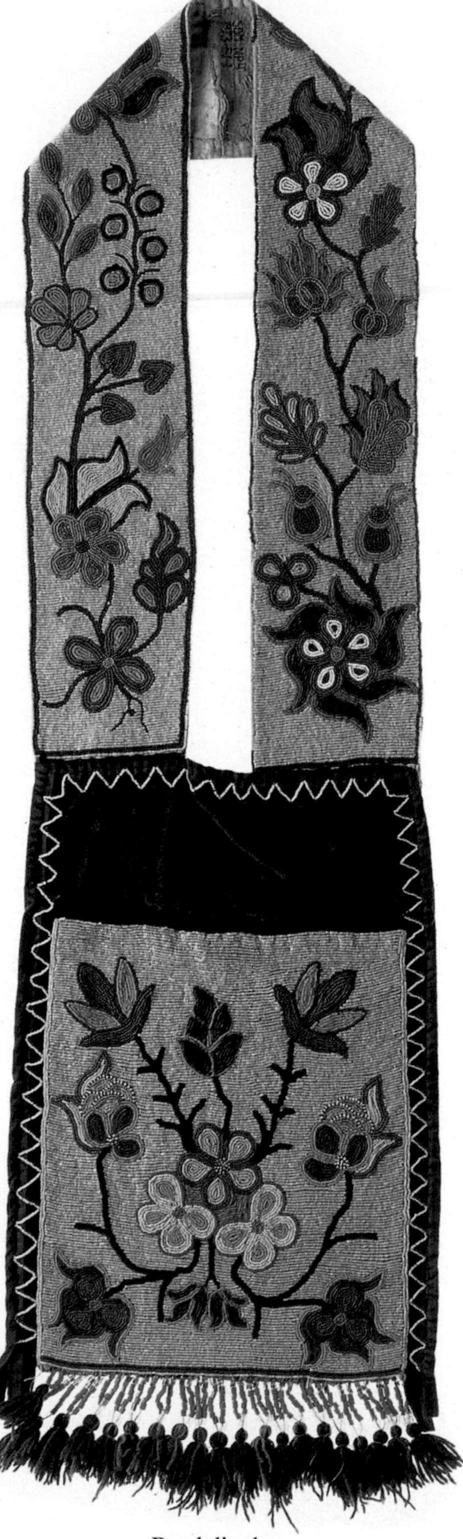

Bandolier bag

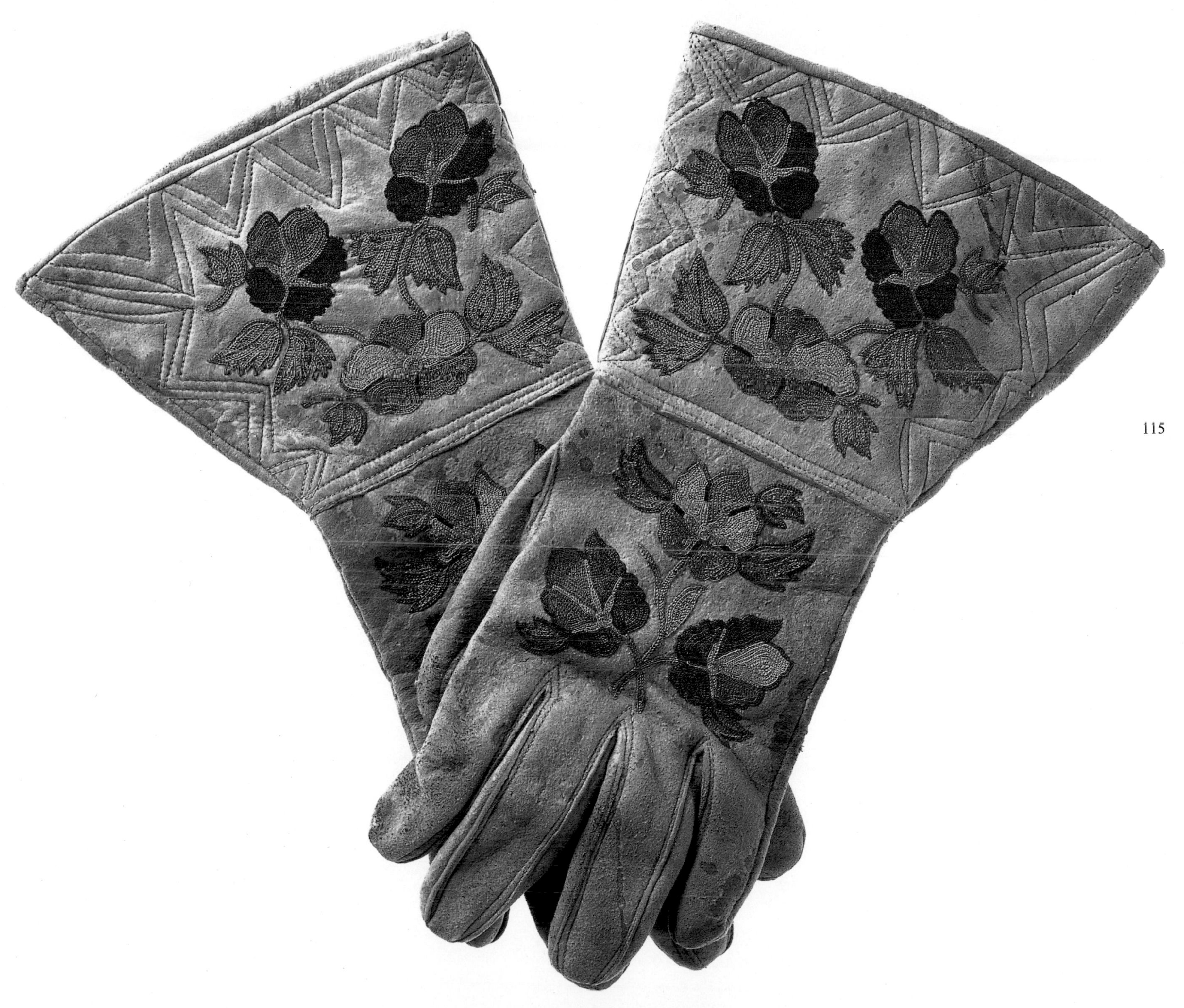

Ojibwa or Cree embroidered gauntlets

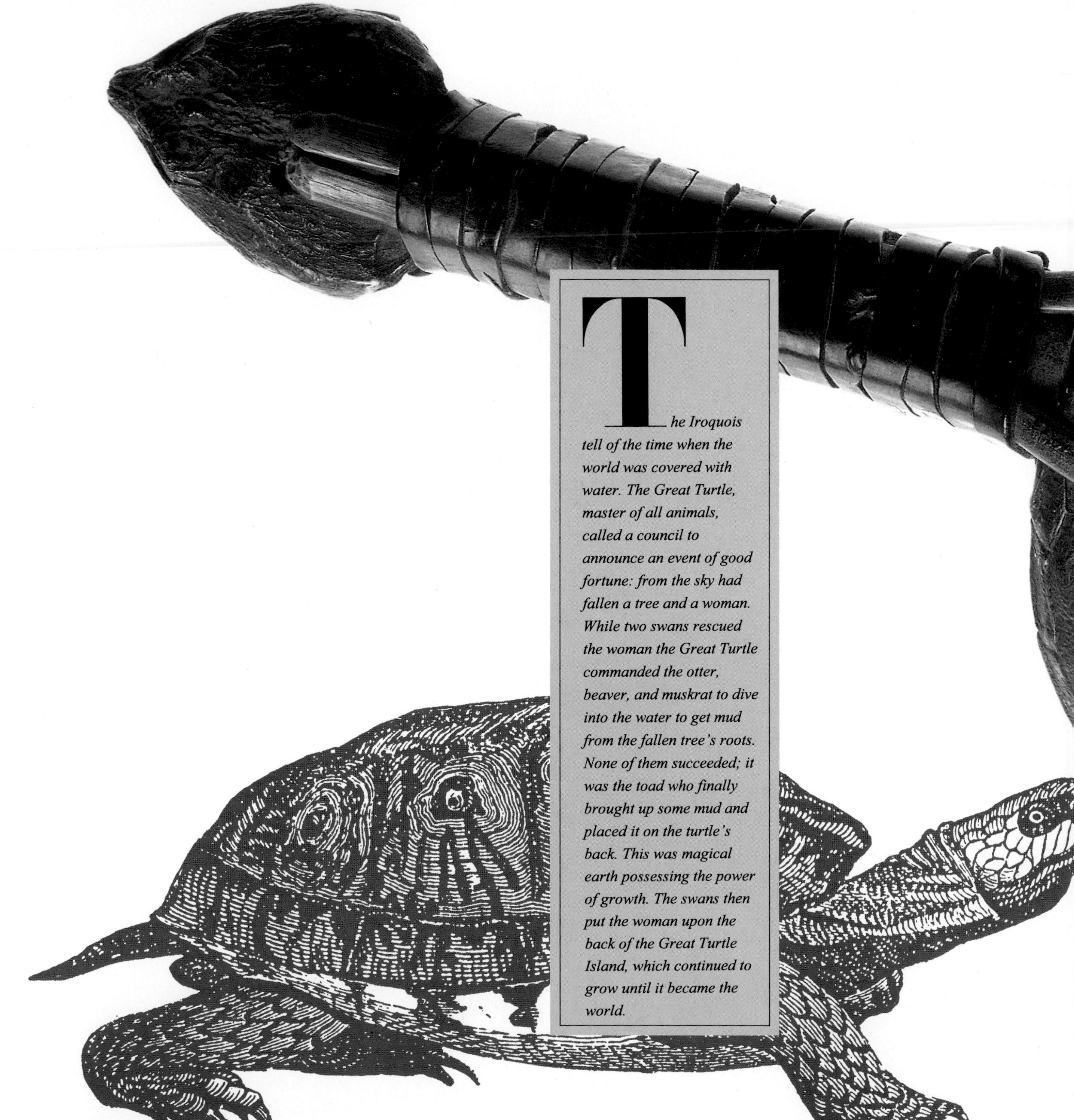

The Iroquois tell of the time when the world was covered with water. The Great Turtle, master of all animals, called a council to announce an event of good fortune: from the sky had fallen a tree and a woman. While two swans rescued the woman the Great Turtle commanded the otter, beaver, and muskrat to dive into the water to get mud from the fallen tree's roots. None of them succeeded; it was the toad who finally brought up some mud and placed it on the turtle's back. This was magical earth possessing the power of growth. The swans then put the woman upon the back of the Great Turtle Island, which continued to grow until it became the world.

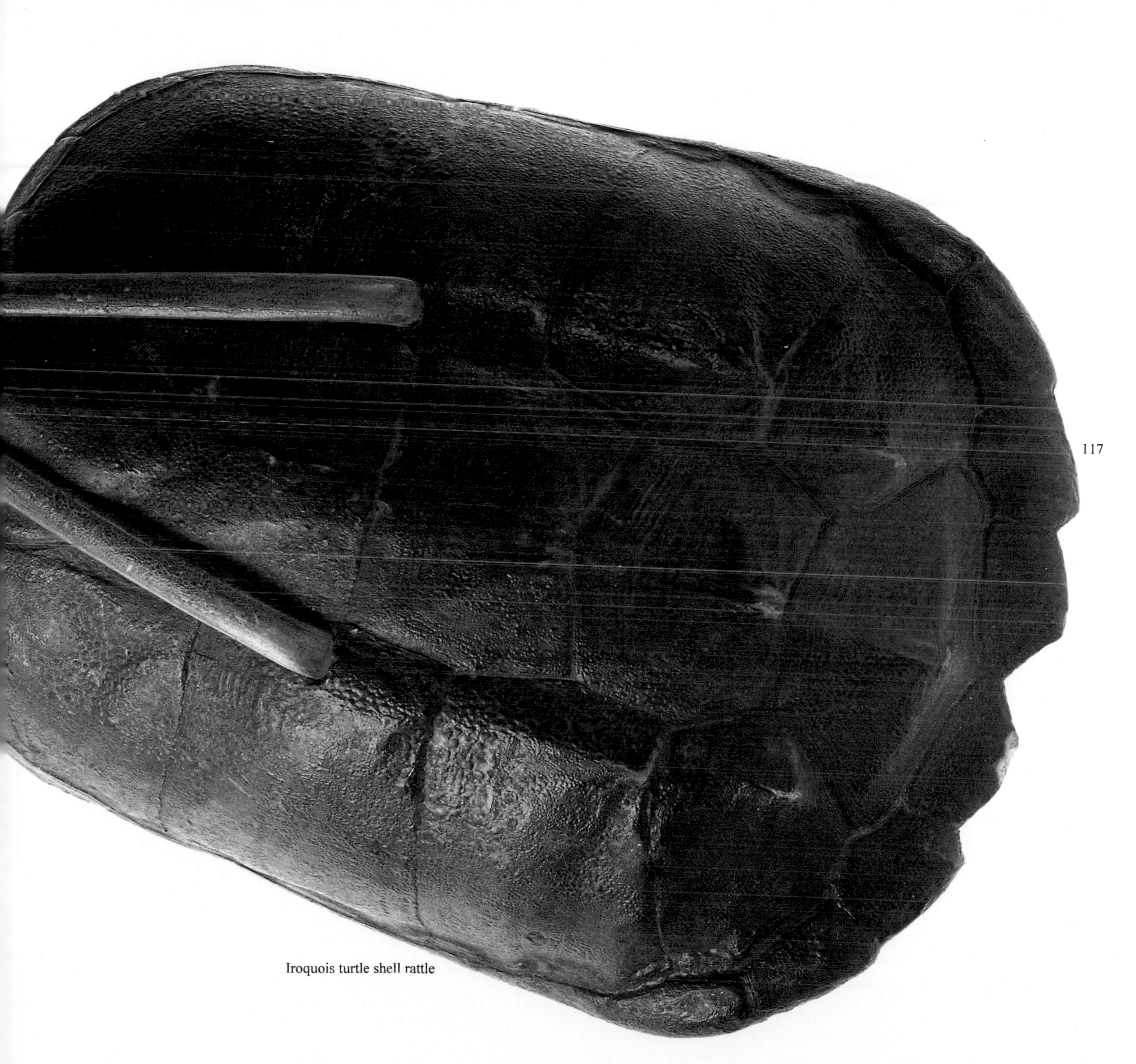

Iroquois turtle shell rattle

INDEX TO ILLUSTRATIONS

San Diego Museum of Man was the source of the artifacts in this book with three exceptions, those on pages 90 and 91 which belong to the Colter Bay Indian Arts Museum, Grand Teton National Park, Wyoming. The artifacts and their museum identification number are listed below, in order of the pages on which they appear.

Photo Credits

Page

2 Monument Valley Tribal Park, Utah-Arizona, Tom Till.

3 Assateague Island National Seashore, Maryland, Tom Till.

4 Olympic National Park, Washington, Tom Till.

6 Saguaro National Monument, Arizona, Willard Clay.

8–9 Alpine Lakes Wilderness, Washington, Pat O'Hara.

10 Three Rivers Petroglyph Site, New Mexico, Tom Till.

13 Sunrise, Arizona, Pat O'Hara.

14 Chief Kadashan Totem, Alaska, Pat O'Hara.

16 Rocky Mountain National Park, Colorado, Willard Clay.

18 Shawnee National Forest, Illinois, Willard Clay.

21 Masked Dancers in Canoes, Qagyuhl, Edward S. Curtis, courtesy of San Diego Museum of Man.

36 Oylmpic National park, Washington, Pat O'Hara.

38 Mount Skokomish Wilderness, Washington, Pat O'Hara.

49 Potlatch or clan house, Ketchikan, Alaska, Pat O'Hara.

50–51 Kotsuis and Hohhuq, Nakoaktok, Edward S. Curtis, courtesy of San Diego Museum of Man.

55 Sunset, Oregon coast, Willard Clay.

59 Carved Posts at Alert Bay, Edward S. Curtis, courtesy of San Diego Museum of Man.

68 Sunset, Nevada, Tom Till.

70 Scotts Bluff National Monument, Nebraska, Willard Clay.

78 Sunset, New Mexico, Willard Clay.

84 Tesuque Buffalo Dancers, Edward S. Curtis, courtesy of San Diego Museum of Man.

92 Nez Perce Brave, Edward S. Curtis, courtesy of San Diego Museum of Man.

94 Shawnee National Forest, Illinois, Willard Clay.

96 Redbud, Illinois, Willard Clay.

111 Swamp marigolds, Texas, Willard Clay.

113 White Mountain National Forest, New Hampshire, Willard Clay.

For further information, contact the museums at the addresses listed below:

Colter Bay Indian Arts Museum
Colter Bay Visitor Center
Grand Teton National Park, Wyoming 83012

San Diego Museum of Man
1350 El Prado, Balboa Park
San Diego, California 92101

BIBLIOGRAPHY

Babcock, Barbara A. *The Pueblo Storytellers.* Tucson and London: University of Arizona Press, 1986.

Bighorse, Tiana, edited by Noel Bennett. *Bighorse the Warrior.* Tucson and London: University of Arizona Press, 1990.

Brafford, C.J., and Laine Thom. *Dancing Colors: Paths of Native American Women.* San Francisco: Chronicle Books, 1992.

Brown, Dee. *Bury My Heart at Wounded Knee.* New York: Holt, Rhinehart, and Winston, 1970.

Bruchac, Joseph. *Native American Stories.* Golden, Colorado: Fulcrum Publishing, 1991.

Burland, Cottie, revised by Marion Wood. *North American Indian Mythology.* New York: Pater Bedrick Books, 1985.

Caduto, Michael J., and Joseph Bruchac. *Keepers of the Earth.* Golden, Colorado: Fulcrum Publishing, Inc., 1988.

——, *Keepers of the Animals.* Golden, Colorado: Fulcrum Publishing, Inc., 1991.

Clark, Ella E. *Indian Legends from the Northern Rockies.* Norman and London: University of Oklahoma Press, 1966.

Colton, Harold S. *Hopi Kachina Dolls: With a Key to Their Identification.* Albuquerque: University of New Mexico Press, 1987.

Davis, Barbara A. *Edward S. Curtis: The Life and Times of a Shadow Catcher.* San Francisco: Chronicle Books, 1985.

Fitzgerald, Michael, Orem. *Yellowtail: Crow Medicine Man and Sundance Chief.* Norman and London: University of Oklahoma Press, 1991.

Gone, Fred P., edited by George Horse Capture. *The Seven Visions of Bull Lodge.* Lincoln: University of Nebraska Press, 1992.

Houlihan, Collings, Nestor, and Batkin. *Harmony by Hand: Art of the Southwest Indians; Basketry, Weaving, Pottery.* San Francisco: Chronicle Books, 1987.

Hungry Wolf, Beverly. *The Ways of My Grandmothers.* New York: Quill, 1980.

Jonaitis, Aldona. *From the Land of the Totem Poles.* Seattle: University of Washington Press, 1991.

Josephy, Alvin M., Jr. *Now That the Buffalo's Gone.* Norman and London: University of Oklahoma Press, 1984.

Kammen, Lefthand, Marshall. *Soldiers Falling into Camp.* Encampment, Wyoming: Affiliated Writers of America, 1993.

Laubin, Reginald and Gladys. *Indian Dances of North America.* Norman and London: University of Oklahoma Press, 1977.

Lobb, Allen. *Indian Baskets of Pacific Northwest and Alaska.* Portland: Graphic Arts Center Publishing Co., 1990.

Lowie, Robert H. *Indians of the Plains.* Lincoln and London: University of Nebraska Press, 1982.

Lyford, Carrie A. *Quillwork and Beadwork of the Western Sioux.* Boulder, Colorado: Johnson Books, 1979.

Madsen, Brigham D. *The Shoshoni Frontier and the Bear River Massacre.* Salt Lake City: University of Utah Press, 1985.

Marriot, Alice. *The Ten Grandmothers.* Norman and London: University of Oklahoma Press, 1977.

Marsh, Charles S. *People of the Shining Mountains.* Boulder, Colorado: Pruett Publishing Co., 1982.

McLuhan, T. C. *Touch the Earth.* New York: Rocket Books, 1971.

McWhorter, Lucullus V. *Yellow Wolf: His Own Story.* Caxton, Idaho: The Caxton Printers, Ltd., 1990.

Medicine Crow, Joseph. *From the Heart of the Crow Country.* New York: Orion Books, 1992.

Monture, Joel. *The Complete Guide to Traditional Native American Beadwork.* New York: Collier Books, 1993.

Niethammer, Carolyn. *Daughters of the Earth: The Lives and Keepers of American Indian Women.* London: Collier MacMillan Publishers, 1977.

Olson, James C. *Red Cloud and the Sioux.* Lincoln and London: University of Nebraska Press, 1965.

Stedman, Raymond W. *Shadows of the Indians.* Norman and London: University of Oklahoma Press, 1982.

Steltenhamp, Michael F. *Black Elk.* Norman and London: University of Oklahoma Press, 1993.

Taylor, Colin P., and William C. Sturtevant. *The Native Americans: The Indigenous People of North America.* New York: Salamander Books Ltd., 1991.

Thom, Laine. *Becoming Brave: The Path to Native American Manhood.* San Francisco: Chronicle Books, 1992.

Walker, Deward E. *Myths of Idaho Indians.* Moscow, Idaho: University of Idaho Press, 1980.

Walter, Anna Lee. *The Spirit of Native America: Beauty and Mysticism in American Indian Art.* San Francisco: Chronicle Books, 1989.